Profiles of
PENTECOSTAL
MISSIONARIES

Other books by Mary Wallace

Total Teaching
He Stands Tall
It's Real
Curtain of Time
My Name is Christian Woman
Pioneer Pentecostal Women Vol. I & II
Profiles of Pentecostal Preachers Vol. I & II
God Answers Prayer
Elly

Profiles of PENTECOSTAL MISSIONARIES

Compiled by Mary H. Wallace

Profiles of Pentecostal Missionaries

Compiled by Mary Wallace

©1986 Word Aflame® Press
Hazelwood, MO 63042-2299
2nd printing, 1988

Cover Design by Tim Agnew

All Scripture quotations in this book are from the King James Version of the Bible unless otherwise identified. Some Scripture quotations from The Amplified Bible © 1965 by Zondervan Publishing House.

Printed in United States of America.

Printed by

Library of Congress Cataloging-in-Publication Data

Profiles of Pentecostal missionaries.

    Contents: The story of Margaret Calhoun / by JoAnn Yonts — The story of LaVerne Collins / by Nona Freeman — The story of Lucile Farmer / by Lucile Farmer — [etc.]
    1. Missionaries—United States—Biography.
2. United Pentecostal Church—Missions. 3. Pentecostal churches—United States—Missions. I. Wallace, Mary H.
BV2595.U57P76   1986   266′.994   [B]   86-15919
ISBN 0-932581-00-5

Table of Contents

Preface

From the upper room experience described in the second chapter of Acts to Azusa Street, Pentecostals have been characterized by conviction, courage and commitment to a cause. Perhaps no group of Pentecostals portray conviction, courage and commitment more than Pentecostal missionaries.

For more than four years I have tried to collect stories of some of these early Pentecostal missionaries but it has been very difficult to grope past the curtain of time and "reconstruct the past and kindle the passion of those former days."

Nona Freeman, beloved missionary and well-known writer, took a keen interest in helping compile these stories and has written several of them in her own inimitable style.

Others have been written by friends and relatives. So here they are—a parade of heroes and heroines, many of whom left the shores of their homeland by faith alone with no Missionary Division, no funding—just sheer faith. They grappled with a foreign language, different culture, loneliness and lack of funding but were "determined and could not be deterred."

They soon carried the Pentecostal message to Japan, China, India, Africa, South America and Jamaica where it still thrives today. Although the Bamboo Curtain shut off China for long years, even there the precious seed that were sown yielded fruit.

Someone has said that the life of a man faithfully recorded is a heroic poem rhymed or unrhymed. Let the stories of these faithful Pentecostals fill your heart with praise and poetry.

1

THE STORY OF

Margaret Calhoun

by JoAnn Yonts

In 1932 America was desperately trying to pull itself out of the morass and deep poverty of the depression. Declaring "a new deal" for "the forgotten man," Franklin Delano Roosevelt was nominated the new standard bearer of the Democratic Party.

At the same time, the creator was also molding a new life that would one day reach out for the spiritually "forgotten man" of Brazil, for on December 6, 1932, Mr. and Mrs. J. N. Calhoun had a baby girl and named her Margaret Sue. How proud they were of her! Life was full and happy for Margaret and her younger brother Jim. Little did anyone realize that into the life of this carefree little girl would some day come a call from God that would change the eternal destinies of many. Only God could know the paths these tiny feet would walk and the labor of love these small hands would perform.

As Margaret matured, preparations were made for her to have the best education possible, so that her life would be enriched with knowledge, refinement and opportunity.

After graduating from high school, she received her Bachelor of Arts degree in Elementary Education at Indiana University. In 1956 she entered Butler University and received her Master's degree in Education and Psychology. Later she studied at the University of Wisconsin.

Adventure seemed to be in the heart of this quiet, refined young lady, who was not content to teach only in the United States, but who also taught in Venezuela, Japan and Libya. These years were filled with family, friends and exciting travels; but hidden somewhere in the inner room of the heart there was a deep, undiscovered longing for "something, somewhere or someone." Someday she would discover exactly what her life was meant to be. It was finally God's divine love that enabled Margaret to make this ultimate discovery.

In the fall of 1964, Margaret moved to Madison, Wisconsin, to accept a teaching position at Phillip Falk Elementary School. She was a first grade teacher and also worked with children who had accelerated reading skills. Having settled in a rented room, she was now ready to find a church home.

The church in Madison, under the leadership of Pastor J. A. Yonts, had earnestly been seeking God for new ways to reach the people of the city with the true gospel message. We had gathered at the church this September night to have a "rather unusual" service. Instead of preaching, we had come to hear a soulwinning tape by Sister Vesta Mangun, and so we viewed with interest and concern the visit of a stranger in our midst. This was the North, where "drop-ins" to a service were rare.

Margaret had not been looking for a Pentecostal church. She was looking for a church her friend had told her about, but it had closed its doors. Seeing the lights on and cars parked in the church parking lot of "Calvary Gospel Church" she decided to come in for service.

As Sister Mangun spoke of baptism in Jesus' name and the baptism of the Holy Ghost, the sweet presence of the Lord filled the room. Oh, yes! He was there—and Margaret knew it! After visiting a little while with the people, Margaret confessed to Pastor Yonts, "I've never been baptized in Jesus' name."

The year before, while teaching in Libya, a friend had witnessed to Margaret about the baptism of the Holy Ghost. Although brought up in a denominational church, she had begun to have many doubts as to whether there really was a God. However, as she watched her friend's faith; she, too, began her search to know God. One day while praying alone, God's presence came very near and she heard herself saying, "Abba Father." She did not know that this was part of a Scripture verse and thought perhaps she had received the Holy Ghost baptism. That day Margaret fell in love with this wonderful "Father" and recognized His loving ownership of her life.

On Sunday morning she attended the church again and after the service told Pastor Yonts that she "was searching" and would possibly come back. In the boldness of truth that sometimes causes a man of God to say something startling, he said, "Margaret, if you are honest, you

11

will be back." Being the refined and cultured young woman that she was, she was shocked, but she was also completely honest. What she did not tell Pastor Yonts was that he had preached that morning on the very Scripture she had been reading."Beloved, when I gave all diligence to write unto you of the common salvation, it was needful for me to write unto you, and exhort you that ye should earnestly contend for the faith which was once delivered unto the saints" (Jude 3). How marvelously God was leading her.

Margaret did come back! And she was baptized in that lovely name of the Lord Jesus for remission of her sins.

After her water baptism, Margaret began to write family and friends of her new found treasure. As it is with so many new converts, she met resistance and rejection. This was very difficult for Margaret because her family was dear to her and she had many friends whom she cherished. The struggles began as she wrestled with "church doctrines" versus the Bible. Many times Margaret would come over to the parsonage confused and in need of scriptural understanding and strength. But truth always prevails! With understanding came the beautiful radiance of joy which she shared with everyone she met.

By this time the first quarter of the school semester was coming to an end. Report cards had to be graded. The beautiful colors of fall had faded away and the great arms of "old man winter" were taking a firmer grip on our busy city. Families now were spending more time indoors. The days grew shorter and dusk enveloped us soon after the children arrived home from school.

Margaret came home to a nice warm apartment, put on some gospel records and settled down to work on report cards. Barren trees dotted the landscape around the apartment, but there was a deeper barrenness inside her heart. She wanted the Holy Ghost. She began to worship.

At the parsonage we were getting ready for our evening meal. A friend of Margaret's, Jan Reger, had stopped by to visit for a few minutes, and we were discussing the burden we had for Margaret to be filled with the Spirit. Jan had been fasting for this, and the days were adding up—but she would not eat until Margaret had her baptism! The phone rings often in a pastor's home—even at meal time—so it was no surprise to hear the jangling of the telephone. As I picked up the telephone I heard a sweet, gentle voice saying, "Sister Yonts, I think I just received the Holy Ghost. I've been speaking with other tongues for about thirty minutes." Oh what rejoicing we all had that night. Needless to say, Jan was especially thankful!

Margaret quickly became a part of the church family and a part of our personal family. She loved the homemade noodles, cinnamon rolls and general "chaos" of the preacher's home. Whether it was painting the walls, decorating the house or tending to the children, she was always ready to help. Our little girl, Valarie, was only three years old at the time. She became especially close to Margaret. Margaret sewed lovely little dresses for her, took her to her apartment, and, when the time came, she taught Valarie to become an excellent reader. Margaret loved all of us, however, and was a very special person to the "parsonage family."

Being kind and thoughtful was part of the very fibre of Margaret, and the Holy Ghost only deepened these virtues. She went "way out on a limb" at times. Insisting that I had a marvelous talent for singing, she often requested me to sing. Unfortunately she was the only member in my "fan club."

I really can not think of any area of the church work that Margaret did not enter into. From very generous giving, prayer, teaching and "reaching" she became involved. She loved the church in Madison, but the severe, cold winters seemed especially difficult for her. When the car will not start at 7:00 a.m. and the hot tears are turning to icicles on one's cheeks, it is easy to long for a warmer climate.

One Sunday Brother Paul Box and Brother Haskell Yadon came to the church for a World Missions service. God's presence had met with us and as the service was ending, Pastor Yonts asked anyone who would someday like to work in missions to step forward. Two young women moved toward the front of the church: Janice Rhinehardt and Margaret Calhoun. The die was cast. From that time forward Margaret's heart belonged to missions.

She and I often did "home missionary work" together. We had a lot in common. Neither of us enjoyed "intruding" unexpectedly at a stranger's door and neither of us could read a city map! But how we longed to reach the lost! One Saturday I discovered that I certainly was not a "Daniel," because even a large dog terrified me, but not Margaret! She quickly made friends with the dog and we proceeded to the door. God knew that behind that door was a hungry family. With follow-up work by Pastor Yonts, God added this family to His church, but the Lord had allowed Margaret and I to give the initial invitation.

Margaret met the DeMerchants while they were doing missionary deputational work. Sister DeMerchant was from the Madison church, and from this brief meeting emerged the desire to visit them on the mission field. In July, 1968, Margaret and another young lady, Sue Pippin, flew to Manaus, Brazil.

It seemed now that God was beginning to set in motion the design for her life. There was a thread running through her life that kept surfacing—her love for children. She longed for a child of her own—a golden haired little girl with frills and curls just like Valarie. When Margaret sat in Sister DeMerchant's Sunday school class in Manaus, tears flooded her eyes. These children—so deprived of this world's best—were so eager to hear about God's love for them. If God would permit her, she would go to Manaus.

Upon their return to the United States after spending three weeks with the DeMerchants, Sue Pippin returned to the local church and showed pictures of their trip at a missionary service. She said of Margaret, "Sometimes I thought I would not be able to bring her home with me."

Meanwhile, Margaret had gone to St. Louis to visit her mother. While there she visited the World Evangelism Center of the United Pentecostal Church and applied for an appointment as a missionary assistant with the Foreign Missions Division. She told them she would go anywhere, but she preferred South America, specifically Manaus.

That fall at the General Conference in Atlantic City, New Jersey, Margaret was scheduled to meet with the Foreign Missions Board. She was visibly nervous and very anxious to receive their approval.

Even in God's work things are not always simple.

Because Margaret did not have a minister's license, it created a difficulty for the Foreign Missions board. Although there were other single missionary women on the field, at this time there was no policy in force to appoint an unlicensed "Christian worker." These men of God, however, sensed the burden and teaching abilities of Margaret and set about to help her. Brother Yonts met with the Wisconsin District board and they granted Margaret a local ministerial license (which was not to be valid if she returned home). This cleared the way for the Foreign Missions Division to appoint her and provided some protection for her with a foreign government.

What causes a young woman in the prime of her career to sacrifice it all for Jesus' sake? Her salary was $12,000 a year (a nice income at that time). As a missionary, she would have a personal income of $85 per month. The words of Jesus rang loud and clear for Margaret, "Take no thought for your life, what ye shall eat, or what ye shall drink: nor yet for your body what ye shall put on. Is not life more than meat, and the body than raiment?"

The church in Madison loved Margaret and missions. Led by their pastor, they willingly pledged Margaret's monthly support and her fare. Oh happy day! She was appointed a missionary to Brazil with the United Pentecostal Church. Farewell parties were given, tears shed, prayers prayed and hugs brimming over with love were exchanged.

And so it was that on July 27, 1969, the Mandley family of Madison took Margaret to New York to board ship. This trip meant a great deal to her, because she felt the love and strength of this godly family. At the docks in

New York farewells were said amidst tears of joy and just a little sorrow; knowing that she was leaving behind her widowed mother, her only brother and his family, and the family of God, which was now so much a part of her life.

Missionary Margaret Calhoun was on her way!

The trip itself was full of adventures. The only ocean going vessels between New York and Brazil were freighters, and passenger accommodations were limited. On August 2, they left the docks of New York, and Margaret was told they would arrive in Manaus in three weeks. But Margaret was learning that Latin America operates on an "about" time schedule. With no definite route, the freighters stop at any port where they have cargo to discharge or pick up.

When they got to Trinidad, the other passengers left and no more came on board. Their "overnight" stay stretched out to five days. The entire crew, including the captain, went out and got drunk.

Margaret wrote to us from Venezuela.

The Lord had a wonderful bonus in store for me. We anchored Sunday off the coast, and that day I was lent a South America travel book. To my joy I discovered that Cumana was only thirty miles from Guanta where we were to dock Monday. The Assarises are our missionaries in Cumana. As soon as we docked I inquired about transportation. Shortly I was on my way—in a sugar truck! It was a lovely 1½ hour drive along the seacoast. The driver chattered a lot and I smiled and tried to enter in the conversation, but caught only about 25% of what he said—in Spanish, of course.

After a few inquiries in Cumana I found the Assarises

*at home. Praise the Lord! What a wonderful thrill to have
Christian fellowship, and a lady to talk to. . . .*

From Belem, Tuesday, August 26th, she wrote:

*Just think, it's quicker to go to the moon than to
Manaus. Well, anyway, I am becoming an expert on the
subject of freighters.*

On September 1, 1969, Margaret sent these greetings
to the church:

Dear Saints,
*I celebrated my "one month" anniversary on ship last
night, but praise the Lord, we should be in Manaus tomorrow morning. . . .*
*Truly I have felt His love and care on all of this trip.
I was longing for company on the ship other than men,
who were courteous, but love their liquor, etc.*
*Something very unusual happened in Belem last Tues-
day. We got five new passengers. I was excited all week
and the time has flown by. I just wasn't cut out to be "one
of the boys."*

During this time the DeMerchants were busy preparing for Margaret's coming. They were going to take the
roof off their house and add a second story apartment
for Margaret. July is "supposed" to be the dry season
in Manaus; so they decided that this would be the ideal
time to remove the aluminum roof.

That night Sister DeMerchant got up to heat some
milk for little three-month-old Pam. What a sight she saw

at 3:00 a.m.! Rain was pouring into their living room, right through the cement slab, light fixtures and all. She and Brother DeMerchant stayed up the rest of the night moving furniture and trying to dry the floors.

By the time Margaret arrived, however, all was complete, except for those special decorator touches such as paint, floor tile and bathroom details. Margaret had a special talent for decorating and they wanted her to have the joy of putting her own "personal" touch on the apartment.

On Wednesday, September 3, 1969, Margaret wrote:

We arrived at 6:00 a.m. yesterday and my eyes were gladdened as I looked through binoculars to see Ben and Theresa on the dock. How I thank and praise the Lord for a safe trip, many chances to witness of His love and the gift of the Holy Ghost and then for my arrival.

This place feels like home to me. It seems like I have been here a long time and I belong here. The Lord is so good to me.

Margaret loved the Amazon, the hot climate, and the Indian people. Several years before she had a dream of Indians dancing and making their war calls and she could not forget them. Even as a young girl she had hoped someday to be "some kind of a missionary." Little did she know what God had in store for her life.

The poverty and needs of the Brazilian people broke Margaret's heart and often caused her to share and go without the things that she needed for herself. God's work was first in her life. If there arose a need for a microphone in the church, or other projects, she was the first to sacrifice with her offering.

Discipline was one of the secrets of this young woman's life. She always arose early to read her Bible and pray. Her apartment was always neat and clean—and replete with unique and "homey" touches. She loved her hot tea (with sugar, please) in the morning and iced tea the rest of the day. Margaret was slender and ate very lightly. A peanut butter sandwich was a meal for her.

Margaret studied Portuguese for eight months before the DeMerchants left for furlough in 1970. Although we at home felt a concern for her, she stayed alone in Manaus during their year's furlough. A young Brazilian girl stayed in the apartment with her and the DeMerchants rented their house to a Portuguese couple.

On Tuesday, January 13, 1970, she wrote to Eileen Mandley:

The thought of being preacher, pastor, pastor' wife, treasurer (the worst job), administrator, Sunday school superintendent, handy-man, is too much to comtemplate, especially in Portuguese. I know Jesus is in charge of this. It is His business and I know He will help me to manage it. I think the money and business part scares me most. Maybe it was the Lord's will for me to be Ladies Auxiliary treasurer in Madison after all. I am not complaining, just shaking a bit, as the possibility gets closer. I appreciate your prayers.

It was a hard task for a single lady, but Margaret did well with the language, administrating the work, and communicating with Brother DeMerchant while they were away. When the DeMerchant family returned, Margaret had their house spotless, repainted and new curtains hung.

Many times Margaret longed for a friend to communicate with on her own level. She tried hard to make friends with Americans of other faiths in Manaus, often giving her testimony of how she had received the Holy Ghost.

Sister DeMerchant and Margaret did visitation together and won an educated Japanese social worker to the Lord. Margaret was so happy to have a friend. However, after having been baptized, this Japanese girl moved south with an unsaved boyfriend. Margaret wept; not only for the soul, but because she had lost such a dear friend.

Many hours were spent traveling on a river boat, sometimes sleeping at night in her hammock, while traveling up the Amazon to the jungle area of Manacapuree. Revival had broken out through the efforts of a Brazilian worker and Margaret would go stay in the homes of the people and teach them of Jesus' love and how that He had died for their sins.

Later, when Brother DeMerchant returned from the United States with the Sheaves For Christ floatplane, he would fly Margaret and her maid to these jungle churches.

How the Brazilians loved her. They called her Margaretche, "Handmaiden of the Lord." A hammock, mosquito netting, cooking utensils and canned food seemed to be sufficient for her. The mosquitos and "outdoor plumbing" seemed no sacrifice compared to the privilege of teaching these dear people God's Word.

One time when Brother DeMerchant was taking her out to the jungle she quickly stepped onto the float and slipped off into the river. She swam back, soaking wet and covered with mud. After that Brother Tenney, our

National Foreign Missions Director, called her "the lady of the mud."

The work was progressing and the DeMerchants were sending some of the Amazon young men to study in the Bible School at Rio de Janeiro. Since Margaret had been a school teacher, she longed to be in school again. The DeMerchants knew that she could be a tremendous blessing to Brother and Sister Norris and made arrangements for her to move to Rio. Faithfully she taught, translated and mailed correspondence courses to students all over Brazil.

Four years had passed and Margaret was going home for a much deserved furlough. It was a joy to see her at the General Conference in Miami. As usual her hands were not empty. She had carried, on the plane with her, the largest piranha she could find for her pastor, Jack Yonts.

After finishing her deputational work, Margaret spent some months at the World Evangelism Center in St. Louis writing and translating for the Foreign Missions Division. During this time she made a dear friend of Catherine Chambers, the wife of our former General Superintendent. This added many cheerful hours of fellowship and joy to her stay.

Brazil was still the land of Margaret's calling and in 1974 she returned to Rio de Janerio for her second appointment. She longed for Brother Yonts and I to visit this land that she loved, but we were serving in Home Missions and felt at the time that it was not financially feasible. The Wisconsin District, however, was sending Brother Yonts to the Jerusalem Conference and we hoped that we would see her there.

On June 21, 1976, she sent these birthday greetings to Valarie:

Dear Valarie,

Greetings in Jesus name. I'm sure you have figured out this is a birthday card. [It was written in Portuguese.] If my calculations are right you will be 15. That is hard to believe. Sister Mandley writes that you are faithful to the Lord and a good witness. For that I say "Praise the Lord." Guess you saw my girls Beth and Pamee DeMerchant recently. Now Beth is too big for me to sew for, but Pam will still do. Brother Norris has a baby granddaughter (now in Manaus) so she will probably be my future sewing victim. I still like to make little dresses.

I've always hoped the Lord would give me a little girl, but so far I am still not a "mother." So last month I finally got a black poodle (miniature-toys cost too much). Her name is Mitzi. She is a doll. A little scamp at times, but a good dog and at least she is company and someone to talk to! I'm really glad I got her. Are you going to Jerusalem? Tell your folks I'm still waiting.

Love,

Margaret

The last sentence of this letter was to come back to trouble my heart many times.

This same year of 1976, the DeMerchants were on furlough in the United States and Canada. Mark Norris and his wife were in Manaus taking care of the work. Their furlough was to begin before Brother DeMerchant could arrive back in Manaus. Sister DeMerchant was expecting the arrival of their third child any day now and it became impossible for them to return as scheduled.

To enable the Norrises to leave as planned, Margaret agreed to fly up to Manaus and care for the work until Brother DeMerchant could arrive.

On August 28, 1976, Brother DeMerchant, his daughter Beth, age 11, and Clayton Goodine (an older relative and pilot), arrived from New Brunswick, Canada in a new Cessna 206 floatplane. This newer Sheaves For Christ plane was to replace the older and smaller 172 Cessna. After arriving, Brother DeMerchant called his wife in New Brunswick to report that he had a safe trip. On Sunday, Sister DeMerchant entered into the hospital at Ft. Fairfield, Maine, for surgery. Meanwhile, in Brazil, they were having a great day of reunion among the three churches at Manaus.

On Tuesday, August 31, Brother DeMerchant prepared to make his first visit, in the new floatplane, to the church in Maues. Brother Jonas was planning a reunion of five churches in the Maues area and Margaret was invited to go along. Brother Jonas was a special person to Margaret. She remembered the young man who came to church in 1970, while the DeMerchants were on their first furlough. His mother had cancer and he wanted prayer for her. Jonas had come from a jungle village, and someone had given him a tract with the church address on it. After prayer, his mother became better. Margaret visited often with them and won Jonas for the Lord. A Brazilian worker then baptized him in the name of the Lord Jesus. After the DeMerchants returned from furlough, Jonas received the Holy Ghost and went to the Bible College in Rio de Janeiro. He then went 175 miles down the river from Manaus and started a work in Maues.

Now Brother Jonas was a successful pastor and presbyter who had developed a large constituency in the lower Amazon region. He had been greatly aided in the work by a diesel powered five-ton boat. This boat had been purchased by the proceeds of the sale of Margaret's car when she had left Manaus.

Although Margaret was supposed to return to Rio de Janeiro that same day, she just could not resist the opportunity to fellowship with Brother Jonas and the dear Brazilian saints in Maues. Surely one day could not make a difference! She could return to Rio the next day.

As Margaret was leaving the DeMerchant's home that day, she said a strange thing to the maid, Dagmar. "Dagmar, if I don't come back to Manaus tommorrow, you can use my airline ticket to go to Bible School in Rio."

At the floatplane ramp Brother DeMerchant checked over the floatplane and filed the flight plan with the local airport. Brother Goodine, Brother DeMerchant, Margaret and Jose Cinque, a Brazilian Bible School student, boarded the plane. Beth decided to stay home with Dagmar as she had homework.

As they took off, in the sheltered water of the cove, Margaret exclaimed happily how beautiful and roomy the new plane was. The plane quickly cleared the cove area and flew out over the rough water of the Rio Negro Bay. At one hundred feet, the new Cessna lost total engine power! Brother DeMerchant struggled to start the engine and manipulate the controls. He glided the plane back to the water in a strong crosswind. The high waves and the wind caused the plane to capsize upon impact. The windshield came out. Upside-down, the cabin immediately filled with dark black water. Brother DeMerchant got clear of the control yoke and seat belt. Working backwards he tried to get the rear passenger's door opened. He felt its handle three times, but the wing flap jammed against it and would not release the door. Working his way around the cabin Brother DeMerchant smashed out a small window with his fist. Out of breath and hoping that the others had already escaped, Brother DeMerchant feverishly worked his way out the window. A sharp piece of plastic glass tore Brother DeMerchant's shirt and back and caught on his belt. Half way out of the window, Brother DeMerchant lost hope of getting out. In an instant he thought of his wife in the hospital, his infant son, two daughters and the work yet to do. He prayed, "Lord, send our angel if you want me to get out of here." He gave two strong kicks and was free, swimming up with his lungs seemingly bursting for air.

On the water's surface, and clinging to the float amidst the over-dashing waves, Brother DeMerchant could see only one head, that of Brother Goodine. A large boat came immediately to the rescue and eight men struggled for half an hour, diving amidst the high waves, trying to get inside the plane. Seeing the hopelessness, the men towed the plane to shore.

Brother "Benny" had taken off hundreds of times before with no problems, but a malfunctioning carburetor had ruined a perfect record. The accident took place about 4:00 p.m. The men stayed on the dock with the bodies of Sister Margaret and Brother Cinque for about four more hours. Brother Goodine and Brother DeMerchant were sick and in shock. It was nightfall before the police and all the investigators came to begin their inquiry.

The next day Brother DeMerchant held the funerals

of Margaret and Brother Cinque at the central church in Manaus. There were a great number of documents to take care of in order to send Margaret's body to Indianapolis (the home of her brother). Missionary Superintendent Robert Norris flew up to Manaus from Rio de Janeiro to help.

During the following three nights after the accident, Brother DeMerchant worked, wept and prayed. Since he was the pilot of the plane, he felt responsible for the lives abroad. Yet he had done everything possible he knew, without success. In the middle of the third night he was awake, tired, and in prayer, hoping that it had all been a bad dream. The Lord then appeared to him in a vision. He came into the bedroom and stood by Brother DeMerchant and rebuked him saying, "Am I not pilot in command of your life? Leave this to me. Get up and go on with the work." Brother DeMerchant woke up singing the victory.

When the phone rang in our home, Brother Yonts answered. I could tell the conversation was serious and went over to sit with him at the kitchen table. An accident. . .someone drowned. . .Brother Jack Leaman of the Foreign Missions Division. . . .

Little flags of danger began to go up in my heart—"Who darling?" "What is it?"

Brother Yonts softly whispered, "Margaret."

Panic, rejection, unbelief flooded my mind. "How could this be, Lord? Margaret is in your care! You promised never to leave us, nor forsake us. She's working for you, Jesus."

"Are you sure, honey? Sure that it's Margaret?"

Quiet tears were coming down my husband's cheeks.

Many tears later, we were among Margaret's friends and relatives in Calvary Tabernacle, Indianapolis, Indiana. We came to pay honor to a valiant soldier of the cross. She had passed through those phantom doors into the shining—and we lamented her absence. The sweet refrain of "I'll fly away, oh glory, I'll fly away" filled the tabernacle as Sister Jean Urshan sang.

Four years have passed since this dear missionary took her "heavenly flight" home. The lives of Sister Margaret and Brother Cinque were like seeds, planted in the earth, which burst forth in much fruit. In Amazonas, the DeMerchants have seen revival as never before. Over 4,000 constituents have been baptized, 80 national ministers licensed, and 53 churches have been started. Today in Rio de Janeiro stands "The Margaret Calhoun Memorial Training and Convention Center" in her honor. Up the Amazon River a thousand miles, stands a church building, filled with people, who owe their salvation to this missionary lady.

If Margaret could have written us after her "homegoing" she might have said something like this. . . .

We arrived yesterday, just at evening time. My eyes were gladdened as I looked through the binoculars to see Jesus—waiting on the dock for me. How I thank and praise the Lord for a safe trip, many chances to witness, and His love; for the Holy Ghost and my arrival.

This place feels like home to me. It seems like I have been here a long time. . .and I belong here.

"In Him we also were made God's heritage and we obtained an inheritance, for we had been chosen

*and appointed beforehand in accordance with His
purpose, who works out everything in agreement
with the counsel and design of His own will" (Ephe-
sians 1:11, Amplified Bible).*

Acknowledgements

With grateful thanks to Theresa DeMerchant, missionary to Brazil; Lena Luke, former missionary secretary
of Calvary Gospel Church, Madison, Wisconsin; and
Eileen Mandley, faithful friend and correspondent with
Margaret. They supplied vital information which made
this story possible. All of us share special love and precious
memories of Margaret.

JoAnn Yonts

A Tribute to my Friend Margaret Calhoun

It was Sunday morning, Mother's Day 1974, in Rio
de Janeiro, South America. In honor of their mothers the
children were proudly presenting each mother with a
beautiful long stemmed red rose. I felt a tap on my
shoulder and turning I looked into the eyes of my dear
friend Margaret. "My natural mother is so far from me
this morning, may I adopt you for the day?" she asked,
as she presented me with a rose. I was far from any of
my own children that day and just a bit homesick for them.
Margaret and I warmly embraced and smiled through our
tears. From that moment on we felt very close to one
another, even though the miles often separated us.

When we visited the missionaries in Rio de Janeiro, she insisted that Brother Chambers and I use her bedroom in the tiny apartment which she rented. We did this very reluctantly as this necessitated making her bed in the hall and sleeping in a hammock. She declared she enjoyed sleeping in a hammock and had become accustomed to it when travelling in the jungle. Sacrifice was a way of life with Margaret. She was well educated and could have held a very responsible and well paying position in the secular world but she loved God fervently and chose to dedicate her life completely to Him and His cause. Giving to others, both naturally and spiritually was her delight.

I will always cherish the memory of my dear friend. The happy times shopping in Rio and our laughing together when she lost her way. The serious talks when we would unburden our hearts to one another and the little surprise gifts and letters she sent my way. I appreciate the framed butterflies from Rio and I especially cherish the framed verses she hand lettered and presented to me before she left on her last term overseas. They spoke volumes and were a source of comfort to me when I received word of her death, for I loved her very dearly.

"Trust in the Lord with all thine heart; and lean not unto thine own understanding.

In all thy ways acknowledge him, and he shall direct thy paths" (Proverbs 3:5-6).

Catherine Chambers

Margaret with friend.

Margaret Calhoun holding Valarie Yonts at a social.

31

Margaret with Rev. & Mrs. S. W. Chambers.

Margaret teaching a lesson.

2

THE STORY OF
LaVerne Collins

by Nona Freeman

No one noticed the little dark-haired girl clutching a heavy black-bound book. The Bee Collins family, moving to spend a few months on Clarence Collins' farm, was trying to load the last of their personal needs and themselves into a horse-drawn carriage. In the confusion, three-year-old LaVerne felt personally responsible for Papa's Bible that usually occupied a place of honor on the sewing machine. It took grit and determination to get there with it, but leaving time found her sitting in the front seat, holding it tightly as though the book was a treasure she feared would be left behind. The family never forgot this first sign of God-consciouness in a life that later was a model of dedication.

The move was typical of kind-hearted Thomas Burdick Collins, affectionately known as Bee. Since Clarence, Bee's oldest brother, and Clarence's wife, Laura, wanted to help in home mission churches, Bee and Virgie moved to their farm for a year with their three young daughters, Thelma, age seven, Louie, age five, and LaVerne, age three. Their responsibilities included the care of their seven-year-old niece, Ida Jane, as well as the livestock and fields.

LaVerne was born July 7, 1913 on a farm near Alpena, Arkansas. Before her birth Bee received a supernatural message, God spoke to him saying, "This child your wife carries will be mightily used of the Lord." He remembered this message when he heard her playing church with her paper dolls. Totally absorbed in the little drama, she knelt among the paper family and prayed so sweetly that tears came to Bee's eyes.

Most of LaVerne's early years were spent on an Ozark farm with cows, horses, pigs, chickens, goats, and plenty of work. Virgie was an excellent mother and organizer, seeing that everyone had a job and did it well. Grandparents, uncles and aunts lived near, so there was no lack of loving attention and interesting visits back and forth.

LaVerne's strong sense of neatness and proper dress was evident early. She was alone on the farm with her sick mother who asked her to go to the spring for a little bucket of water. Virgie heard her crying in another room and although she was weak, she went to investigate. She found LaVerne futilely trying to brush the tangles out of her baby-fine hair. "I can't go after water with my hair not combed!" she sobbed.

When LaVerne was four, Dorothy Lorene, another sister, was born. Two brothers, Willie and Glen, arrived later. Blonde Betty Lou completed the family. She came when LaVerne was away at high school.

A visiting teacher was amazed to hear LaVerne reading at age four and urged for her education to start at once. Though that was not possible, she was a good student from the first grade and had an avid hunger for learning.

There was also eagerness in spiritual matters. When she learned Thelma and Lou were planning to be baptized, she insisted on being immersed too, even though she was only six years old.

Sometimes the girls would walk to the store with eggs or cream to sell. When LaVerne was eight she made one of those trips with Thelma and Lou. When time for the long walk home came they discovered the sky was extremely dark even though it was early afternoon. As heavy rain set in the girls reluctantly agreed to spend the night with the owner's family who lived upstairs over the store. The five girls were to sleep on mattresses on the floor, but LaVerne tossed and turned and couldn't sleep. Finally, she slipped out of bed and knelt on the floor in silent prayer. One of the girls whispered to Thelma, "What is she doing?".

"She is praying. At our house Papa reads the Bible to us and we all pray together before we go to bed at night. She can't go to sleep until she has prayed!" Thelma replied.

During LaVerne's grade school years family life revolved around church and school, both of which were about two and a half miles distant. Sometimes Bee walked with the older children to church leaving Virgie and the little ones at home. But more frequently, a horse-drawn carriage until later replaced by the trusty Model T Ford, took the whole family.

On one of those church nights LaVerne joined in singing a song about Jesus. Suddenly she thought, "How can I sing that song when Jesus doesn't live in my heart?" Convicted of sin she wept in true repentance.

There was a sweet closeness in the family that was irretrievably lost when the older girls had to leave for high school near Branson, Missouri. As the students worked in the summer for their school term tuition, this meant many months away from home. How they looked forward to those too brief, but delightful vacations on the family farm.

While in high school LaVerne wanted to take piano lessons, but there was simply no money for luxuries. Resourceful LaVerne and willing Virgie found a way: Mrs. Hayes, the music instructor, had some quilt tops; Virgie got out the quilting frames and traded her artistry with the needle for piano lessons. To LaVerne playing for the church song service was a source of great satisfaction and another avenue of service to the Lord.

Louie was the sister nearest LaVerne in age and they were very close. One day, Louie found her studying the solar system with her customary deep concentration. "LaVerne, why are you so interested in the stars and moon and all that celestial stuff?" she asked.

"It's God's creation," LaVerne replied. "I want to learn more about His handiwork." Even today, when Louie glances at the heavens, she remembers her little sister.

Bee and Virgie were strict, God-fearing parents with high standards for their family. The only time LaVerne deliberately displeased them is when she came home from school with matching jacket, riding pants and boots and went horseback riding with a boy friend. Bee said sorrowfully, "Virgie, I never thought one of my girls would do such a thing." The riding outfit was never seen again.

Her last year in high school, LaVerne roomed with Loretta Crowe, now the wife of Rev. Earl Wilson. Loretta's godly influence was a turning point in her life, but the big change came in early 1938. Jim Smythe held a revival that lasted several weeks at Denver, Arkansas, where Daniel Lyn pastored. LaVerne was one of many who received the Holy Ghost. Realizing how small her understanding was when she was baptized as a child, she requested to be rebaptized in the name of Jesus. A high bluff in the background made the Long Creek Bridge a beautiful site for that precious experience.

The remarkable difference in the new LaVerne was evident to everyone. She dedicated her life to the Lord for Him to use her however He willed. Much time was devoted to prayer and Bible study with Verna Epley Johnson, a dear friend. When they realized that Verna's young daughter Halene felt left out and that she was having to do more than her share of the work, Verna lightened the work load, while LaVerne told Halene stories of Bible characters with unforgettable enthusiasm. LaVerne had a lot of practice at that. Many of her pupils at Sunday school and school remember how she made Bible people as vivid and familiar as next-door neighbors.

But, all was not always easy for LaVerne. Several years later she told Lou, "Not long after I dedicated my whole future to the Lord one trial and problem after another confronted me. If they had all come at once, I

37

could not have held on, but the Lord did not allow more than I could bear at one time."

After high school came college in Springfield, Missouri. She took a live-in job taking care of two small boys morning and evening. Her duties ended when they were bathed and asleep. On the first night she went to the mother looking for something else to do. When the mother could not think of anything, LaVerne offered to darn socks. The lady, surprised and pleased, said, "You are the first person I've had that asked for more work."

Summer vacations were spent helping at home with whatever needed doing. LaVerne was excellent at redecorating and improvised when money for needed supplies was not available. She once papered her bedroom with brown paper bags and cleverly made a striking border with strips of brown paper decorated with crayons. As Virgie was a good seamstress LaVerne always came home with remnants and yardage. While she worked on the house, Virgie transformed all the material into neat, well-made blouses, skirts and dresses.

After qualifying, LaVerne found her life's work-teaching. She was a gifted teacher and loved each individual pupil. Teaching country grade schools, however, was no picnic. The teacher had to go early, for she was also the janitor. In winter the large stove in the middle of the room had to be well fired by the time students arrived as some of them walked as much as three miles. In summer upgrading her teaching certificate was a necessary nuisance for several years and she greatly rejoiced when the courses were completed. She hated to think of missing a revival or camp meeting.

Questioned why she never married, she answered, "I

didn't want anything to hinder me obeying God."

During World War II she felt a tremendous burden for the young men of that community in the service. A blackboard was dedicated to them and their names listed on it. Each name was prayed over in every church service. When the war was over, everyone whose name was written on that blackboard returned safely.

LaVerne decided to enroll in the Bible college at Tulsa, Oklahoma, directed by Rev. and Mrs. C.P. Williams. After the first year her father became very ill, so she returned home and spent the summer caring for him and helping her mother. When he passed away, LaVerne picked up his Bible the next evening after the funeral and said, "Everyone gather round!" In spite of tear-shiny eyes and a shaky voice she led the family in Bible reading and prayer as he had always done.

It was not easy to leave her mother, two teenage brothers and a little seven-year-old sister to struggle on the farm, but a compelling dedication made her feel she must return to Bible college. She loved bringing friends home with her during holidays and school breaks to share her family and taste Virgie's delicious, farm meals cooked on the wood stove. However, life on the farm became too difficult without Bee, and Virgie moved, first to Denver and later to Tulsa.

Pauline Gruse, a fellow student at Apostolic College, spoke often of the need for dedicated teachers in Liberia, West Africa. LaVerne applied to the Foreign Missions Board for appointment while they were still in school together, but, was refused on the grounds of frail health.

When Bible college was behind her, LaVerne continued teaching in rural grade schools, "occupying until."

She was a quiet person who exerted a tremendous influence in her home church, with continual efforts to turn her students' attention toward Bible salvation.

The year 1944 found her in charge of the small school in Center Point Community, boarding with her dear old friend, Halene, while producing and directing many plays and programs for special occasions. One Christmas play was unforgettably embarrassing. A group of students were to sing "Beautiful Star of Bethlehem, Shine On!" The lights were turned out to let a large star shine impressively in the darkness. But, since the singers couldn't see the words, the youngster holding the light in the star removed it to illuminate the music. The children sang with fervor but the star didn't shine!

When school closed, part of the Collins family made a memorable trip to Urbana, Illinois, taking Willie and Glen to visit Louie. The two young men, soon to leave for military service, got some advance endurance training. There were six travelers in the one-seated car and the speed limit was thirty-five miles per hour all the way!

The highlight of '44 was LaVerne's purchase of a small cottage in Green Forest, Arkansas, for her home base.

LaVerne was a vital participant in a tremendous revival at Denver, Arkansas, in 1945. In September of that year she was thrilled to be given the eighth grade class at Omaha, Arkansas. This was more challenge and an enlarged scope for witnessing.

In 1946 she made the last payment on her cottage and could not help but feel grief over the old family farm being sold. It was the site of so many tender memories.

May saw seventeen of her pupils, "a mighty sweet

group to give up," graduate from the eighth grade. She involved her heart with students to such extent that her joy of their success was deeply edged by parting's sorrow.

Vacation time saw another tedious problem solved in a series of appointments as her deteriorated teeth were replaced with dentures. "No more toothache, hallelujah!" she exclaimed.

Between other duties and obligations she cleaned, painted, papered and arranged her little house into an exquisite haven. She always knew the grand purpose of her life was still to be revealed. But while she waited for the revelation, no time was wasted. Her cottage was near Aunt Clara Carpenter, a very devout lady. Between them, home prayer meetings were held, people were saved and the church grew.

During the summer, 1947, LaVerne was housemother to a group of boys at an orphanage in Farmington, Misouri where her cousin, Norma Collins, worked. LaVerne relieved her and learned a deeper love for children that made her influence even more Christlike in the classroom and on the playground.

She spent a heart-satisfying Christmas with her family, but 1948 began with heartache. Willie, only twenty-five, died suddenly on New Year's Day with a heart attack, leaving a young widow and an eighteen-month-old son, Wayne.

But life must go on. LaVerne's continued as a study in faithfulness, ever gleaning spiritually from special services, camp meetings and conferences.

On a cold winter night in early 1954, Pauline Gruse knocked on her door. LaVerne was now teaching at Hill Top, ten miles south of Harrison, Arkansas, a place not easy to locate. "How did you find me?" LaVerne exclaimed.

"The Lord has directed me to your door—He needs you in Liberia," Pauline replied. She had opened a mission station and school in remote Fasama, five days' walk from Bomi Hills and the road to Monrovia, Liberia. The need for a teacher was urgent. "We are working on an airstrip. By the time you can get there, it will be ready and you can fly instead of walking," the missionary continued.

The decision was hard to make. It involved giving up security, her beloved little home and more beloved family. But wasn't this what she waited for? Once decided, there was only one answer to every argument, "I was sent for and I must go!"

In spring, 1954, she resigned her post with the Arkansas Teachers Association and sold her home, furniture, and car, keeping only a few items that held special memories. LaVerne couldn't take a piano with her so she bought an accordion and took a few lessons. After the sale, her affairs settled and supplies bought, $700.00 cash was left. Her family begged her to save this for an emergency but she felt it should go to missions.

Halene and her husband took LaVerne to Virgie's in Tulsa where final packing and planning for her future in Liberia was made.

Virgie sewed the sturdy clothes LaVerne needed with a heavy heart. "I lost my son in '48, now, only six years later, I'm losing my daughter—she won't come home alive, I know." Virgie could not stem the premonition that assailed her so she sewed and tried to hold back the tears.

Her sisters vainly tried to comfort and assure their

mother. As LaVerne packed, Lou said, "I don't see why you have to go. There's work for you to do here."

LaVerne, radiating joy, answered, "Don't you understand? The sooner I get there, the sooner I'll get home!"

Many of her friends and family came to escort her to the train station December, 1954. Others were waiting to greet her there. After boarding the train she looked out the window at those she loved. Tears rolled down the face of little Wayne, her orphaned nephew; niece Betty Jean smiled and waved. Mother's face was sad: The train moved slowly, last waves were given and kisses were blown. The window that was bright with loving faces turned to darkness. She buried her face in her hands and wept.

She reached New Orleans about 9:00 p.m., took a taxi to Brother Johnny Thomas' church and came in just after I stood to preach. This was my first meeting with LaVerne, but it seemed we had always been friends. We spent the night together at the Thomas' home, but there was no sleep. We talked all night. She shared her heartache about leaving her family and the secure routine of her life and tried to explain the compulsion that said repeatedly, "You must go, you must go!"

Well acquainted with these things, my understanding seemed to help a little. We spoke long of the need for workers in the harvest and the privilege of being chosen to meet a small portion of that need.

When I went on my way to the following appointment the next morning, LaVerne thought she would be sailing that day. But it was December 10 before the cargo *Del Sol* moved slowly away from the New Orleans wharf and she waved "goodbye" to the Thomases. While unpacking her suitcase and making the cabin ready for her journey, she suddenly realized a song was singing in her heart. She paused to listen. It was one she had not thought of or sung in a long time. "I'm as happy as a true soldier can be!"

The true soldier battled seasickness in a rough storm, while clutching a pillow to a rolling stomach and burying a dizzy, aching head in another. Christmas Day brought her first glimpse of Africa when the boat docked at Dakar, Senegal. She was thrilled by beautiful flowers, gorgeous shrubs and trees and amazed at a baobab tree which was twelve yards and ten inches in circumference.

She felt tremendous excitement all day December 26 because the next stop would be Monrovia.

On Red Letter Day, December 27, at 5:00 p.m., the boat allowed passengers to disembark at Monrovia Harbor. Missionaries, Jean Bailey, whom she knew from Tulsa school days. Valda Russell and Hubert Parks met her enthusiastically. Jean took her luggage to Bomi Hills Mission while Valda escorted LaVerne to the necessary offices, bank and business houses. By nightfall the next day she had a pair of badly blistered feet. On December 29 she registered with the Department of Education and the teacher's exams. After a pleasant four-day interlude with Jean at Bomi Hills, she returned to Monrovia for a three-week course.

Finally, on January 31, a small charter plane deposited her roughly on Fasama Mission landing strip. She was the first missionary to use this new facility. She appreciated the tremendous bird's-eye view of impressive and somewhat ominous jungles on the way up, but ever so thankful to be on the mission at last, declared, "I'd be happy to stay on the ground for the rest of my life."

Pauline was overjoyed on the arrival of her colleague and helper. LaVerne was impressed by the neat buildings and the purposeful atmosphere of the mission and felt a sense of fulfillment immediately. Routines evolved cordially with duties shared and companionship was mutually enjoyed by two brave ladies. Installed in the classroom LaVerne did not expect to love the students so quickly and couldn't believe how soon they took the place of the ones she loved so dearly in Arkansas.

Her letters home expressed contentment. She loved the walks they took at sundown listening to the songs of exotic birds. It was so gratifying to teach and train and watch God at work, bringing light and joy to lives that had only known darkness.

On her forty-second birthday, July 7, 1955, LaVerne wrote her mother an animated account of a surprise birthday party:

Dear Mother,

I am forty-two years old today. And what a birthday party I had last night! I'll try to tell you just how it was. We always leave the lanterns on the screened in porch when we come in from church. Sometimes I turn them out and sometimes Pauline does. I went in the living room, lit a lamp and sat down to read. Then I heard Pauline on the porch pumping up the lantern! I wondered, "Why is she pumping up the lantern instead of turning it out?" Then she said, "LaVerne, someone to see you." I went out and all the mission children came crowding in the front door and put gifts on the table. Then I remembered; My birthday! Grusie came out with a cake she had baked and hid while I was at school. I wanted to cry, but didn't. The children had worked after closing time to have money or earn things from Pauline to give me. I made a little speech and unwrapped my gifts. Here is a list of what I received:

2 pencils

a pkg. of envelopes

1 roll film

7 nickels

1 dime

1 flower(made from hose someone had given her)

3 belts (the children made from native material)

1 handbag

1 chicken (from the African teacher)

I cut my cake in twenty-nine pieces and made a bite for every one. Cake is a very unusual treat for the children.

All my love,
LaVerne

The climax of her adventure in missions is widely known by those who love Pentecostal history. By the last week of July, LaVerne was desperately ill and with her friend Pauline Gruse standing by, her earthly story ended August 1. She was only on the field seven months, but her work was done. In the wisdom of God, He called her home.

Embalming facilities were not available then, nor now in Liberia. Pauline sent runners for help. They shortened the five-day walk somewhat but last respects could not wait. As the tropics demand quick burial, only the mission family grieved with her when Pauline, broken hearted, laid her dear friend to rest.

Joe Yarpar, who grew up at Fasama Mission, remembers lessons that LaVerne taught and the impression she made on the jungle community. The responsibility of Fasama is his today. He spoke to me one day about LaVerne.

We've had many missionaries who came, changed locations and left, but Mother Collins in love, has remained with us. When I walk by that white cement slab, I feel the trust she committed to us. Lying there she continually reminds us to be faithful. We are better men and women because she came and most of all, because she stayed!

She being dead, yet speaketh!

Back home, LaVerne's family grieved and a small marker commemorating her was placed in the family plot in Denver Cemetery. One day Lorene knelt at the marker, weeping bitterly, when a hand was laid on her shoulder. She looked up to see Vera Miles, a grade school friend of LaVerne's. "Don't weep," she said. "No one knew, but she and I made plans to be missionaries in Africa when we were children together. She went and fulfilled her dream. She made it; I didn't. LaVerne would not want you to grieve."

I made my first visit to Fasama in 1971 arriving late in the evening. I wanted to see where LaVerne rests, awaiting the first resurrection. Early the next morning I hurried to the white slab I had seen in pictures. A tree loaded with lush pink blossoms reached its lovely branches toward the marker. I remembered vividly our night-long talk and all that we discussed. There was a question in my mind, and I had to ask—however foolish it might

47

seem. I knew she couldn't hear me, but I wondered if maybe the loving Lord would let an angel whisper an answer.

"Oh, LaVerne," I asked, "You were so eager to come and it was all over so quickly. If you had known the way it would end—if you knew your time was so short, would you still have come? Would you do it all over again? Was it worth it, LaVerne?"

Reason coldly said there would be no answer, but I waited quietly in the soft African sunrise listening to bird calls and the murmur of beginning activity in the village across the stream and down the hill. Somehow, soft waves of peace rippled through my heart and the question that had been there so long was answered. I did not hear an audible voice, yet, assurance was as clear as the sun surmounting the tall trees behind me. Confirmation will only come when we meet again face to face, but I know what I felt is true. I cannot even explain how the knowledge came, but it was crystal clear and triumphant:

"Oh, yes! Even if I knew what the end would be, I'd still do it again—it was worth it!"

LaVerne on ship from New Orleans.

Lt. to Rt. Louie, Thelma, LaVerne.

LaVerne Collins.

49

This building contained LaVerne's room, the church and the native teacher's homeroom.

LaVerne with students.

Lt. to Rt. Thelma, Virgie and LaVerne.

3

THE STORY OF
Lucile Farmer

by Lucile Farmer

I was standing on the steps of a little country store
in the midst of the steamy jungles of western Ecuador.
As I waited for my companion, a Colombian girl, who was
taking me to visit some of the few Pentecostal churches
which existed at that time, my mind flashed back to a
scene on June 8, 1943 exactly twenty one years earlier
to the day. That was the first time the Lord had ever
spoken to me about my being involved in missionary work.

I do not know why the Lord chose that particular day
to speak. I was extremely tired. A friend of mine had just
been through a difficult thirty hours of labor before her
first baby was born at home. Finally only the doctor and
I were left. One by one, all the other members of the family left. After the doctor was gone, I went to my mother's

house to pick up Hugh, my six month old son. My responsibilities were to care for the new mother, her newborn, and my own baby, besides doing the cooking and other housework.

While I was standing at the sink, washing dishes, the Lord began to speak to me about working as a missionary. I had always enjoyed the missionary services in our church, perhaps more than any of the other services. Several years passed before I ever mentioned to anyone what the Lord said to me that day.

My husband had left me a few months before, leaving me with three little girls, two, three and five years of age besides my baby boy. I shall never forget how my brother, Elmo Darrah, and my mother helped me in those days. Because my father had died a few months earlier, my oldest brother was left with the responsibility of providing for our mother, the two younger brothers, and also partially for me and my four little ones.

We all worked at whatever work we could find, but I was not trained to support myself in the business world. As I had thought only of getting married and making a good home for my family, I had never considered taking business training. I had always lived a very sheltered life, both before and after my marriage. After my husband left, it was quite a shock to me to go out and meet the world head-on for the first time. The only work I knew how to do was housework and cooking, so that is what I did until the Lord opened up other possibilities for me.

The Lord was precious to me in those days. Just as He promised in His Word that He would be a husband to the forsaken woman, so He became that to me, especially in my times of feeling so alone in a cold and unfriendly world. Even through these trying and lonely times, I often thought of the things the Lord had laid on my heart regarding my future work as a missionary. Many times I would think, "This experience that I am passing through now will be a help to me some day when I am a missionary." I did not say much to anyone, besides my mother, about the thoughts which I carried in my heart. However, the Lord was leading me, in His own way, toward that goal.

When my children were two, four, six and eight years old, the Lord opened up the way for me to go to Superior, Wyoming to help a friend of mine, Bernice Davis, who was trying to establish a Sunday school in that little coal mining town. We had many interesting experiences there, and succeeded in establishing the first United Pentecostal Church in that state.

Because of her father's ill health, Bernice left Superior after five years. The work was going well, and I stayed on another two years. Then I felt the church was large enough that they needed a man as pastor. We were having close to one hundred in attendance, and I persuaded Brother George Eads to hold a revival for us. While he was there I talked to him and Sister Eads about taking over the pastorate. After praying about my suggestion and talking to the people of the church, they decided to accept. At the time we were having meetings and living in an old house which had once been used as a boarding house. Brother and Sister Eads were later able to build a regular church building.

During these years, I occasionally had an opportunity to attend a district conference or fellowship meeting. A few times I had encountered Brother Wynn Stairs, who was at that time the Missionary Secretary (Director) and I talked to him about my interest in becoming a foreign missionary. He said, "Sister Farmer, you have a job to do. When you have finished that, then you come and talk to me." The "job" he referred to was raising my children.

The years passed, and finally my children were all through high school and on their own. Two of my girls were already married. Finally I wrote to Brother Stairs and told him that I was ready to go. He answered my letter and said, "I'm sorry, Sister Farmer, but we have changed our policy. We are not sending single women any more." That was a great blow to me and to my visions of going to the foreign field. Instead, I decided to go to Gallup, New Mexico and help my brother, David Darrah, and his wife, who were working with the Navajo Indians at that time.

After being there about nine months. I received an urgent telephone call from Montesano, Washington, saying that my oldest daughter, Lora had suffered a "movement of the brain," which was supposed to be fatal. She was unconscious, and the doctors had given her only a few hours to live. I was naturally quite shocked and saddened by the news. I could hardly believe that this had happened to her. She was a spiritual girl and her husband, Russell Marrow, had recently become pastor of the United Pentecostal Church there, and everything seemed to be going well for them, then this!

I spent several hours crying and praying; then the Lord very clearly spoke these words to me, "This sickness is not unto death, but for the glory of God." At the time, I didn't remember where this verse of Scripture was found, but the next morning I found it in the story about

Lazarus, After I had this "word" from the Lord, I immediately felt a peace in my heart about my daughter.

"I must go to her," I thought. "But how can I?" I had just taken out a loan from the bank where I worked so I could send $100 to Conquerors Bible College for my daughter, Ann, who was attending school there. She had not found employment during the three months since she entered the school. I knew the check had not been paid at my bank yet, so I decided to use that money to go to my daughter, Lora. I called the college and explained that their check would not be paid because of my need to go to my daughter, Lora. My air fare was $104.00; I had just the right amount for my plane ticket.

My daughter regained consciousness before I arrived at the hospital in Tacoma, Washington and, through a series of miracles, was able to return home after just one week in the hospital. I stayed on with Lora and her family so I could help during her recovery. After about six months, however my son-in-law decided to resign the church and move to another town. The members of the church then asked me to stay and become their pastor.

A few months later, I was talking to Ann, who knew how disappointed I had been when I received a negative answer from Brother Stairs. She made the remark to me, "Mom, why don't you just go on your own; Jerry and I will help what we can. I know all your children will help. You have lots of friends, and there must be some who would also want to help you." About two days after she had said this to me, I received a letter from a missionary friend of mine. She wrote, "This is not official, but if I were in your place, I would just pack a couple of suitcases and go."

I began to pray about it and felt that perhaps it was the Lord's will to send me. I did not have any debts except the payments on a house trailer which I had bought for my mother two years before. By the end of that year, 1963, I could have my Mother's trailer paid off, with perhaps a little money put away for my trip, and also I should receive approximately $350 as my Christmas bonus at the bank where I was working. With this in mind, I began thinking, praying, and planning my trip. I had visited the Lewis Morleys in Colombia in 1959 and had some idea of what the work and living conditions would be like.

I had not mentioned my plans to the church yet. But one day I heard of a man who might be available to take my place as pastor. This was August, and I had not planned to leave my work at the bank until the end of the year. But rather than miss this opportunity for a replacement, I decided to talk privately to the adult members of the church. They were in favor of Brother Christmas, so we contacted him and made arrangements for him and his family to move into the parsonage right away and to take over the church.

Brother and Sister Christmas insisted that I stay in the parsonage with them, since there was plenty of room for all of us. They had two sweet little girls, named Carole and Merry Christmas.

When our District Superintendent, Brother Orion Gleason came to have the installation service for Brother Christmas, he asked what my plans were for the future. I had asked the members of the church not to mention to anyone what I planned to do because I did not want anyone to try to talk me out of going to Ecuador. So I said casually to Brother Gleason that I wanted to become involved in "some kind of missionary work."

He did not ask me any more questions at that time. After the service that night, however, he came to me and said, "Sister Farmer, I want to know just exactly what kind of missionary work that you have in mind to do." I knew then, that someone must have told him about my plans, and so I told him how it all came about.

He didn't say any more that night, but the next morning after breakfast, he walked over to where I was seated, pulled a ten dollar bill from his pocket and said to me, "This is all I have. I wish it was more, but I've just come from camp meeting so I happen to be pretty broke at this time. I want you to take this money as a token from God that He will supply all the money you need. I have been a member of the Foreign Missionary Board for seven years and have just recently resigned my place on the board so that I could become the superintendent of this district. I am almost certain that the missionary board will give you an appointment to Ecuador if you go to the conference in Memphis, Tennessee next month."

Brother and Sister Christmas went not only to the members of that church, but also to some of the neighboring churches and raised enough money for me to pay off all my debts, to buy my bus fare to Memphis and back, and still have some money left. Just before this, I had asked for a three week leave of absence from the bank where I worked, so I could give myself to fasting and prayer concerning some problems in the church. Consequently, I did not feel free to ask for more time off. Instead I felt the Lord was telling me just to quit my job then and there and to trust Him for the future. That is what I did.

I went to the conference and was appointed. I spent the next four months visiting my children and waiting for the call to go. Brother Paul Box, the Foreign Mission Secretary, called me the last of March, 1964 and told me I could go. I spent the next six weeks visiting churches in the Northwest and California.

I did not spend any more time on deputation because Sister Morley, missionary to Colombia, had invited me to visit them on my way to Ecuador, so I could brush up on my Spanish. It had been thirty years since I had studied Spanish in high school. Because Sister Morley was planning to have some dental work done about that time, she would not be doing any travelling for about a month, and would be free to help me with the language.

After an enjoyable visit with the Morleys and the believers there in Colombia, the time arrived for me to go on to Ecuador, the land of my calling. It was July, 1964.

Two days before I was to leave for Ecuador, I received a telephone call from the airline, stating that I had lost my reservation for that particular day, but that I could go either the day before or the day after. Because I did not have time to notify the pastor who was to meet me at the airport in Quito, I decided to go to Ecuador one day before they expected me, rather than cause worry when I did not arrive on the appointed day. Sister Morley gave me the address of Brother Limone's home, and so I arrived in a strange land with no one to meet me. However, I found a taxi driver, showed him the address, and we arrived at the pastor's home without further incident.

When I visited the Morleys in 1959, I became acquainted with a Colombian girl in her early twenties. After I saw her in Colombia, she went as a missionary to Ecuador, the same day I arrived in Quito, she did also. She, at Sister Morley's request, was to travel with me to visit the seven churches that she and a Colombian couple had opened in the five years they had been working here. She was ready to leave the next day on our travels. So thanks to Argemira Parra, I plunged right into missionary work from the day I arrived in Ecuador.

On that, my very first day, of missionary travel, I made one of the most important contacts of my entire stay in Ecuador. At the church in Santo Domingo in the central part of western Ecuador, Argemira introduced me to a Lino Cedeno, a young man who had a problem. He had been attending services in the church there in Santo Domingo, which was a three hour bus trip from his home. He wanted very much to be baptized in Jesus' name and to receive the baptism of the Holy Spirit. But he, like so many poor people in Latin America, was not married to his "woman." She was willing to marry him, but she did not share his interest in this "new religion" that the Colombians were preaching. So for that reason, Brother Lino was reluctant to marry her, although they had two darling little girls (twins) who were six years old.

When he heard that we were planning to go to Emeraldas, a small coastal town on the northwestern tip of Ecuador, the next day, he said, "Why don't you stop at my house on your way? It is right on the road to Esmeraldas, at Kilometer 207." He promised to invite all his neighbors if we would stop for a night service there.

When we arrived, the neighbors began trickling in by two's and three's until there was no more room in the house, not even on the floor. Thirty-five were there that night. All showed a good interest, Brother Lino asked if we could come back to his house for services once a week. Argemira and I discussed it, and at her suggestion, we told him that we, or at least I, would come as often as possible. I lived about six hours away by bus, and Argemira lived seven hours away. However, we would talk to the pastor in Esmeraldas, who was only about three hours away. Perhaps he would be able to visit every week. The pastor agreed, and so my first church was officially opened.

I was not able to return for three weeks because I had been robbed while trying to board a city bus in Quito. The thief had taken not only my purse with my Ecuadorian money, but another folder which contained my temporary resident visa and some American dollars. I was forced to apply for another visa, this time a permanent resident visa.

After three weeks, I returned with Argemira to visit the new church. When we walked toward the house, we found a very changed Brother Lino. He had a look of sadness, but also a radiant clean, peaceful expression. After three weeks of meetings in his house, all his family—including his "woman," two little girls, father, brother and cousin—walked out of his house on the same day. The next day he traveled to Santo Domingo where a Colombian pastor baptized him, and the following day, Sunday, he received the baptism of the Holy Spirit. We arrived at his house two days later and found a young man who was at the same time both sad and happy. But he knew he finally had what he had been looking for, peace in his soul.

My first week in Ecuador, I visited the Colombian missionaries there, Brother and Sister Miguel Pena, who lived in the large coastal city of Guyaquil. Brother Pena told me, "I'm going to turn the mountain section over to you, and I'll work here on the coast." Almost all of their works were in the densely populated area around Guyaquil. Only two small outlying works existed—one in Quito, where I was to live, and another one in Esmeraldas, which was quite a distance from any of the other churches. The white-haired brother continued, "I'm going to turn these churches over to you, and you can supervise them if you wish. I'm getting too old to travel to these far out places." I found out later that he was six months younger than I!

I was happy to have these two churches to start with, even though it meant a lot of traveling. When I first went to Ecuador, most of the buses were very old. It was a long, tiring, thirteen-hour trip from Quito to Esmeraldas. Later, after they got newer buses, the trip was shorter—only nine to ten hours.

We began services in the town of Quininde, near Brother Lino's place, so that we could reach more people. The pastor in Esmeraldas agreed to hold meetings in Brother Lino's house, but after the first six months, he was transferred away by Brother Pena. Consequently it was up to Brother Lino to do the preaching, and he took over the church six months after his conversion. He did very well and the little church grew. Many people were baptized in Jesus' name and received the Holy Spirit.

Brother Lino began to get restless. He was not content to be pastor of one church; he wanted to witness to people at little stops along the road where there were banana plantations. I encouraged him to do this.

When Brother Lino came into the church, he could neither read nor write. He so wanted to read the Bible that he fasted and prayed until the Lord Himself taught him how to read. He also learned to write some. Eventually he acquired five different kinds of Spanish Bibles, and he enjoyed reading all of them. When I left, over five years later, Brother Lino was supervising twelve churches that he himself had helped to establish.

The pastor in Quito, Brother Crisogono Limones, not only liked to be pastor, but he also liked to go out and evangelize. After I had been there a little while, I saw that he was quite a good evangelist, and encouraged him to hold revivals in other places in order to encourage workers, especially those in faraway places. I encouraged him to go where there was not much fellowship and hold special meetings for them in order to bring in new people and to strengthen the churches.

When I first went to Quito, Brother and Sister Limones made arrangements for me to live with a young couple in their church, Jaime and Yolando Yanez who had two children. The Yanez family lived in two small rooms, but with my help to pay part of the rent, we were able to get a small, three-bedroom apartment.

Brother Lino wanted to be married, and prayed a year and a half that the woman who left him would serve the Lord. She did come occasionally to the services, but she never did give her heart to the Lord. Instead, she began living with Brother Lino's cousin and had a baby by him. Finally, Brother Lino saw that she was not going to come to the Lord, and began praying for the Lord to send him the kind of wife he needed to help him in the work.

About this time, a eighteen year old girl named Cecilia,

was in a convent, studying to be a nun. She came out of the convent for a ten-day vacation in order to visit her family in Santo Domingo before taking her permanent vows. While she was there, some of the Pentecostal believers witnessed to her.

Cecilia was baptized a few days later and then went to the yearly convention in Guayaquil that Brother Pena conducted. While at the convention, she received the Holy Spirit. Brother Lino observed Cecilia at the convention and decided that it was God's will for him to marry her.

After Cecilia returned to Santo Domingo, she found work in a grocery store. One day Brother Lino went here and publicly proposed. She accepted and soon afterwards he came up to Quito to ask me to help him buy her trousseau for it is customary that the man buy the wedding dress for the girl.

They planned their wedding for the last day of October. Cecilia had come out of the convent, been baptized in Jesus' name, received the Holy Spirit and was married all in the month of October!

I had been wanting to move from Quito to the west central area of Ecuador because there were more people down there. Moreover, the work was easier there than in the mountains as the people there were much more open to the gospel. After Brother Lino was married, I talked about moving to Santo Domingo. He said, "Why don't you come and live with us? You can teach my wife what she needs to know to be a pastor's wife." I gladly consented to live with them.

I was somewhat concerned, however, about one thing. In the jungles there are tiny insects which are a torment, especially to people who are allergic to them. I called them "carniverous gnats" because I felt like they were "eating me up." Some people call them "no see ems." Some of the women and girls wear pajamas on their legs to protect themselves from these pesky things. I have seen many people, especially women and girls with huge scabs on their arms and legs. I soon learned to wear mosquito repellent so that they would not bother me so much. It lasted about six hours and was sticky but it was better than bites. To live in Santo Domingo, I would have to use the mosquito repellent constantly, which would be not only messy and inconvenient but also expensive. I definitely felt that I was in God's will to go there, so I just decided to leave this problem in His hands.

On the day I arrived, I was so concerned about getting all my baggage off the top of the bus before the driver decided to go on his way, that I forgot to put on the mosquito repellent. After I was safely inside the house with all my baggage, I suddenly remembered those bugs! Always before, as soon as I put one foot on the ground, they were there in full force. That day, it was different, I could look around me and see lots of them, and some of them even landed on my skin, but not one bite! I could not thank the Lord enough for this most welcome miracle.

This divine protection continued for the entire time of my stay there. On the morning of my departure, however, I was sitting on the front steps of Brother Lino's house watching for the bus. During the twenty minutes or so that I was waiting, these little insects gave me a royal send off. Also, every trip I made back there, they were out in force to greet me.

I lived with Brother and Sister Lino for the first two months after they were married. I taught Cecilia Scripture verses. In Ecuadorian testimony meetings, everyone quotes a verse of Scripture learned especially for the service. Some would quote a whole psalm at a time. Cecilia began memorizing Bible verses and learning choruses and hymns. One month after she was married, Cecilia was leading hymns and choruses in the services.

Life was not easy in the middle of the jungle. Hardly any fresh meat and no fresh milk was available. For a few days I bought milk in the morning, and before noon it would be spoiled. Finally, when I went back to Quito I managed to get some powdered milk so I would have milk for my oatmeal.

One day I felt strongly impressed to make a trip to Quito. I had already moved down to Quininde, planning to stay there for some time. Brother Lino was going to build me a bamboo house. Because much more was going on in that part than in the mountains in Quito. Nevertheless, I felt strongly impressed that I should go up to Quito for some reason. I thought that perhaps I had some important mail up there. I went to Quito that night and early the next morning I went to the post office and there was a telegram.

Brother Oscar Vouga, the Director of Foreign Missions, was coming. He had sent the telegram three or four days earlier, but of course, I was not in Quito to receive it. He was arriving the very day I received the telegram. I barely had time to hurry in a taxi to the airport to meet him.

He stayed a few days, during which time we visited some of the works. Brother Vouga said to me, "Sister Farmer, I know you are interested in the work down in the middle of the jungles, but you must come back to

Quito. This is the capital. We have to establish a strong work here before we can branch out into other places. I want you to work here in Quito until this work grows; then we can think about going out into other places."

I was somewhat disappointed about these instructions because Brother Limones in Quito had difficulty in accepting me as his missionary supervisor. They all highly respected me, were kind to me, and treated me as a member of the family, but because I was a woman, he could not accept me as his supervisor.

As a result, I did not know how I was going to work with Brother Limones. He was a man of prayer, a good pastor and an especially good evangelist, but I did not know how we would work together. The Lord worked the situation out later, so the move was for the best, after all.

One day a new believer came to me while Brother Limones was out of town preaching in an outlying church. She said, "I have a neighbor who's been sick for sixteen years, and she has not even been out of bed for the last four years. They take her to the hospital every so often and give her fluid in her veins because she has trouble with her liver. She vomits constantly and her vomiting has so weakened her that she has been unable to get out of bed for four years." The believer continued to tell me that this woman had four children from three years to fifteen years old, and she could not even cook for them. She had to supervise them and let them do the housework while her husband was gone.

They were a very poor family with only one room where they all slept and a little lean-to for a very crude kitchen. They cooked over an open fire.

When the believer asked me to visit this woman, I

took a Colombian girl who was staying with me temporarily, and the three of us went. As I entered the room, I remembered something I had learned from one of the pastors when he prayed for the sick. The first thing he did when someone asked him to pray for them was to look around and see if there were holy pictures on the wall or images anywhere. Then he would say to that person, "Are you willing to give me those pictures, that I might take them and destroy them?" If the person was willing, then he would pray for the person. If they were not willing, however, he would not pray because he did not expect the Lord to heal them as they were violating the Second Commandment. The Bible tells us not to make images of anything in heaven, in earth, or beneath the earth and not to bow down to them. These poor people in their ignorance did not know this was written in the Bible. In fact, it is omitted in one kind of Bible that they used.

I read a few verses of Scripture on healing, made a few comments on healing and asked the woman if she would like for us to pray for her. She said she would. I then asked her about the pictures on the walls; she had three pictures on the wall and a beautiful white statue of Mary beside her bed. I told her I could not pray for her unless she would give me these things so that I could take them and destroy them. To my surprise, she readily gave them to me. So we prayed a simple prayer there for her healing. Then we left her in the hands of the Lord.

As we were going to make several other visits that same day, we left. The sick woman's house was in a low place and we had to go up about 100 steps to the street. As the three of us were standing at the top of the stairs, talking about where we should go next, I happened to turn

67

and looked behind us. Coming up that long flight of stairs was the woman we had just left. She had gotten up, dressed, and was walking up the stairs—every one of them—to where we were. She was perfectly well; the Lord had touched her and healed her!

We were preparing to hold an open air campaign and told her about it. It was a three-week campaign, and she came every night with her four children. Later she suffered some persecution from her husband because of her attendance at the Pentecostal church. I advised her to be patient with him and to pray for him, even though he was being cruel to her. One morning about eight o'clock, she appeared at my door with her children. She asked if she could leave her children there until she could find a place to take them, for her husband had ordered her out of the house. I invited them in, and after talking to the pastor, told her that she could stay with us and sleep in part of my big room, which I curtained off with sheets.

She stayed with me about five months until I moved from the city. She was a big help to me, cooking all the meals and keeping the house, as she was very appreciative of my help in providing food for her children. She did go out and work some, but she did not know to do anything except housework. The wages for a household maid were so low that a woman like her could not possibly pay rent and furnish food for her children.

When I had stopped to visit the Morleys on my way to Ecuador, I had met a very dedicated young lady. She had been a nun, but she had come out of the convent, been baptized in one of the Colombian churches and received the baptism of the Holy Spirit. Later she went to live in the same town where the Morleys lived and attended the church there. Day after day she prayed in the chapel and fasted seeking God's will for her life. Not long after I arrived in Ecuador, Sister Morley wrote and asked if I would like her helper, at least for awhile. I answered affirmatively, so Sister Oliva came to help me there in Ecuador.

She was an excellent helper traveling with me on the buses and witnessing everywhere she went. She was humble, sweet, quiet, very ladylike, and loved by all the believers. Many times, on the buses, we would start singing choruses. I did not have the nerve to do it alone, but together we would sing Pentecostal choruses on the buses. Everyone else would stop their chatter and listen. When we finished, we would pass out tracts to the people on the buses. Everyone who received the tracts seemed to be glad for them and they had plenty of time to read them, while on the bus. This was a very fruitful time of my ministry.

After Sister Oliva was with me for about six months, I had trouble getting her visa. Because I did not have enough money to get her residence papers, I had to send her back to Colombia. A young evangelist there said he had fallen in love with her the first time he saw her. He tried to get her to marry him when she was first in Colombia, but she did not think marriage was for her. When she went back to Colombia this time, however, he succeeded in persuading her. They were married, and I lost my last little helper.

During my stay in Ecuador, I was privileged to witness many healings and miracles among these simple, trusting people. In one open air campaign, which ran nightly for five weeks, we usually had in attendance 400 to 500 people. Brother Limones was the evangelist. The

Lord blessed mightily with many receiving the baptism of the Holy Spirit. During this campaign a certain miracle happened for the first time.

Several people, especially the wife and the mother of one of our young preachers, said they could feel the presence of the Lord walking back and forth in the crowd. There was a beautiful fragrance in the air when His presence was near them.

I did not disbelieve their accounts, but I wanted, just one time at least, to experience this myself. The Lord granted my request. Some of the other believers were a little skeptical about this experience (perhaps they were a little envious), but when they talked to me, I could tell them it was real. This happened occasionally in other meetings, especially when the presence of the Lord was very real in the service.

A similar miracle happened to Lola Mendez, a very poor widow who always wore black. She was about my age and worked very hard to make her living. She never complained and always had a friendly smile for everyone. While traveling on the buses, she would witness to anyone who sat down next to her. On several occasions, the person sitting next to her would begin sniffing the air and ask what kind of perfume she was wearing, because the fragrance was so beautiful. This opened the way for her to give her personal testimony and to tell them about Jesus. She was a good soulwinner.

During the first six months I was in Quito, I lived with a young couple, Jaime and Yolanda Yanez, and their two children. Shortly after I went there, she received the Holy Spirit one night in a prayer meeting in our apartment. Yolanda was an only child who had been pampered by her mother. After she was married, her husband continued spoiling her, so that even after she received the Holy Spirit, she was still a rather carnal Christian having a hard time making the consecration to give up her makeup and her earrings.

One night we went to church, and Sister Oliva, the Colombian girl who was formerly a nun, was leading the testimony service. Suddenly, Yolanda broke into the service, saying loudly, "Pray, everybody, pray; Jesus is here!" She told me later that, instead of seeing Oliva standing by the pulpit, she was astonished to see Jesus standing there. She started crying and fell to her knees, praying in a loud voice and repenting. Everyone else joined in for a season of prayer.

During this time of prayer she fell on the floor, evidently in a trance. After a little while the pastor continued the service. When the service was finished Yolanda was still in a trance. We gathered around to pray some more with her. Once in a while she would open her eyes and look around at us and say to us, "Pray, pray; Jesus is here." Then she would lapse into a trance again.

We finally decided to take her home in a taxi. I was a little embarrassed thinking that the taxi driver would suppose she was drunk. Jaime later told that the trance ended about three o'clock the next morning. Yolanda talked to us and told us that Jesus had taken her up to heaven and how beautiful it was there. When she came out of the trance, she was crying because she did not want to come back to this earth. She said, "Oh, it's so dirty here, so filthy here. You don't realize how dirty it is here until you've seen heaven. I didn't want to come back. I just wanted to stay with Jesus."

For about three or four weeks, after that she was very quiet, and had very little to say about her experience. I felt in my heart that Jesus had probably talked to her about making a deeper consecration.

One of the believers in the church, a nurse, was very skeptical about Yolanda's experience in seeing Jesus. A few days later, this nurse had a similar experience, except that she only saw Jesus from a distance, and she felt very much reproved then for her disbelief.

A similiar occurrence happened in the same church in Quito a year or so later. One night, an Indian woman who had recently started attending services brought her grandson, who was about eight years old. The service was very good that night, and several received the baptism of the Holy Spirit, including this little boy who had never been in a Pentecostal church before. He spoke for quite some time in other languages; then he lay there as though he was in another world. Some of the believers were concerned, because he had lain so long on that cold cement floor. One man picked him up gently and laid him on a wooden bench nearby. The boy didn't open his eyes but made some movements with his hands, then it seemed that he was eating something. Occasionally, he smiled, and at the last, he waved, as if telling someone goodbye.

Finally, when he opened his eyes and looked at us, I asked him what had happened to him. He told us then that two men in long white robes had carried him high into the sky, and there he saw another Man who was very friendly and who smiled at him. He offered this little boy an apple and some candy. Then He asked the little boy if he would like to ride on a horse. They wandered through beautiful places filled with flowers and trees, and the streets were yellow like gold. After a while, the Man told him, "You must go back now because your grandmother is waiting for you." This little boy had never heard any stories from the Bible, so could not possibly know about the biblical description of heaven. To say the least, this experience was very inspiring for all who witnessed the scene that night.

My oldest daughter Lora and her husband Russell Marrow had been living and working in Kodiak, Alaska. In 1967 they decided to come to Ecuador for an extended visit.

They were with me several months, until August, of that year. They were all a blessing to me in various ways. It was so good to have some of my own family in the house. My daughter organized a Sunday school class for the children which had about thirty-five attending before she left there. She, with her limited Spanish, taught the class with the help of an eleven year old girl in the church. My oldest granddaughter, Nathalie, had entered school in Kodiak in September, was taken out of school in November when they left Kodiak and was not able to enter school again until the first of February in Ecuador. She finished that year—first grade—with honors, having learned to speak and to read Spanish during her short stay in Ecuador. When her family moved back to the States, she passed her examinations for entrance into the second grade. Her brother and sister, David and Debbie, five year old twins, also attended school. They did not get too much out of that except to learn Spanish. My son-in-law was the first to return to the States to find work and to send for his family. Just before my daughter and the children left to join him in Florida, something very precious happened.

Before our services in Ecuador, we always had an hour of prayer. One Sunday night all of Brother Limones' children and four of my grandchildren were praying at the altar when the power of the Lord came down in a wave of glory. The children were still praying with all their hearts when the time came to start the service. My daughter took her children into one of the Sunday school rooms so they could continue praying.

I always sat by the back door of the church to pass out the hymnals. Before long I could hear sounds of victory coming from the Sunday school room. When I went to investigate, I found David, Debbie and Nathalie with their hands raised in the air, praising the Lord in other languages as they were filled with the Holy Ghost. What a blessed going away gift this was for me and for my family. It was also a wonderful birthday gift for the twins, who were six years old the following day.

During an open air campaign in Quito, I saw a tall man standing to one side, leaning against a telephone pole. He looked very tired and sad, and seemed to be "at the end of his rope." At the close of the service, the pastor asked me to talk to this man while he prayed with those who had come forward for prayer. He would come as soon as possible.

The man was in deep financial trouble, having just experienced an entire crop failure for the third consecutive year. He was about to lose everything; besides that, he had an infection in his body so that he could not walk very far or stand very long. I told him we would pray with him about his physical condition and his financial problems.

He stayed and talked to us until about two o'clock in the morning. The next evening in the service, he stood in the same spot as the night before, but with much happier expression on his face. As soon as the service was finished, he told us God had healed him. He never missed a service after that and nearly always stayed to pray and discuss the Bible.

One night we were praying with several new believers and five of them received their baptism. Jose Guevara was so interested in and curious about this experience that he knelt beside some of those people who were speaking in other languages so he could hear clearly what they were saying.

After everyone else was gone, he said with tears in his eyes, "I have been searching for God all my life in cathedrals, in the mountains, and by the seashore; but I never really found Him until now. Here among these humble, uneducated people I can see the hand of God moving. Some of these people are not educated, so they could not possibly speak these languages under their own power. Oh, that I could receive the same experience!"

It was not long until he did receive that very same experience. On a Sunday night, during a communion service which we had especially for all the newly baptized believers, he stood along with the others while we prayed. Although he had been a proud man, was well educated, and had much money, he felt very humble that night. In fact, he admitted to the Lord that he was nothing better than a piece of garbage in the street, but even so, he begged God to be merciful to him, a sinner. In that moment, the power of God struck him. He was embarrassed to fall down to his knees, and tried to stand again, but he could not because all strength had gone from his body. At the same time, his jaw began moving, and his lips and tongue began forming strange words. Then he lifted his head, allowing the praises to go forth, glorifying God in other languages. For half an hour, I watched as this man rejoiced in his new-found salvation.

He grew rapidly in matters of the Spirit, ever anxious to learn more about the Bible and about the ways of God. His financial matters were not any better and eventually he lost everything he owned. The Lord, however, was using him in a great way to witness to many people about this wonderful experience. The Lord later used this man in many wonderful healings and miracles. I have seen from time to time all nine of the gifts of the Spirit manifested in his life.

One morning he came to me to ask me a question. A few days before this he had given a post-dated check to a local bank as security for a loan. The bank had promised to hold the check for two weeks, according to the date on the check. However, while in prayer that morning, Brother Guevara had seen in a vision a stack of checks with his check on top. I told him this was probably a warning from the Lord that the bank would try to cash his check. I explained that often the gift of knowledge works in this manner.

He left and went to the bank to see about his check. Sure enough, just as he had seen in his vision, there was his check on top of a stack of checks, ready to be presented for payment that day. This could have been a serious matter if he had not caught the check before it left that bank. In this way he learned about the gifts that God gives to those who wait for Him.

Soon after this he asked Brother Limones and I if it would be a good idea to start a branch work in another part of town. We agreed so Brother Limones asked some of the believers to help Brother Guevara make contact with new people in another part of town. Thus Brother Guevara opened his first church under the supervison of Pastor Limones and me.

All the offerings which came from this work went to Brother Limones to help pay the rent for the second church. After several months of experience with his branch work, Brother Guevara felt led to work in another part of Ecuador. We sent him away with good wishes and prayer. The Lord blessed his work and granted a number of outstanding healings.

On one occasion, Brother Guevara told me about a new work that he was opening. He wanted me to be there if possible for the first baptismal service in his new church. Brother Guevara and his wife, another pastor and his wife, and I planned a trip to the southern part of Ecuador to the province of Loja where, as yet, we had no works. On this trip we first stopped at the new place where several were waiting to be baptized.

When we arrived, we found fifteen people ready for baptism. As we were starting towards the river, there appeared two old men who had a pole and hammock on their shoulders. We stopped to see what they wanted. They put the hammock down on the ground and pulled the covering back. There we saw an older man who appeared to be at the point of death. The two men who were carrying the hammock had brought their father, who was 125 years old, so he could hear the Pentecostal message before he died.

The old man's eyes were rolled back in his head, he appeared unconscious. Brother Guevara took his hand as we all gathered around to pray for him. Then Brother Guevara began to speak to the old man. The old man finally focused his eyes on the preacher and seemed to understand what he was saying. It was necessary for Brother Guevara to speak in a very loud voice, practically shouting, because the old man was extremely deaf.

Brother Guevara took the old man's two hands, raised him to a sitting position, spoke a few more words to him then lifted him to his feet and commanded him to walk in Jesus' name. The old man began to take a few faltering steps. The farther he went, the more strength he gained. All the while, Brother Guevara talked to him about salvation, explaining how to repent. Brother Guevara told him we were going to a batismal service, and invited him to come and watch. The old man said, "But I want to be baptized too." I offered to take him in the car, but he declined, "I'll walk with the others."

During the baptismal service, Brother Guevara questioned each person to make sure that they were ready for baptism, leaving the old man to the very last. The people were all standing in the water, waiting to be baptized. I watched the old man closely because. I was afraid he might not have enough strength to stand, so I was ready to catch him in case he fell.

He did not fall but when Brother Guevara put him under the water in Jesus' name, the old man came out of the water with a shout of victory. The Lord had restored his hearing.

We then walked back up to the meeting place, which was a bamboo house, like most other houses in the jungles.

This house did not have ordinary steps leading up to the front door, only a sort of a ladder, made of bamboo, with no handrails. The old man walked up the ladder just as if he were on level ground, whereas I had to hold onto the wall to keep from falling.

In that room were simple benches without backs. The old man sat on the first bench in the front, clapped his hands during all the songs and thoroughly enjoyed himself. About six weeks later the old man passed away, but not until he received a wonderful infilling of the Holy Spirit.

The believers in that town also shared a prayer request with us. There were three men in that vicinity who were a law unto themselves. As it was far from any large town, there was little interference from legal authorities. For instance, when one of these men saw a pretty girl on the street, he would go to her father and offer to buy her for a small amount of money. If the father refused, the man would come with some of his friends and take the girl by force. He would live with the girl until he tired of her, then he discarded her, just as he would an old piece of clothing. The girl would then be unfit to marry anyone else according to their customs, since she was no longer a virgin.

Because the leader of these three men had been threatening some of the believers, all the believers, were quite concerned. They asked us that night to pray especially for them.

We went on our way the next day to Loja and returned after about three days. The believers told us what had happened in the meantime. One of the evil men had an argument with a neighbor, so he came one evening with a group of his evil friends to kill this neighbor. The neighbor knew why he was coming, and went out with his gun ready. The two men shot simultaneously, so both of them died together. The other neighbors knew the Pentecostals had been praying, so this put a little fear into them. That was the last time believers had trouble.

About a year and a half before I left Ecuador, I started a prayer and fasting service on Saturday. At first we gathered in the church for this, but it was very cold there, especially for those who were fasting. There were not too many in our group, so I asked them to come to my apartment where it was much warmer. During the day we fasted, prayed and read and discussed the Bible. About five o'clock in the afternoon we ended our fast together with a big pot of soup that I made for that occasion. We enjoyed some rich times of fellowship, both with each other and with Jesus, who made His presence felt in our midst. Three of the most faithful ones attending this meeting were Rosa and Felipe Ramache (Quechua Indians) and Lola Mendez, the little widow who always wore black and had a smile for everyone.

There were many victories and many souls won for the Lord and filled with the precious Holy Spirit. There were also many adversaries, which is true in every case of genuine revival. The work goes on however, and God is saving more and more souls in Ecuador as the revival fires continue to burn.

Lucile Farmer in 1963.

Leaving for Ecuador in 1964, Lucile Farmer and mother.

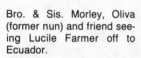

Bro. & Sis. Morley, Oliva (former nun) and friend seeing Lucile Farmer off to Ecuador.

Bro. Lino with his ''woman'' and their six-year-old twins.

Bro. Lino after he was baptized in Jesus' Name.

Bro. Lino with believers in Tobuchila.

Lucile Farmer's daughter Lora with husband and children in Ecuador, 1967.

Couple Lucile lived with during first year in Ecuador, Jamie, Yolanda and son.

Lucile Farmer's last and prettiest apartment in Quito, Ecuador.

Bro. Vouga, Bro. Chambers and some of our Ecuadorian pastors.

Oliva Maria Buero, former nun with Bro. Zuniga, Colombian pastor.

Lucile Farmer

Oliva, Lucile's helper.

Pastor Limones baptizing near Quito.

Marta and Lucile grinding corn for bread.

Felipe and Rosa Ramache, Quechua Indians, started the first church among the Quechuas.

Lino and Cecelia Cedeno.

4

THE STORY OF

Frank and Elizabeth May Gray

by Olive Gray Haney

David Heath agonized as his eldest daughter told him of her burden for Japan.

"Oh, May, I cannot bear to give you up. Our family would be too lonely and bereft. You know we have already lost two of our dear children. Baby Mabel, and then three weeks later, before we could even reach him, our Walter died in college. Please don't go."

"But, Papa, God is calling me, and I have so wanted to work for Him."

"Dear May, surely you can find a work to do for the Lord in this country; besides, I have never even seen a Japanese. What kind of people are they? Are they barbarians or cannibals?"

"Dear, dear Papa, I must go. The burden for Japan is great. They worship many, many ugly gods of fear, and the great masses have never even heard the name of Jesus. I hear them calling me night and day. Though I love you dearly and it almost breaks my heart to leave all my family, the call of God is strong. I must go."

It was 1902, May Heath, a single lady, at age twenty-five, was going to far-off Japan, the field of labor she felt the Lord had put on her heart. She had always been hungry for the Lord and had a deep desire to serve Him.

Born in 1877, May was the oldest daughter of eight children that graced the home of David and Mary Jane Heath. Theirs was one of two Protestant families in the little Catholic town of St. Mary's, Pennsylvania. Often the nuns who taught in the schools tried to persuade May to become one of them as they saw her love and devotion to God.

Graduating from high school in 1893, she planned a teaching career and attended Normal School (teachers college) at Lock Haven, becoming a kindergarten teacher. Being consumed with a burden for mankind, she forsook her career, and at about twenty-one years of age volunteered for slum work in Philadelphia. Edward Whittaker, a well to-do business man and president of a missionary society, wrote the following about her in a religious paper:

Miss May Heath, whom I had the privilege of seeing accept Jesus as her "all in all," about three years ago, taught school in Elk County, Pennsylvania, and anticipated following that profession as her life's work, but the Lord has led her in a way that she knew not of. Both Miss Heath and her senior worker labor among the outcasts of society because of their "love for souls," and give their time without money and without price. Every dollar given for this work goes right direct to the cause, as there are no salaried offices.

The work on "Middle Alley" was a two-story and attic home. The first floor housed the mission where services were held every evening but Wednesday. The second floor had two rooms, one for the matron, named Clara and May, and the other a kitchen. In the attic were six beds to house for two weeks (or longer if necessary) women who had expressed a desire to forsake their degraded life and embark on a new one.

When May first came, Clara, met her at the door and said, "May, you are too frail for this kind of work, and I really don't need or want you." But May would not be deterred. Finally Clara said, "You know we don't receive any remuneration whatsoever."

As May had been under the impression that she would receive twelve dollars a month, this statement greatly surprised her. Before she realized what she was saying, she replied, "My Father supports me." Of course she meant her heavenly Father, as no money would be forthcoming from her earthly one. Until the day that May left "Middle Alley," Clara did not realize that May received no regular income. God met her every need. Often her purse was empty. When Clara would say that they must take the streetcar to some of their duties, May would insist that they should walk, saying they needed the exercise. In reality May did not have the carfare.

Before May left she told Clara of God's faithfulness in meeting every need. It broke Clara's heart. She wept bitterly, for she had come to love May dearly and felt that many times she could have made things easier for her. But the faith lessons learned were very great. Not every want was supplied, but every need was met. This was all the more precious because it came from God. It is an enriching experience, and none other can quite take its place.

In 1900, May, feeling the need of more Bible training, attended Nyack-on-the-Hudson, and Missionary Alliance school founded by the famous Dr. A. B. Simpson, who was strong on faith, healing, sanctification, and the missionary cause. God gave May a burden for Japan, and she felt she must go to those "heathen beyond." Even though hurting with her father's grief, the call of God was strong on her life and had priority.

On October 13, 1902 May, with a friend, Pearlie Ague of Pittsburg, Pennsylvania, left for the land of "flowers." Though tears flowed from her eyes during the long train ride from Pennsylvania to San Francisco, California, and though she was deathly seasick during the three to four week boat trip, she was full of zeal and determined to do the will of God.

First, she studied the customs and the language in Hiroshima. Then she went on to Kobe and opened a prison work. She also ministered in Tokyo among the soldiers and sometimes went far into the interior where many of the natives had never seen a white women. A native Christian "Bible woman" was necessary and accompanied May, who needed help with the language and customs.

May greatly missed American food. Japanese staples were mostly rice, fish and beans. She longed for good American bread. At that time the Japanese cooked over a very low brick stove. Somewhere May obtained a five gallon can and had a door cut in the side making it a sort of Dutch oven. Buying some wheat flour, she made some biscuits. How delicious! It satisfied that terrible craving for bread.

Even while learning the language, she preached and taught the best she could. Not being fluent, she would occasionally make mistakes. One day at the close of her message a Japanese approached her asking, "Where can I get some of this Jesus soap?" In speaking of the blood of Jesus that washes whiter than snow, she had used a wrong word, giving the impression that "Jesus soap" would make skin white. It grieved her that everywhere she went there were Singer sewing machine shops, and yet the majority of people had not even heard the name of Jesus.

As she watched the terrible fear and despair in the eyes of the masses as they worshiped their idols, it broke her heart.

Standing before one ugly god, she observed huge multitudes approach. Reaching into their large kimona sleeves, they would pull out small pieces of paper. On this paper they would write their requests and then form it into a spit-ball which they then threw at the idol. If it clung to the idol, they would go away rejoicing, feeling assured their prayers were answered. But if it fell off they went away weeping, wailing and beating their chest, down cast because their god had denied their request. All of their gods were gods of fear, but May happily told them of Jesus, the God of Love, who loved so much that He gave His Life.

On one occasion May, with her Bible woman, was invited far into the interior of Japan to a feast which was given in her honor by Japanese officials. As all eyes were upon her, she glanced down and saw on her plate what looked like a huge eye. Her Bible woman instructed her that this fish eye was a great delicacy and was given just to her, the honored guest. "I cannot eat it," was May's comment. "You must," said the Bible woman. This debate continued for a few minutes until the Bible woman said, "You can never tell them of Jesus if you disregard their ethics code and do not accept the honor given you," That settled it. Somehow with God's help she was able to swallow it. She could always rely on the help of the Lord.

The strain of kneeling around a long, low table for the two-hour feast was severe. When, as the honored guest, May should have arisen first, she was unable to stand up. So after all others had reluctantly left she pushed herself around to the front porch. Sitting there she allowed her feet and legs (which were numb and asleep) to hang over the side. The pain was terrible. Even after she was able to manipulate them and start for home with her Bible woman, she suffered and cried most of the two-mile walk.

While May was in Japan another terrible tragedy struck the Heath household. Bertha, her youngest sister, a beautiful, happy-go-lucky, sixteen year old, was burned to death in a gas explosion at home.

May knew a well-to-do Japanese family that wished their daughter to be educated in America. Arrangements were made to send her to the Heaths. Even though she spoke no English and they spoke no Japanese, the barriers were gradually broken down and the Heath family came to love her as another daughter. She helped fill the lonely place that was caused by Bertha's death. Also they came to appreciate the people to whom May had gone to minister.

May had always thrown herself whole-heartedly into whatever she did. It is no wonder that the combined effect of the climate and hard work on her frail health was too much for her heart. The doctor said she must return to the United States.

One day before leaving, she received a tract in the mail. It told about the Holy Ghost outpouring on Azusa Street in Los Angeles, California. Her hungry heart said, "Lord, this is what I am looking for. How can I go there and see about it?" God always satisfies those that "hunger and thirst after righteousness" (Matthew 5:6).

Fearing the long boat trip would be too much for her, the doctor declared she must go by slow train through China, Russia and Siberia, then cross the channel to England. Resting there would allow her to recuperate until her health permitted her to cross the Atlantic to New York. The slow pace discouraged her, for the soul that weak body held could hardly rest while one person did not know of Jesus, especially her beloved Japanese.

May was full of plans and drive, and this same spirit is evident today in her grandson, Kenneth Haney, pastor of Christian Life Center, Stockton, California. The God who does all things well was in charge of the situation and leading the way. She needed power to fulfill the God-given tasks and responsibilities before her.

Improved somewhat in health, May eventually arrived in Pennsylvania and was re-united with her dear family. Her father summoned a physician. After some time the doctor announced that he could do no more and made the suggestion that, if at all possible, David Heath should send his daughter to a milder climate, probably California. May said to her mother, "Papa and the doctor think they are sending me to California for my health, but God is sending me there to get the Holy Ghost."

Accompanied by her mother, May arrived in Redlands, California. When health permitted she began searching for Azusa Street. She was greatly distressed when she found the correct location, but learned that the group had disbanded. She had no idea where to look next. This was no problem with God; He already had a plan.

One day a young lad selling horseradish came to the door of their home. Upon being told that they were not interested, he replied, "I don't care if you buy any or not; I just use selling as an opening. What I really want to know is if you have heard about the wonderful Holy Ghost?"

What a spiritual feast May had as she assured him that she had come halfway around the world to hear about and receive this glorious gift! The young boy told her of a nearby Pentecostal church and asked her if she had ever heard any one speak in tongues. Of course she had not. Never before having met a Spirit filled person as far as she knew. Then right on her front porch he began to praise God and was soon speaking in tongues and glorifying the Lord.

May then attended this church and later received this experience for herself.

In her missionary days May had encountered some experiences that made her realize she should never return to Japan as a single lady. She had told her mission board that it was not right at that time to send a single woman out alone to this country, but that a woman must have the love and protection of a husband. On her thirty-second birthday, May 8, 1909, her mother gave her some beautiful white material for a dress. It seemed God spoke to her and said, "This is your wedding dress." "Me get married?" she replied, "But, Lord I don't know anyone I love or would consider." But God, in His forsight, had plans to change all that.

May's father, David Heath, had worked for thirty years as foreman of the molding department in a foundry in St. Mary's. A breakdown in his health prompted him to come west seeking improved health. He, with his family (including May) located in Pomona, California, where he became the much loved custodian of the city hall. It was not long until May found a Pentecostal church here and became part of that Holy Ghost company.

* * * * *

Frank Gray was born in Sullivan County, Missouri, in 1877. When he was four years old his family migrated to the state of Washington in a covered wagon. It was an exciting trip for him, though sometimes lonely at night. Since he was an only boy with five sisters, he slept under the wagon. Years later he was given a certificate which reads:

> *This membership in the Society of Covered Wagon Folk is hereby presented to Frank Gray, descendant of pioneer forefathers who share the hardships of the stalwart men and women in carrying America westward.*
> *Signed—Walter Knott, Chairman*
> *Founder of Knotts Berry Farm*
> *Buena Park, California*

The family settled in Spokane, Washington and joined a group called "Hard-Shelled Baptist." This was a close fellowship which did not believe in the evangelistic thrust. As Frank grew older he too felt a burden to work for God and attended far off Nyack Bible Institute in New York to prepare himself. His name, along with many others, is on the roster of their twenty-fourth commencement, May 24, 1906, the year that May returned from her first trip to Japan.

After Bible school Frank moved to California and began to attend the Pentecostal church in Pomona. Here Frank met May, and it was not long until he knew of his deep feeling and love for her. He was confident also that she was God's choice for him.

May, however, was not so sure. When he proposed she asked for time to pray about it, which he willingly gave her. She wanted to be confident it was God's will for her. Then, too, she was not positive she loved him enough to marry him. Nevertheless, he had a call to Japan and was an extremely good man with a heart of gold, one she could completely trust. Yet she could not marry him without love, so she asked God to give her a deep love for Frank if this was His choice for her. Also she asked God to make it plain to her, just as he had to Eliezer in searching a wife for Isaac.

The following Sunday, being a returned missionary she sat on the platform at church. As she looked over at Frank, it just seemed like a bucket of sweet honey poured over her heart for him.

Ordinarily Frank came over to see May on Thursday nights. The next week, however, she planned to go shopping in Los Angeles on Thursday. Since she was going by streetcar, she was afraid she would not be back in time for his visit. As he worked hard as a farmer all day and then had to come quite a distance by horse and buggy, she asked him not to come, for she did not wish him to make the trip in vain. On Thursday morning she awoke feeling ill and decided to postpone her trip. A prayer formed in her heart, "Dear Lord Jesus, if Frank is Your choice for me, have him come over tonight even though I told him not to." That evening about six o'clock when she answered the door, there Frank stood with a bouquet of roses in his hand. "Why Frank, how did you happen to come over? I told you not to," was her greeting. His reply was, "May, I know you did, but as evening came on I couldn't help myself. I had such an urge to come; I felt you would be here."

They were married January 4, 1910 and lived in a tiny tent-house the first year of their married life.

In 1914 they sailed to Japan, the land of their calling, taking the Holy Ghost message. Only May had received the Holy Ghost; Frank received the Holy Ghost in 1920. He was such a good man he had not felt an urgent need; also he had seen some fanaticism that had hindered him.

While in Japan word reached them of a new doctrine: Jesus-name baptism and the Oneness of God. Immediately they began studying the Scripture and became convinced of the truth. Frank felt it was important to baptize their converts in Jesus' name, but wanted to first be a partaker. He said, "If it's the truth, I had better walk in it." But who would baptize him? He succeeded in finding another missionary who admitted that he too saw this truth and agreed to baptize him. Meeting at the agreed place Frank was thrilled that he would now obey the Word of the Lord. Great was his consternation to hear these words, "Holy Father, bless this man as I baptize him," as he was plunged into the lake.

"Barney, you didn't use the name of Jesus. Why not?" Frank demanded.

"Frank, if the folks at home hear of it, and haven't accepted it, they will cut off my support."

"What if they do? God will take care of you," was Frank's reply.

Frank and May had an opportunity to prove that statement, for when the Upper Room Mission, who had sent them out, heard about their stand on this issue, their support was truly cut off. They were now true faith missionaries: there was no church board or organization behind them, but Jesus never failed.

George B. Studd, a godly man and brother to C. T. Studd the famous missionary to China and Africa, was used of the Lord to collect money from various individuals who wished to support foreign missions. He disbursed the money as God laid it on his heart, or if it was stipulated for certain missions, he sent it there. God used him and other friends to meet the needs of the Grays, and they were able to get a solid work founded in Nara. However, they had to wait until they came back to America to be baptized in Jesus' name.

In January 1916, at the age of thirty-nine, God gave May a miraculous delivery at childbirth, and I, Faith Olive, made my appearance. The doctor had made some dire predictions since May had already had two miscarriages, but she felt that the Lord had told her to take communion and in doing so to claim the strength of His body for her.

Nearby missionaries administered this, and before the doctor could arrive I was safely delivered. On May 6, 1917 a son, David, was born. He is now pastor of Revival Tabernacle in San Diego, California.

At this time May became known as the "Mother of Pentecost in Japan." She was more fluent than Frank in the Japanese and was a better public speaker and preacher than he. Frank was a great Bible student and his was a teaching ministry.

They came in contact with a successful British business man, Leonard W. Coote, and expounded the Word of the Lord more fully to him. At this time he was a very honest, humble and zealous man for the work of God. So when May's health again failed, they turned their work over to him and in March, 1919 returned to the States. This was the real beginning of L. W. Cootes' work in Japan. May's physical problem was leakage of the heart plus an enlarged heart.

Upon their return they visited the Upper Room Mission, which had at the first sent them out, and were completely ignored. After the service, when Frank went up to speak to the pastor, who formerly had been their friend, he tried to avoid them. The pastor finally said, "Frank, you are not welcome around here any more since you have accepted the Jesus name heresy."

Their homecoming was made sad by the illness and subsequent death of May's dear father. He was considered one of Pomona's most highly respected and loved citizens. May and all the family deeply felt their loss, but the God of all comfort comforted her.

At the age of forty-two it was not easy for Frank to find employment in the States. He not only had a sick wife, but two young children and a third on the way. He felt keenly his responsibility. Finally he took a position in an abalone factory while going to night school to learn carpentry. He became a very fine finish carpenter and often used this acquired talent in the work of the Lord.

In December, 1919, the Grays' third and last child was born. He was a boy and they named him Paul. Their three children were all given Bible names because the parents' great desire was that each one would live and work for God.

Because of ill health and the weight of responsibility in raising and educating their three children, after seeking the Lord, both Frank and May felt that for a time they would remain in the States. Though for many years they gave up their work on foreign soil, their labor of love by letters, prayers, offerings and the sending of missionary boxes continued. May Gray's motto had long been:

Only for souls my life's work shall be,
Only for souls till death shall set free,
I'll strive as those striving after earth's goals,
Only for souls, only for souls.

author unknown.

May's heart was deeply burdened for all who had never had the privilege of hearing about Jesus even once, while most in America had heard the old, old story over and over again. So amid the struggle of trying to make ends meet for the family, May and Frank continued to reach out to the unsaved. Everywhere they moved they tried to locate Japanese to reach them with the Gospel and teach and train them for Jesus.

They also kept close contact with the work in Japan. In the terrible earthquake and tidal wave around 1926, they worked for the relief of their beloved Japanese, sending finance as well as boxes of clothing and bedding. Also they solicited help from anyone who would do the same.

Our home was permeated with a godly spirit and prayer. Always somewhere in the house was the motto, "Prayer changes things." Many a morning I was awakened before dawn, hearing their prayers from their bedroom across the hall from me. We children never saw either of them lose their temper or have a serious disagreement.

Money and time were both very scarce, for Frank had to work long, hard hours to make a living for his family during the depression years. (He refused welfare or token work.) May contributed by her economical ways—cooking good, nutritious, low-cost foods, and "making over" most of our clothes. Also she made candy, which Frank sold on his vegetable route.

In spite of all this they took time for us children, with family games plus nightly reading of stories of outstanding godly people such as: the fantastic tale of Evangelist Jeffries, a preacher during the Welch Revival who on two or three occasions while preaching had a lamb appear on the wall behind him; the incredible story of Smith-Wigglesworth, who stood his dead wife against a wall and commanded life to enter her body; the thrilling account of "Holy Ann," an Irish saint, whose nose was eaten away with cancer, but went about pointing to the hole in her face saying, "See my new nose," until God did give her a new one; the terrible tale of Madam Guyon's imprisonment and ruthless treatment by her own family for Jesus' sake; and the up-to-date story of Dr. Yokum's deliverence from morphine upon coming to the Lord Jesus Christ. All these true stories and others gave us our heroes and heroines and enriched our lives. Sunday was altogether given over to spiritual things. Church, Bible stories and games culminated with hot chocolate served in a beautiful Japanese pitcher and other goodies.

Yes, my parents lived what they preached every day of their lives. When my father paid off the school bill at the Christian school to which they had sent my brother David and me, the principal said, "Brother Gray, you are the first minister who has sent his children here and paid his bill in full." May was in great demand among the ladies in whatever neighborhood we lived. They came to her with their problems and troubles. She advised, counseled, prayed with and pointed them to a better life. Many of them in eternity will rise up and "call her blessed."

Still their hearts were in Japan. In 1935, six months after I was married, they returned to the land of their calling at the age of fifty-eight, planning to work with Leonard Coote. My brother David was almost eighteen and, feeling the call of God on his life, entered Harry Morse's training home in Oakland, Calfornia. Paul was fifteen and could go with them. Frank and May were both thrilled and excited by this open door.

Terrible disappointment awaited them when they reached the field. Great changes had taken place and they saw so much inconsistancy that refused to be rectified, that they felt they must leave that area. Their support had been guaranteed in this particular place, but now they would again step out on faith with no visible means of income.

They returned to Nara where many years earlier they had labored. The field in Japan was hard, they fought against the strongholds of Satan. The Japanese had their own gods and idols which they claimed had never failed them for thousands of years and had seen to it that they had always come out victorious. They believed their first emperor came down from heaven, the son of the sun god. Consequently, the Japanese had no desire for the "foreign devils' " God.

Another great enemy that seemed to escalate during these prewar years was Shintoism or ancestor worship. Everybody, whether Buddhist or Christian, was practically forced to bow down at Shinto shrines. This was very strongly ingrained into the people and even Christians had a difficult time breaking these ties. The government required that churches have Shinto shrines at their entrances. The Japanese first had to bow down at these shrines before going into the church to worship God. Much suffering and persecution occurred at this time, especially to native pastors who would not subscribe to this custom. Eyes were plucked out, ears were cut off and other atrocities were committed against those who would not comply.

It was a traumatic time for missionaries and Japanese Christians alike. The Japanese people did not glibly and lightheartedly accept Jesus. They knew the terrible price they might be called on to pay if they did. This picture greatly changed after World War II, when in defeat the Japanese lost faith and confidence in their own idols and gods and were wide open for the true God. This opened the door for the Christian message, and General MacArthur pleaded with the United States to send missionaries.

Nara was a very high class, professional part of Japan.

One way that Frank and May Gray could get a fresh start there was to have English classes. Doctors, lawyers, engineers, officials, teachers and many other professional people desired to learn English and attended these sessions. They paid for their lessons, which gave Frank and May a living. The Bible was the text book, and thus the seed was planted. Though some did not accept the gospel, many did and were baptized and received the Holy Ghost. In fact in 1954, when May laid down her armor and joined the heavenly ranks, scores of letters were received by Frank, bemoaning the death of "Mama-san-Gray" and in desperation asking where they could turn for help and encouragement and who would care and pray for them.

In 1938, Sister May Iry of China invited Frank and May to visit her in the summer, saying she would pay their way. However as May was not well and felt unable to make the trip, they declined the invitation. In the spring of 1939, a young missionary who was with Sister Iry, Katherine Hendricks, became very ill with tuberculosis of the throat, and the doctors ordered her to return to the States. Sister Iry brought her as far as Japan and saw her on the steamer bound for America. She then encouraged Frank and May to return with her to China for a couple of months. This was a unique and enjoyable trip for them and they were permitted to share in the work of the Lord in another needy land. Though the fields in China were white and the laborers few, their first love was Japan and in the fall they returned to Nara.

Less than a year after their return from China they were forced to leave Japan because war clouds were hanging low. They sailed for America in July, 1940, after five and one-half years of love service to the Japanese. It was a happy day for me when I again saw their dear faces. God gave my mother fourteen more years of life and my father nineteen, which were packed full of ministry and service.

During the war years when the Japanese in America were in concentration camps the Grays lived in and took care of a well-to-do Japanese business man's home in Los Angeles. At that time we were pastoring in Pasadena, about twenty-five miles from where they lived. They generally came up every weekend to help us. Later when we built the new church building at 390 South Rosemead Boulevard in Pasadena, my father donated hours and hours of labor for days on end to that edifice. He was a finish carpenter and did beautiful work. My mother made many articles which she sold and contributed the money to help finance the project.

The Pasadena church allowed Frank to build themselves a home on the back of the church property for their retirement years. At their death this house was to return to the assembly. There were three rooms downstairs plus a bath and service porch and one large room upstairs. This upstairs room was May's workroom, in which she had her sewing machine. She made hundreds, and perhaps thousands of garments and various items. These she sold and, while some money was given to the local church, the bulk was sent to Japan to further the work of God there. A motto on the wall of this room was, "Serve the Lord with gladness."

We grown children were hardly ever permitted to enter this room. It was unfinished and was filled with garments they had collected, which May could sort, wash, iron and mend for rummage sales. There were mattresses from which she would extract cotton for items she made for sale. One-woman rummage sales would be conducted and the proceeds from this went for the work in Japan.

This was their life and the midnight oil burned early and late. It was for their people and if they could not go, they would give and send. They never sought or desired any honor, credit or acknowledgement. Their deeds are written in "a book of remembrance." The day of rewards will surely come, and the master will say to them, "Well done, thou good and faithful servant" (Matthew 25:21).

The District Superintendent at the time the late Odell Cagle, told of an incident late one night he was supposed to meet some ministers in an area nearby. Somehow or another signals got mixed and connections were not made. He waited late and began to wonder if the rapture had taken place. He thought, "I'll drive over to Brother and Sister Gray's and see if there is anyone there." Arriving there about four or five in the morning, he was greatly relieved to see a light shining through the upstairs window and the shadow of May Gray walking around.

Between 1946-1948 Frank Gray suffered a stroke and his mental and physical abilities were impaired. He was never again able to work under his own initiative, but under May's instruction he still continued to keep busy and do many things to forward the kingdom of God.

May continued to keep as close contact as possible with the Japanese people. Constant letter writing, encouraged, instructed, corrected false teaching and advised. The letter writing went on and on. Day after day prayers were made without ceasing. The Japanese were as dear children to them. They lived very frugal, self-sacrificing lives in every way possible, so that they might have more to give to these loved ones.

My parents continued to live in the home they built in Pasadena even after we moved to Stockton, a little over three hundred miles away. Occasionally they would visit my two brothers, one in Lakewood and the other in San Diego, or they would come up to Stockton and spend a couple of weeks with us. They were always working helping us, the church or the Japanese.

We could see my mother's health deteriorating, but she would not slow down. Her last visit with us was in August 1954. We took them the three hundred or so miles home and though it was extemely hot, she could not get warm. We had to return to Stockton as Bible school was starting shortly. In October, while visiting my brother Paul in Lakewood, my mother became seriously ill and was hospitalized. Immediately I, with my baby Joni, took the train to Lakewood.

By then Mother had returned to my brother's house from the hospital, too ill to be moved to her own home. I went into my bedroom there and told God He could not take her, for I needed her. That night as I was changing her night clothes for perhaps the fifth or sixth time, (from light weight to heavy and back again) as she was cold and then hot, she said to me, "Olive, please let me go. I so want to go." So in the morning I once more sought my room and gave her to God for whatever was His will. She left us that evening for heaven.

Just a day or two before her departure she wrote to her beloved Japanese and also made arrangements for someone to carry on her work, including her correspondance.

My father, Frank, came and lived with us for about

four and one-half years before he too crossed over to glory. Both are laid to rest in a beautiful cemetery in Pomona. On their tomb stone are these words: "They rest from their labors. . .and their works follow them" (Revelation 14:13).

If we could converse with her, we might ask, "May, do you ever regret going so far away and leaving your home and loved ones? Do you begrudge the sacrificial years of labor and self-denial that took such a toll on your health? Are you sorry you did not spend more time and finance for yourselves that would have enabled you to live a more pleasant and comfortable life?" Her answer would thunder back to us, "No, no, a thousand times no. My only regret is that I did not have more to lay at my Savior's feet. I would gladly have given one hundred lives for my dear Jesus and His cause."

After May Gray's death, Frank received many letters from Japan—tremendous expressions of sorrow and also appreciation for her labors. Many wondered how they could survive without her encouragement and understanding. She left a mark on us children also. Her very life, more than what she said, often convicts and challenges me to follow more closely to Jesus. She found her Lord precious and sweet and more and more expressed to me the necessity of not just working for Him, but taking time to seek Him and be with Him, not for His gifts, but because we love communion with the Giver. Yes, this "Mother of Pentecost" for Japan, set an example that should stir all that knew her. She could truly say, "Follow me as I follow Christ."

May Heath in Japanese costume, on first trip.

Frank and May Gray's first home.

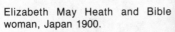

Elizabeth May Heath and Bible woman, Japan 1900.

Frank and May Gray shortly after marriage.

Frank and May in Japan around 1915.

Business men's class in Nara about 1938.

Frank and May Gray with converts in Japan about 1939, Nara.

Frank and May Gray around 1948.

Frank and May beside boxes they were shipping to Japan.

5

THE STORY OF
Carl and Mable Hensley

by Fred Kinzie

"Put up your hands and come forward one at a time," came a stern command from a gruff voice out of the darkness! As she cautiously approached with hands up the barrel of a rifle, with bayonet attached, suddenly loomed menacingly just inches from her face. "Who are you and where are you going?" spoke that same gruff voice, slightly more harshly now.

"Well, we live at the mission house and we're just going home, that's all," she answered softly, "I've been helping take care of a sick woman, one of your own Chinese women. She was giving birth to a baby and sent for me. I've been helping her, and we're going home."

"No, you're not going by here. Just take one more

step and I'll kill you!" bellowed the harsh voice as the man cocked his gun. She heard the click of the gun and at once recognized she was facing a soldier who meant business. He ordered another soldier to put a bayonet to her side.

Mable Hensley, a Pentecostal Assemblies of the World missionary to China, stopped dead in her tracks as she felt the pressure of the bayonet against her ribs. Confident that God would handle the situation, and gaining courage as she breathed a prayer to Him, she faced the soldiers and said, "You can't kill me unless my God lets you!"

"I'll show you I can kill you!" retorted the gruff-voiced man.

"You can't unless it's my time to go and God has a purpose in it. Otherwise, you can't kill me! Your gun can't kill me. Cock that trigger if you want to, but your gun can't kill me!" Mable Hensley spoke boldy.

The other soldiers yelled out, "Kill her! You've got her; kill her!"

She turned and said to them, "He can't kill me! My God won't let him!"

The gruff-voiced man peered at her momentarily, then turned to the soldier whose bayonet pressed against her side and said, "Put your gun down. These foreign devil women aren't afraid of anything!"

Where did the courage to face such a challenge come from? God takes us through many experiences designed to teach us to trust Him. Before this mission field experience, Mabel had gazed down the barrel of another gun in an extremely frightening situation.

When Mable was ten years old, she was constantly praying with people. One night while in the prayer room, a black brother came running in and said, "Sister Mable, Sister Mable, come quick, come quick! My sister is at the altar seeking the Lord and her husband is here with a gun to kill her. Come quick and help us."

As she hurried after him she wondered why he came to her instead of one of the brothers. Later he explained that he felt that seeing a child defending this lady would affect the gunman more than a man. He was right!

Standing between this man and his praying wife, Mable, with tears streaming down her cheeks, pleaded, "Please don't do it! Please don't do it! If you kill her, she'll go to heaven. God will see to that, but you'll go to hell for certain! Do you want to spend eternity in hell? Do you?"

As she spoke to him, he turned the gun away from his wife and pointed it at her. With tears still flowing she pleaded with him! Suddenly, pressing the gun into her hands, he fell to the floor begging God for mercy. In a very short time he received the Holy Ghost, even before his wife. Forty years later she learned that this man became a preacher and was faithful to God unto the end of his life.

Who is this Mable Hensley? Where did she come from and how did she get to China?

She was born Mable Lowe, the second of seven children born to Elmer and Sallie Hilbert Lowe, on April 8, 1902 at Coxville, a small mining town near Terre Haute, Indiana. When she was three years old the family moved to San Pedro, California at the coast.

Her grandfather, Benjamin Lowe, an old fashioned circuit-riding Methodist preacher, received the Holy Ghost quite some time before the outpouring in the early days

115

of the twentieth century. Her grandmother was frightened when she first heard him speaking in tongues, not knowing what it was. When she later became accustomed to it she confided to a friend, "I don't know what it is, but I will admit that after every time I hear him doing this, he preaches better than ever!"

Mable's father, Elmer, grew up in the Methodist Church but drifted away from it. Later he had a dream three nights in succession that he was being shaken over the bottomless pit of hell. It so frightened him that he repented and turned his heart back to God. Her mother came to God at the same time.

The Lowes attended a holiness church. One night while praying at the altar the Lord blessed Elmer to the extent that he quivered and shook all over. The minister took him aside and expressed his displeasure and forbade any further demonstration in his church. Brother Lowe remarked, "Why, I've never been so close to heaven in my life!" They soon left this church and sought one where they could feel free to worship God.

Because of the sickness of Mabel's small brother, Homer, the doctor suggested that the Lowes move to Azusa, California, which was away from the coast and had a much drier climate. The boy died, however, soon after they moved. A neighbor then put them in touch with the Azusa Street Mission twenty-five miles away in Los Angeles. Their daughters, Mona and Faye, both very ill were healed when they took them to the mission. Subsequently the whole family received the Holy Ghost there, including Mable, who was almost ten years old. Mable gave herself completely to the Lord, keeping her heart open to the leading of the Spirit.

In the meantime Brother William H. Durham came to Los Angeles from Chicago and became the pastor of a large group of those who had received the Holy Ghost at Azusa Street. He enlisted a young man, Frank Ewart, to assist him with the church. Sometime later Brother Durham took a leave of absence to return to Chicago, fully expecting to return to Los Angeles and continue to pastor the church. While in Chicago, however, he contracted tuberculosis and died. Brother Ewart then became the pastor.

About this time, the Lowe family moved back east, returning to Los Angeles one year later. While they were gone, Brother Ewart received a scriptural understanding of Jesus name baptism and the oneness of God. Upon their return, God opened the truth to them and the whole Lowe family including Mabel, was baptized in the name of the Lord Jesus Christ, in 1914. Brother Lowe then became Brother Ewart's right hand man. Mable soon became the church pianist.

When she was a teenager she arrived late for service one night. Only one seat was left—halfway back through the crowded tent. When testimony service began she stood to testify. As the Spirit moved on her, she stepped out into an aisle, then to the front of the tent. With her eyes closed, she preached, walking back and forth across the front of the tent. Witnesses testified that when she came to tent posts, she walked around them, never touching a one. When she finished twenty minutes later, Brother Ewart gave the altar call and many people flocked to the altar. This is the way her ministry began!

Carl Hensley came to the Lord in another city and church but was dissatisfied there. Two young men from the Los Angeles church met him in Taft, California, his home town, and invited him to Los Angeles. He came and in his first service at Brother Ewart's, a tent meeting, he received the Holy Ghost and was baptized in the name of Jesus Christ. His mother, a school teacher, was a very devout Christian. She taught mostly at country schools and usually started Sunday schools in these buildings. His maternal grandfather was a very devoted minister.

Carl was a meticulous dresser. That afternoon he was wearing a neatly-pressed, dark suit but ended up lying flat on his back in the sawdust. The Lord knew exactly how to humble him.

On his second trip to Los Angeles, Mable met him for the first time, and he kept coming back often after that! After a short courtship they were married and three months later he was drafted into the army during World War I.

Before their marriage, Mable had experienced a missionary call one morning while Brother Andrew Urshan was speaking at Brother Ewart's church. It was a moving experience. As she sat on the front row weeping profusely, Brother Urshan pleaded, "Someone here is receiving a call to be a missionary, and I want you to come forward."

Several came, but not satisfied, he said, "There is still one who is not obeying." Finally, when Mable, still weeping profusely, knelt submissively at the altar, he said, "No more come." He knew to whom God was speaking!

After their marriage, that call intensified within her. Although she often wrote to Carl in the army, she did not mention this. When he wrote back one time, he urged her to say "yes" if God was speaking to her.

Shortly after he returned from the service, a missionary to China, Sister Addell Harrison and her daughter, were visiting in the Lowe home where the Hensleys were staying. One day out of nowhere Sister Harrison said to her, "Mable, why don't you two go to China with me?"

"China!" Mable cried out. "Sister Harrison, China? I'm scared of the Chinese!" Immediately she heard a voice saying, "You didn't ask Me about this, did you?" Smitten in her heart by this question she knew was from the Lord, she turned and ran into her bedroom and threw herself across the bed weeping uncontrollably. After weeping and praying for quite some time, her husband came and putting his arm around her, said, "Honey, whatever the Lord is asking you to do, say yes!"

Startled, she turned to him and asked, "Where did you come from?"

"I was lying on the bed listening to you pray. I had been praying before you came in. Mable, if God wants us to be missionaries, we'll have to go. So both of us must say, 'yes.' " Kneeling at the bed together in humble submission and prayer, both knew they would be going to the mission field.

A message in tongues and interpretation came in the missionary service that night: "Don't hesitate to accept My leading for it is I, God, Who is speaking to two people in this congregation tonight. You, to whom I am speaking, know who you are."

As Mable listened to the interpretation, her experience the morning Brother Urshan had preached at their church while she was still unmarried, came back to her forcefully. She stood to her feet and said, "Yes we know who has been called. Carl and I must go to China!"

She then told the congregation about the resistance she had expressed to Sister Harrison about going to China and how God had spoken to both her and Carl.

As she spoke she had a vision. She saw Chinese people as far as her eye could see. She was standing among them speaking with her arms outstretched toward them. When the vision diminished and she came to herself, she was speaking in tongues. Later, when she was in China and had learned the language, she realized she had been speaking in Chinese in that vision. She commented, "Oh what a beautiful experience!"

Immediately Mabel and Carl started planning for China. Sister Harrison wanted them to return with her as she desperately needed help. They did not promise, but determined to wait for direction from the Lord.

At the next Pentecostal Assemblies of the World Convention, Brother and Sister Hensley were ordained over the objections of their pastor, Brother Ewart, who finally acquiesced by saying, "I don't want to lose them!" He would not help them, however, when they left—no offerings, not even a goodbye. This whole situation crushed the Hensleys, but the call of God and the vision prevailed. No doubt, this was a severe test to see if they really meant it or not.

They decided to embark from San Francisco. One problem, however, needed a quick solution: They had no money for the trip to San Francisco, let alone to China! What were they to do? There was but one answer, prayer, and that is what they did. The Lord was teaching them to trust Him long before they ever left America.

Mable was invited to speak at the Baldwin Park church where her father was pastor. The church gave them an offering of one hundred dollars. When they returned home that night Brother Hensley found two twenty dollar bills in his coat pocket, which he was sure was given by three Swedish brothers. With confidence that God would furnish the finances, they started up the coast, stopping at Lodi, Visalia and other churches on the way.

Arriving in Oakland they stayed in an apartment rented by Sister Harrison. Brother Hensley went to make reservations on a boat to China, but learned the boat was completely booked. Confidently he said, "I know we are going on that boat. They don't have any room, but I know God wants us on it and He will make a way for us!"

Brother Harry Morse, pastor in Oakland, said he was going to have a missionary rally. "I've never done this before," he said, "but I feel like doing it now. I'll invite the other churches in the area of the rally for we'll have a love feast together. We've got Sister Harrison and her daughter, Sister Elizabeth Stieglitz, both veteran missionaries to China, and Carl and Mable Hensley, new missionaries to there. We'll have a time of great fellowship and I'll promise not to take an offering."

It was a blessed meeting with all of the missionaries speaking. Sister Hensley was the last to speak. As she spoke the Lord showered blessings on the place. "It was wonderful!" Sister Hensley remarked.

When Sister Hensley finished, Brother Morse, with tears in his eyes, stood and said, "I must apologize to everybody here tonight. I promised that I'd not take an offering, but God has smitten me. I have to ask you to forgive me, for I must take an offering. The offering will be for the Hensleys. I don't know what they need. They have not said a word to me. They may not even need it.

121

But I don't believe that for God would not have told me to take it if they didn't need it!" At that point they didn't have their fare even if they could have gotten passage on the boat. "I want this couple to come and stand down here in front and as you pass by and shake hands with them, give them an offering," Brother Morse instructed.

As the people went by shaking hands and giving them money, Brother Hensley stuffed his in one coat pocket and she put hers in the other. Seeing the pockets filling up, Brother Morse grabbed his hat and said, "Here take this, you need more than the pockets it looks like."

The offering was just enough to meet their fare. Brother Morse asked, "I want to ask you a question. Did you have the money for your fare?" He said it loud enough for everyone to hear.

"No," they replied, "we didn't."

"Now will you forgive me for taking this offering?" he addressed the congregation. "The Lord has provided!"

The next morning Brother Hensley again headed for the ticket office. "I've come to purchase the tickets for China," he addressed the clerk.

"I'm sorry," she replied, "I told you we don't have passage on that ship for two. You'll just have to wait for the next boat!"

"No," Brother Hensley replied, "the Lord has let me know we are to go on this ship, and I believe Him."

"I'm sorry," she reiterated, "but there is still nothing available."

Slightly distressed and discouraged that nothing had materialized, he started toward the door. Just as he reached it, the phone rang. "Wait a minute," the clerk said as she answered the telephone. Hanging up the telephone, she said to Brother Hensley, "Sir, that phone call was a cancellation by a woman. If your wife will travel with the woman in this room and you with a man in another room, I'll sell you the tickets."

"Oh thank you," replied Brother Hensley, "I felt sure we would be going on this ship. By the way, there's a missionary going to China on this boat. Is there any way you could rearrange accomodation to put my wife with her? They are good friends and it would be real convenient for them to travel together."

"What's this missionary's name?" she asked.

"Elizabeth Stieglitz," he replied.

"Stieglitz?" she questioned thoughtfully. "I believe that's the room where the lady cancelled. Wait a minute and I'll check it out." Flipping through her files she finally looked up with a smile on her face and said, "That's the room where the lady cancelled. Yes, your wife can share that room with her!"

Carl Hensley walked out of that ticket office with quickened steps, praise on his lips and victory in his heart.

The accomodations were very special to Sister Hensley as she was pregnant with her first child, Eloise, who later was born in China. Their ship steamed out of the port of San Francisco in May, 1919, but when the boat docked in Japan, Carl and Mable were able to travel the rest of the journey together.

God had miraculously provided the means to get them to San Francisco, then on to the Orient, but what about after they arrived? Funding programs such as Faith Promise and Partners in Missions would not be around for another fifty years. What was their means of support?

"We had to trust God. Our means of support were

letters from the homeland. God had to lay it on people's hearts to send us money. We never knew where it was coming from. It took one month after the money was mailed to get to us in Hong Kong," Sister Hensley recalled.

"Sister Hensley, very few people knew you were going to China. How did they find out about it to send you money?" I asked.

"Brother Haywood knew," she replied, "and his secretary sent us money—and my father helped a lot, along with several California churches that knew about us. We had a very difficult time at first when bills piled up on us for six months. The grocery store proprietor, our landlord and our Chinese language teacher all said they believed we'd get the money somehow and took a chance with us.

"To complicate things Brother Hensley took malaria and was very ill. I had to take care of everything. Out of money to meet expenses, I went one day to the post office where I met another of our missionaries, hoping for a letter from home with money in it. When the mail from the first boat arrived there were a couple of letters with a few dollars in them, but far short of our needs. I was so disappointed. But as there would be another boat yet that day, we all waited. When it came there was a registered letter from my father. The other missionary prophesied, 'There's one hundred dollars in it.'

" 'Not from my father. He doesn't have a hundred dollars to send,' I stated. When I opened it, however, there was a hundred dollar bill in it. Father explained that he had been in Texas and a pastor asked him to receive a missionary offering. It came to $4,000.00 and the pastor gave him this hundred dollar bill for his daughter in China.''

On her way home Sister Hensley stopped at the grocery store, paid her bill, and bought groceries to last for quite some time. She had enough money left to pay both the language teacher and the landlord, even paying a couple of months rent in advance. This turned out to be the most severe financial test of their entire missionary work. God was teaching them how to trust Him! The only other difficult time they faced was during the bitter depression in American when money came very slowly.

Their first stop in China was Kowloon where they studied the language. After studying six months, Mable was asked to play the organ and help in a mission not too far from their apartment. Usually it took two years to be able to speak Chinese fluently enough to preach in it. One night, however, as she was speaking at this mission through an interpreter, she noticed he incorrectly interpreted what she said and corrected it in Chinese. It so angered the interpreter that he sat down and she had to finish in Chinese. When her language teacher heard about it, he insisted she speak only in Chinese. From then on that is what she did.

Brother Hensley's malaria weakened him to the point that he took tuberculosis, asthma and then pneumonia. With his life endangered, she decided they would return home. The year was 1922. The doctor warned that she might have to bury him at sea or at one of the ports along the way. She cabled home for money and as soon as it came they were on their way.

He had a coughing attack on the boat that looked like the end. The ship's doctor warned her that he might not make it through the night. Reaching Japan that day, the Jergensons, a missionary family, whom she had previously met, boarded the boat. Sister Hensley asked Brother Jergenson to pray for her husband. He prayed a short simple prayer, "Father, this is your child. You love him more than we do. Please heal him and let him rest. In Jesus' name, amen."

She awakened the next morning to find Brother Hensley up and shaving! Cheerfully he said, "I'm going to get my breakfast." God had healed him during the night. When they walked into the dining room everyone just stood and stared. They could not believe what they saw. The passengers were so thrilled about his healing that they had a birthday party for him and gave him almost one hundred dollars. To his dying day neither asthma nor tuberculosis ever bothered him again.

Both of their fathers were surprised when they met the boat! They fully expected to carry Brother Hensley off, but he had already gained five pounds and was feeling great. He was soon traveling throughout the United States preaching and promoting the missionary cause. A lot of the traveling was in very severe weather, but he never even had a cold.

While they were home, Brother Hensley's father had a stroke. Consequently they settled down, pastored a church and took care of him. Sometime later he had another stroke and died. The Hensleys then traveled again getting acquainted with churches across the land.

Because of civil disturbances in China, Brother Hensley returned to China in November, 1925 by himself; Sister Hensley stayed in the States doing evangelistic work. Part of the time she traveled with Mattie Crawford, a very popular lady evangelist of that time. After two meetings with her, in Twin Falls, Idaho and Portland, Maine, Sister Hensley sensed something was not quite right. They returned to Twin Falls, Idaho, where Mattie was to preach, but because it was such a small place, Mattie left and went back to Los Angeles. Sister Hensley stayed in Twin Falls and took care of the eight people who had been saved in their earlier meetings there. She continued the meeting and God added souls. Her father came and they had services every night for three months. There were then 300 baptized members in the church. Later, Brother Lowe came to pastor the church. In February 1927, fifteen months after her husband had returned to China, she boarded a boat to return also. Doloros, their second child who was born in Oakland, California while they were home, had the measles, but she managed to get through that ordeal without too much inconvenience.

Upon their return to China they went into the interior to Sainan, a city north of Canton, staying there with a couple by the name of Kelly, who were Assembly of God missionaries. This so infuriated other Assembly of God missionaries in China until Brother Kelly finally resigned from that organization. Later, he returned to America and while walking down a street one day in San Francisco praying, the Lord spoke to him and said, "You've been suffering for the name of Jesus, why don't you take a stand for it?" God revealed the truth to him in a greater measure as he walked. Soon he was back in China, preaching the Jesus name message and was faithful to it until he died.

In Kunyui the Hensleys lived close to a river where

natives dumped their garbage and sewage. Also lepers and people with tuberculosis and other contagious diseases bathed in it. Yet this was their only source of drinking water. They had to filter out the mud, then boil the water for twenty minutes to kill the germs.

Superstition in China was rampant. If a person died in a house, no Chinese would ever live in it again. They rented these houses to the "foreign devils" such as the Hensleys. They wondered why these foreigners did not die while living in them.

The Hensleys started a Sunday school in their home and before long they had a large group of children attending. Their language teacher's wife also opened a Christian school. The children really liked the Hensleys. They started taking the message home to their parents. In spite of the parents' warning against the Hensleys, they came anyhow.

One bright, six-year-old boy took the message home to his almost blind father. Soon the father came asking for one of those books his son talked about. They gave him a Chinese Bible. He could not read, but his son quickly learned and read to him. The boy soon wanted to be a Christian and asked to be baptized. Shortly thereafter his father came, along with a cousin, and was saved. That is how revival broke out in that town. The Hensleys were amazed at how easy it was to have revival there.

One day when Sister Hensley was in Canton she met a Swedish missionary lady who told her that at one time she had gone to the city of Kunyui and one Chinese lady came to the Lord. Because of the opposition they were forced to leave without establishing a church. She pleaded for the Lord to send missionaries back there. The

Hensleys felt sure they were the answer to her prayers. They judged that this missionary's prayers had been a great factor in the revival they were having. Several missionaries came from different areas to see how they had revival so soon after being there.

Brother Hensley's manner of ministry was to walk to another town as far as twenty-five miles away early in the morning, stand in the market place and preach, distribute literature, then walk home again. He did this sometimes five days a week. He covered ninety-six towns in this manner.

Soon their area was enveloped in civil war, which created many dangers for them. The account at the beginning of this story took place during this time. The Japanese-Chinese war added to their distress. Their lives were often endangered, but God was good, delivering them from every explosive situation.

During this time, Sister Hensley became very ill with hepatitis and was taken to a hospital in Hong Kong. She spent three months there and the doctor finally recommended she return to America. Although she did not want to leave their work and the girls behind, finally she agreed. God touched her body so that she could make the long journey home. On the boat trip she led her roommate to the Lord. Shortly afterward her girls returned to America also.

At this time, in the spring of 1936, Sister Kinzie and I became acquainted with Sister Hensley. We had just come to the Lord in a small Union church in La Paz, Indiana, and she came there to preach a series of evangelistic meetings. Since she stayed with Sister Kinzie's mother, it afforded us a great opportunity to become well acquainted with her and their work in China. Only God knows how much Sister Hensley helped us in the few weeks she spent in our vicinity.

Brother Hensley was planning to return home also but was detained by the Japanese-Chinese war. The Communists were infiltrating the Chinese army at that time. Trouble was brewing on every side. The authorities told Brother Hensley he would have to flee. He tried to get to Hong Kong, but failing he fled inland.

This turned out to be a blessing, for he was requested by the government to build a hospital for the Chinese. Two days before the hospital was opened the city was bombed by the Japanese. He then left and went further inland. The government then asked him to form medical teams for the army. This afforded him a wonderful open door to witness to the workers he recruited. Many were baptized.

The Hensleys were never able to return to Kunyui because of the war. They heard the town was almost completely destroyed, but all of their people were safe.

Brother Hensley, still in China, was named the secretary of war relief work and was asked to return to America to raise money for it. From the interior, it was necessary to fly over the Himalayan mountains into India and then home via a military plane. He and Sister Hensley traveled for some time in the United States raising the money. She wanted to return to China with him, but was denied because of the war.

He boarded a freighter in New York before it was loaded with ammunition but he was not allowed off anywhere on the trip for fear that someone would disclose what was aboard. They went through the Panama Canal and headed on a zigzag course for Australia. From there they steamed into the Indian Ocean, heading for the Persian Gulf. Fourteen hundred miles out their refrigeration failed and they returned to Australia for repairs.

On a beautiful moonlit night, fourteen hundred miles out of Australia, the captain received a coded radio message that two ships were looking for them.

They were certain someone had discovered what they had on board and where they were headed, then alerted the enemy. Brother Hensley stayed on deck until after midnight talking to a man from his home town of Taft, California, in an endeavor to win him to the Lord. He went to bed and at about 3:00 a.m. he heard an explosion and shooting. He kept the travelers' checks, the money he had raised, in the pocket of a sweater laying on a chair close to the bed so he could grab it in an emergency. He jumped out of bed, dressed quickly, grabbed his sweater (the wrong one) and headed for the deck. There he learned they had only ten minutes to get into the lifeboat. Fortunately the ammunition had not exploded, but the ship was on fire and going down. Everything was lost!

The ship had two lifeboats and one of them was lost when they attempted to put it into the water. Those who had survived the explosion, which included the captain, chief engineer and navigator, twenty-two men in all, loaded into the other boat and rowed feverishly to escape the pull of the sinking ship. The waves were high and fortunately they got far enough away. Taking stock of their supplies they saw one barrel of water had been lost and the food supply was not sufficient for so many men. There were many holes in the boat and all of the able-bodied men climbed overboard and stayed in the water while the holes were being patched.

"Let's head for Ceylon," the navigator suggested. "We might be able to get there in about forty days." All of the men became extremely sore from sunburn and the overcrowded condition added to the distress of the situation. Water was rationed to four ounces per man per day, given out morning, noon and evening. Food was allotted very sparingly, hoping against hope that it would be enough to survive. They caught and cooked one fish, but were never able to catch another. A few jumping fish landed in the boat, and they were eaten raw by those who caught them. The water supply ran out and for two days no one had anything to drink.

Brother Hensley remarked afterward that he thought he would not make it. His tongue swelled, almost closing off his throat. But then, it rained. A part of the boat had canvas on it and they caught enough water to fill up one of their tanks—enough to finish out the journey. Three men died during the trip and were buried at sea.

When some of the men started swearing, the captain forbade it and declared anyone caught stealing food would be thrown overboard. Someone had to pump water out of the boat night and day. Also they found a helmet which they used to bail out water. Everyone had to take their turn in both pumping and bailing. The boat rode so low in the water that waves were constantly washing overboard.

It was a happy, thrilling moment when the lookout cried out excitedly, "I see land in the distance!"

"Everyone stay at your post and don't move!" the captain called out, fearful that they would become so excited they would overturn the boat. They landed on a barren stretch of beach, but fortunately two men were close enough by to tell him where they were. It was India and help arrived soon. There was a hospital within eight miles where they could all be treated. All of them had dysentery and had to be fitted with native clothes. The salt water had rotted most of theirs!

In the meantime, Sister Hensley was helping her father build a new church in Fort Wayne, Indiana. One day as she prayed she saw her husband standing on the deck of the ship with his arms stretched out in a manner that suggested danger. She prayed anxiously for him and then dismissed it. However, she recalled the prayer-vision a few days later when word came from the shipping company that the ship had been torpedoed. The letter had no information as to what had happened or whether there were any survivors. In the anxiety of that hour, however, one of the saints in the Fort Wayne church reassured her that everything was all right. "I had a vision of Brother Hensley struggling in the water and I prayed for him until victory came." After a long time Sister Hensley finally got word in the form of a telegram that her husband was safe in Calcutta, India.

Her husband returned and after he had recuperated and the war was over they were ready to return to China for another term. They were on the west coast in 1949 getting everything ready. Brother Hensley went to San Francisco to put their trunks on the boat, but was involved in an accident in which he received a fractured knee and a brain injury. This forced delay set them back several months. In the meantime word came from China that it was not wise to return there as the Communists were taking over and all missionaries were ready to leave. So the

Hensleys headed for Hawaii and spent the remainder of their missionary days working with the Chinese people there.

While they were in Hawaii they attended a Governor's reception and were honored by Madame Chiang Kai-shek as being very sacrificial and important to the Chinese people. They felt very humbled by that experience, but it certainly helped to know that even the Chinese government knew and honored their labors! It made it all worthwhile.

Both Brother and Sister Hensley were members of the Pentecostal Assemblies of the World when they went to the mission field. Brother Hensley remained with the body throughout his life, but in 1941 Sister Hensley became a member of the Pentecostal Assemblies of Jesus Christ. When that group merged into the United Pentecostal Church she retained her license with it.

Brother Carl Hensley went to meet the Lord on September 24, 1973, with Brother Fred Reed of Troy, Michigan, and I officiating at his funeral. It was an honor to do so. Sister Hensley lives with her daughter, Dolores Priege in Clarkston, Michigan. When possible, she attends the Apostolic Church of Christ in Pontiac, where Brother Roland Baker is pastor and Brother William Parent is Bishop.

Carl and Mable Hensley were faithful warriors, doing their work well and thoroughly. His course is finished, but she, along with many others of us, is awaiting that day when our bodies shall be fashioned like unto His glorious body! (Philippians 3:21).

Carl & Mable Hensley missionaries to China.

Carl Hensley after 30 days in lifeboat.

Carl Hensley after a few weeks rest.

Survivors from shipwreck gather beside hospital in Madras, India, July 17, 1943.

6

THE STORY OF

Aaron and Pearl Holmes

by Mary H. Wallace

"Twenty-five acres of land free!" Aaron Holmes, a tall sharecropper from Florida was excited by the marvelous offer from the government of Liberia, West Africa. "And we can buy more for just a few cents an acre." So with high hopes for a better life Aaron Holmes, his wife and two small children left America and sailed 7,000 miles to Africa.

Clay Ashland near the coast, however, was disappointing with its pseudo-Western look and tiny corrugated-zinc houses not nearly so cool and comfortable as the thatched roofed houses. "There must be better places," Aaron thought as he explored the verdant green hills. But a still greater disappointment hit the farmer two years later when his American wife died.

While looking for a better homesite in the Gola country, Aaron met a beautiful American girl from Arkansas who was a teacher in a Baptist mission. "This is Pearl Graham," a friend introduced Aaron. "And this is her six-year-old son. Pearl's husband is dead." After a whirlwind courtship of only two weeks, the two lonely persons were married.

"I've got our new home all ready," Aaron assured Pearl. "It's high on the bank of the Po River."

But Pearl Holmes, later affectionately called Mother Holmes, was more than an ordinary housewife and mother of three, and she was more than an inspired teacher. She was also a Spirit-filled Pentecostal. Soon she converted her Methodist husband to the Pentecostal faith. "We must have church," they decided. "And we also must teach these children book learning," Pearl insisted.

"But first I must master this Gola dialect," Aaron reminded his little wife.

"Well, I can interpret," Pearl responded firmly. So church services began and plans for a mission school were discussed. The villagers were tremendously excited about the possibility of educating their children.

"We can build mudhuts," someone suggested. "How about a rice farm. They'll need rice for food," another added.

Soon forty students crowded into the Zoradee Mission. The rice farm flourished and Holmes augmented the rice diet with wild pig or deer on special occasions. His early days in the Everglades in Florida had given him good training in marksmanship.

"Good hunting, dear, but let's also hunt for souls," reminded Pearl, ever the enthusiastic evangelist.

And souls *were* filling the mud-and-thatch church—

men in native homespun robes, women in more colorful dresses along with lots of children. No chimes or church bells rang here, but Aaron called the saints to worship on Sunday with a curved cow's horn. The same horn reminded the school children of their classes on weekdays. Then when the men needed to "palaver," the horn was blown again.

"We'll raise more of this good rice," the Holmes planned. The former Floridian wanted citrus—grapefruit and large lemons. "If I can grow a good crop of sugar cane, I think I know where I can get a cane mill," he said. Dreams became reality when a Florida friend sent the mill. From miles around the natives came to make pungent, thick brown molasses which they sold in town for a dollar a gallon.

The Liberians practiced "farm hopping"—a wasteful practice of cutting down valuable timber then making a new rice farm each year. But on the mission farm, the Holmes demonstrated that it was possible to plant rice year after year on the same land.

"Let's plant a large crop of sweet potatoes," the energetic farmer-minister motivated the Golas who had been content with a few hills at a time.

"I can make bread with those sweet potatoes and molasses," Pearl planned and when the aroma of fresh baked bread brought neighbors in, she shared her recipes as she also shared the gospel.

Other children blessed the Holmes home—their own and adopted ones too—so a bountiful harvest of food was a top priority. But the fertile jungle had its problems— pests sometimes destroyed entire crops. Sand-filled winds from the Sahara played havoc with chickens and livestock.

Inside the zinc-roofed house on three-foot mahogany stilts, a rag wick sputtering in a tin plate of palm oil lighted the family table. Then came the day when pests and bad weather hit the mission a devastating blow. But ever resourceful Mother Holmes roasted the pests—locusts—and Daddy Holmes changed his grace from "Father, we thank thee for what we are about to receive. . ." to "Father, *make* us thankful. . . ." And daughter Eugenia Holmes recalled how the children burst into laughter then washed the locusts down with lemonade.

The Golas were a thankful people. There was the unforgettable Sunday when the saints had brought cassava, rice, plantains and chickens for the Sunday morning offering. Boymah the leper crept down and placing the collection bowl carefully on the mud-floor, climbed into it. All he could give was his own diseased body. This sacrifice touched the Holmes deeply.

"I'm leaving tomorrow for Monrovia to be ordained as a minister," he told Mother Holmes firmly.

So he walked sixty-five miles from the Zoradee Pentecostal Mission to Monrovia. In lieu of seminary training, he offered twelve years of ministerial work, and was ordained.

The church was the top priority with the Holmes. On at least one occasion Brother Holmes' demonstration of faith caused his family some anxiety.

The family had gone to a nearby village for a weekly Bible class but when they arrived they were horrified to discover a beautiful young girl tied to a post with her hands covered with straw. She had been caught stealing and the villagers were about to punish her by setting her hands on fire. Brother Holmes knelt by the girl, untied her hands then ordered Mother Holmes, "Tie me up instead."

"Now set my hands afire!" he roared.

"But you did not steal," the villagers protested.

Then while still tied to the post, Brother Holmes began to tell the old story of how Christ was without sin yet He offered Himself for the sins of the world. This dramatic presentation of the gospel made an impact, and the rulers of the village agreed to release the girl.

Such incidents also had influence on the Holmes children as they saw their parents apply gospel principles to everyday problems. Whenever the children were sick they were anointed with oil according to James 5:14 "Is there any sick among you? let him call for the elders of the church; and let them pray over him, anointing him with oil in the name of the Lord." According to Gene Holmes Ashburn the doctor was only called once. Mother Holmes was shocked when her daughter ate poison mushrooms so she sent for the nearest doctor who was forty miles away.

"James said, 'The prayer of faith shall heal the sick,' " Brother Holmes reminded his wife. "Besides that doctor is a dentist."

"Faith without works is dead," Mother Holmes quickly retorted. "That means our faith without the skilled work of a doctor," she insisted. "Even a dentist might have something for mushroom poisoning!"

"In the meantime where's the oil?" Brother Holmes then anointed the girl and prayed. Long before the doctor arrived sixteen hours later, the girl rallied and called for her pet monkey.

In the forties Mother Holmes traveled to America for the very first time after forty-five years on the mission field.

When Georgia Regenhardt from Mississippi was appointed on March 27, 1946 to Maheh mission, Mother Holmes was ready to return to Liberia. Georgia joined her at La Guardia Airport. Their Constellation took off at 11:00 p.m. with thirteen passengers and twenty crew members. They reached Moncton, New Brunswick where a steward cooked eggs and bacon for them but Georgia envied the crew with their fur-lined jackets and hoods.

"I'm so thankful we're together," Georgia confided in the veteran missionary.

"Well, we'll see more of each other when they get the road to Maheh built," Mother Holmes reassured her.

When they arrived in Monrovia, Mother Holmes took charge. "My headquarter's here," she explained as they came to a very old three-story building. "My daughter has a beauty shop here."

Later in July 1947 Mother Holmes again planned to be hostess to another United Pentecostal Church new missionary, Gladys Robinson from Tennessee who was appointed to assist Georgia Regenhardt.

"I'll meet her," Mother Holmes promised but transportation problems delayed Gladys' arrival until August 11 so Mother Holmes had to give up and return to Zoradee.

In the fifties Zoradee had eighty-five students, two teachers, a matron and gospel workers. This thriving work needed additional funds so Brother Holmes set out for America to visit their oldest daughter in Brooklyn and then to raise money for the mission.

Back home in Liberia Mother Holmes said, "I need to go to Monrovia for more supplies. I'll have to go by hammock to Clay then I'll take a truck to the city." So the small, energetic elderly missionary climbed into the hammock carried by four men. In her younger days she had walked and now she dreaded to be a burden on the carriers. "But I'll repay you," she assured them. But the carriers loved the little gray-headed missionary.

Later in Monrovia she sent for the hired men. "God has blessed me and I have already got the supplies. I need to stay here a few days to rest and wait for parcels in customs from the saints in America. You boys go on to Clay by truck then walk on to Zoradee," she instructed then waved goodbye.

As she walked away she slipped and fell on the sidewalk opposite the Postmaster General's home. Her right leg bent back under her body as she fell backward. She tried to pull herself up but fell again harder.

Upstairs in the Postmaster's home a lady saw the accident and called for help. "Come at once. Call my boy to bring my car to take Mother Holmes to the hospital. She's hurt."

When they picked Mother Holmes up she said, "Take me around the corner to my cousin's place. Her cousin, Pearl Teasley, and Rosa Lee Wright from Chicago, who had spent many years on the mission field at Cape Palmas, Liberia, along with other missionaries gathered around Mother Holmes and began to pray.

The leg was swollen from the ankle to the knee. "Are you in pain?" they inquired as they bathed the leg and bandaged it.

The pain was almost unbearable but Mother Holmes asserted, "This is only the work of the enemy, but my God will bring me out." Then the Lord reminded her of the Scripture in Isaiah 41:10: "Fear thou not; for I am with thee: be not dismayed; for I am thy God: I will strengthen thee; yea, I will help thee; yea, I will uphold thee with the right hand of my righteousness."

Although her friends and relatives advised, "You had better go to the hospital. That leg may be broken," Mother Holmes refused to go.

"If I'm going to get well, God will heal me. I put my case in Dr. Jesus' hands." She was determined to let the devil know that God's Word was forever settled in heaven.

Her adopted son, Freddie Holmes, a native doctor who worked only on broken bones, came to help. He said, "Mother, we are sorry to see you in this condition. My father and I will heal your leg and in a few months you will be able to walk. We don't want you to give us a penny. We only want to see you well again."

"Freddie, I know you love me as your own mother, and I thank you so much for your kindness. But, Freddie, I have put my case in God's hands and won't take it out. I'm going to practice what I preach."

Not everyone had Mother Holmes' kind of faith, however, and they whispered, "Very seldom do old people recover from such falls as that."

But down deep in her soul Mother Holmes thought, Is anything too hard for God? And the answer came ringing back, No!

When Brother Holmes received the letter which told of the accident, he wept then answered the letter saying, "Pearl, I was very sorry to hear of your accident, and I prayed at once for God to touch and heal you, and Pearl, I don't see you swinging on a crutch, but I see God, Oh glory, healing your leg and you'll walk again without a crutch, for there is nothing too hard for our God to do."

A few months later just before Brother Holmes set out on his fund-raising tour, he suffered a fatal heart attack.

In Liberia the message of Brother Holmes' death caused an outpouring of sympathy to Mother Holmes now seventy-three years old. Hundreds of tribesmen sat on their wailing mats with hair loosened and ashes rubbed on their bodies. Then they began to chant the life history of the American man who for forty-four years had lived among them and told them the old sweet story of the Christ of Calvary.

Although crippled from the fall and grief-stricken that she could not even attend her husband's funeral, Mother Holmes turned to the eternal God for refuge and rested on His everlasting arms.

Missionary friends, however, saw that the veteran missionary with over sixty-three years of service needed a rest and they began to plan. "We believe that if you go over to America and go to some of those large healing campaigns, that God will heal your leg and you will walk without a crutch.

"Children, God doesn't have to wait until I am in a large crowd to heal me. It is not the crowd, it is the Lord that heals. He did not say, 'Where there is a large crowd there am I in the midst to heal and bless.' He said, 'Where two or three are gathered together in My name, there am I in the midst to heal and to bless.' God is going to heal me whether I am in a crowd or with just a few. I know God will heal me!" Mother Holmes knew in whom she believed.

The small, ninety-eight pound, aged missionary arrived in Brooklyn, New York swinging on her crutches but full of faith in God. Bishop R. C. Lawson invited her and her son and his family to visit in their beautiful home in Panamela, New York.

While there Sister Lawson invited Mother Holmes to a missionary meeting in Connecticut. At the meeting Sister Lawson said, "You all know that Mother Holmes is not strong, and she has just arrived from Africa a few weeks ago. She can only talk for a few minutes as she is not too strong yet. But after she has greeted you, I want you all to gather around Mother Holmes and pray until God touches and heals her feeble body."

Missionaries and elders gathered around the frail veteran missionary then the power of God fell and touched her crippled leg which began to shake. "Mother Holmes, what's the matter?" asked Sister Lawson.

"What's the matter? God has healed my leg, glory to His name!"

When she left church that night someone said, "Mother Holmes, here is your crutch. What must I do with it?"

"That old crutch belongs to Satan. It's not mine!" she said as she stepped out in faith.

Although both Brother and Sister Holmes have now gone on to their reward, Zoradee Mission still stands as a silent witness to the sacrifice and faith of these early Pentecostal missionaries.

Bro. & Sis. Sheets, Mother Holmes & Zula.

Summer of 1950, Sister Pearl Holmes, Zula and Bro.
& Sis. Sheets in New Brunswick, Canada.

Aaron James Holmes.

7

THE STORY OF
Mae Iry

by Nona Freeman

"Someday, Lord, someday," Mae whispered as she dragged a cumbersome mop across an office floor. She paused to stare out a dark window, past twinkling lights below with unseeing eyes. "I know you have called me to China, and I will go—when my children are grown enough to take care of themselves. Someday, sweet Jesus."

A widow with limited education, Mae Iry thanked the Lord for her janitorial job that kept her four children in school and food on the table. God led this Michigan-born lady to Chicago to benefit from William Durham's ministry and the Bible truths he taught. Evidence of the divine hand on her life moved Bishop G. T. Haywood and the elders to ordain her at a conference in Indianapolis.

Childhood polio left Mae with the right half of her face paralyzed. She spoke and ate with the mobile left half of her mouth and charmed everyone with an infectious one-sided grin. She forgot the lonely years of struggle and toil when the time came for her dream to become reality. In preparation to go she visited churches sharing her burden for China and returned briefly to Michigan.

"Joy! Joy! Joy!" she responded to heartwarming news; her daughter Alice and her husband, Robert Sonnenberg, offered to go with her. The trio visited churches across the land, trusting Jesus to supply their fare and their future support. Mae laid down guidelines. "We will never tell or ask anyone for our needs. We will trust in Jesus, who cannot fail, to provide for us."

Leaving time brought more sorrow than the sadness of parting. Forty-five year old Mae had to commit to God's mercy a son serving time in a Louisiana prison.

They reached China in 1921. While they studied the language at Ta T'ung, Elizabeth Stieglitz, a missionary for eleven years, offered to accompany them to a new area. The quartet went north across a rugged range of lofty mountains and chose the town of Taiyoah for their base.

Many days of tedious labor were necessary before they could renovate and occupy the run-down group of buildings that became their mission compound. Language study remained a major concern, but with Stiegie (as her friends called her) services began immediately. Slowly, Robert and Alice gained more fluency in Chinese, while Mae almost dispaired of ever learning it.

Then a strange thing happened, though at first she couldn't make herself understood between services, when she began to preach the Holy Ghost touched that twisted mouth and she gave the Word with anointing and remarkable fluency. Those who knew her on both sides of the world remember an exuberant expression she often gave while preaching, in English or in Chinese; "Joy! Joy! Joy!"

During the language struggle time, Mae walked into the "downside kitchen" where the Chinese cooked their food. An old lady threw herself into Mae's arms weeping in urgent prayer. Suddenly, she broke into English as she received the Holy Ghost, praising God in a language unknown to her, but well-known to the missionary. The Lord spoke to Mae explicitly through the old lady and gave her promises that she would stand on as long as she lived.

From the beginning, an unusually sweet presence of the Lord hovered over Taiyoah Mission and "the Lord added to the church daily such as should be saved" (Acts 2:47). Mae had a special affinity with the poverty-stricken Chinese. She often went to the threshing floor, and sitting on a millstone taught the Word to believers while she cut off the heads of Egyptian corn or maize.

After a year, Mae and Stiegie felt a burden to reach out. They left Alice and Robert in charge of Taiyoh and moved sixty miles away to pioneer a mission at Kwo Hsien. Again, the good seed sown with diligence produced a harvest of souls.

Stiegie went on furlough in the mid-twenties leaving Mae over Kwo Hsien Mission. Soon after Stiegie's return, Alice and Robert asked Mae to relieve them at Taiyoh while they furloughed. As the Sonnenbergs did not return to China, Taiyoh became Mae's mission. The two missionary ladies delighted in taking a few workers with them and holding special services for each other, bringing great spiritual benefits each time.

On her way to Kwo Hsien after furlough in 1933, Stiegie waited a few days in Tientin for Ardley Reynolds, a young man coming from California to help Mae.

Ardley's complete dedication to God's will made him a splendid helper and he learned the language with amazing ease. February, 1934, Mae and Stiegie exchanged revivals again and saw a unique outpouring of the Holy Ghost on both missions. Mae collapsed a few days later from total exhaustion. She had been on the field for thirteen years, helped to start two missions from scratch, and had given herself unsparingly. She did not want a furlough, but one became necessary for survival.

In a letter July, 1934 she stated:

This will be my last letter from China for this term. I say farewell to Taiyoh on August 26th and to Kwo Hsien on the 30th, and sail from Tientsin September 14. Expect to arrive in San Francisco, October 10.

God has been very faithful, always supplying our needs and manifesting His sweet presence in our midst. Oh, how I hate to leave, but God has opened the way, and my health warns me every few days that I need a rest. Of course, America holds those who are dear to me in the flesh. It hurts to leave our dear Chinese, but Ardley Reynolds has succeeded with the language and I believe God will prosper the work in his hands.

A sixteen-year-old deaf-mute is the son of a widow, one of our Christians. Against her will he went to a theater and he came home possessed of a demon. He bit, scratched, kicked, tore his clothing and would hardly eat. He had to be watched day and night. They had to tie him hand and foot to bring him for prayer.

God gave perfect deliverance, now he works on the farm, is kind to his mother and she rejoices. To God be the glory.

Thanks for your faithfulness through the years and hoping by His grace to see your faces. I am very sincerely yours, in His sweet service.

Mae Iry

In 1934 Brother W. T. Witherspoon wrote in the *Pentecostal Outlook* urging all saints to cooperate with the "mite box" plan. "Take a box home and return it with at least a thirty cents offering in it." He said the mite boxes had increased the missionary offerings by one hundred per cent.

On July 13, 1936 Mae wrote:

The days of my furlough are now speedily drawing to a close and what was only pleasant anticipation a short while ago is becoming a sweet but painful memory. I am glad, glad to go back, but parting with friends and loved ones pulls the heartstrings. I will sail from Seattle, Washington, August 10 and reach Tientsin August 31.

I think of Him, who though sinless, suffered the righteous judgment of God to be made perfect through suffering. This cheers my heart, keeps me full of joy and I feel the tug of the cable that reaches to the anchor fastened within the vail. And my love for the Chinese constrains me.

My health is completely recovered. Truly God is good, but the great disappointment now is that no one is going back with me.

Mae learned again that Jesus has His own way of working things out and He is never late. At the last possible minute two young ladies, Kathryn Hendricks and Virginia Weddle, miraculously procured passports, packed their trunks, raised their fares and met Mae at Seattle just in time to board the boat with her headed for China. Kathryn told Mae an unusual fact, "My parents went to Brother Opperman's Bible Conference in Eureka Springs, Arkansas, when I was a tiny baby twenty years ago and you dedicated me to the Lord!"

On reaching China, they went through customs and transferred to a boat going up the Yellow Sea to Tientsin. A train took them from Tientsin to Peking. Rickshas transported them to handle business in the capital city and to the train station.

"Since this will be an overnight ride, girls," Mae said, "I'll book berths for us in a compartment." The compartment turned out to be a small closet-sized room with a tiny aisle and three shelves (the berths) on each side.

Two hefty Chinese men smoked opium on both top bunks and caged pigs, ducks and chickens occupied another one. A lice-infested blanket and the wild scramble for a seat on the delapidated bus that brought them the last forty miles made the humble mission quarters seem a haven of peace and cleanliness.

Excerpt from a letter written in June, 1937 reveals:

The government sent three thousand soldiers to our town and surrounding villages. They are to leave in six months unless war breaks out. There is no actual war that we know of at present.

Thanks to those who helped us pray for our young men

learning to be village workers that were taken by the army and trained to be soldiers. They released them unexpectedly at the Chinese New Year season and five of them are now working full time in the villages and report good interest.

We have a new open door to the mountain villages. Pray much. This is an opportunity among a better class of people. They are not poor enough to come hoping for material gain. The joy and peace of the Christian faith appeals to them.

The Pentecostal Outlook published a clipping in September, 1937, of Marshal Chiang Kai-shek's bid to destroy idolatry, beginning in Canton. Idols, incense stands, joss sticks and joss papers were gathered in large quantities and burned for a beginning. The next step should have been converting a thousand temples into hostels and schools to benefit the public.

Civil unrest and the Japanese invasion defeated the Christian leader's noble plans. Though Mae did not know it when she wrote the letter, an assault on China's borders had already begun in earnest. All government resources of men and means had to be channeled into belated defense against the ominous hordes poised to overthrow the Republic of China.

A letter from Brother and Sister Dan Sheets published in November 1937 said:

The northern part of China lies in ruins, and thousands of lives have been taken. The crash of cannons and bombs shake the earth and homes.

Our American Consular has sent us three urgent let-

*ters to get out and go to a place of safety. Since we do not
know where that would be, we feel to plod on amidst danger
that lost souls might be saved.*

*New souls are coming in, in spite of war, famine, cho-
lera and floods.*

Undeclared war broke out in early July. The Chinese
began retreating by the end of August. Looting, rape and
forced labor became rampant as soldiers left sorrow and
distress in their path. Ardley and a native pastor brought
sixty Christians to the mission for safety in spite of an
armed guard threatening to shoot them. On September
11 three Japanese bomber planes flew over Taiyoh. The
Lord gave Mae a Scripture.

> *"Yea, the sparrow hath found an house, and
> the swallow a nest for herself, where she may lay
> her young, even thine altars, O LORD of hosts, my
> King, and my God. Blessed are they that dwell in
> thy house: they will be still praising thee" (Psalm
> 84:3-4).*

The Japanese bombed Taiyoh the next day. Steel
splinters from bombs landed in the mission compound,
but without harm to anyone. A Christian Japanese general
stationed in Taiyoh told them later that pilots had been
ordered to bomb the mission with its conspicious white-
washed walls. As the planes approached, a dark cloud
moved in, obscuring the pilots' vision. They flew over the
cloud and dropped their bombs on another place. When
the pilots looked back at the cloud they plainly saw a thick
cluster of angels hovering over the mission. The fright-

ened pilots asked not to be ordered to bomb the mission again.

The mayor of Taiyoh and a number of prominent community leaders came and asked Mae what could be done. She said, "Let us pray." Some of them were nominal Christians and together they knelt in prayer asking the Lord for guidance. After prayer, she advised them to welcome the invaders with gifts. Mae and Ardley accompanied the Chinese with a welcome banner and gifts and food when an armada of Japanese armored cars arrived on the 16th of the month. This strategy averted the wholesale slaughter meted out to towns that resisted them.

The Japanese accepted their welcome and took over. The calvary came on September 26 and the big army entered the city the first of October. No one could understand their language and confusion reigned. Young women and older girls fearfully hid in vegetable cellars, under stacks of grain stalks or any place they could find. Many ran to the mission for safety, as a systematic search began for Chinese soldiers.

Older parents who had hidden their daughters and the young women of their households feared they would be found and molested. They begged Mae to round them up and bring them to the mission, afraid of reprisals if they tried.

"I went, being an old woman, and having God with me," Mae said. Few of the militia spoke either Chinese or English and had every right to keep her out which they tried to do with both guns and swords levelled in her direction. "But, Jesus gave me favor," Mae continued. "I went from house to house and brought them in. The officers helped me, showing the courtesy they reserve for the aged. . .my crooked mouth probably helped too," she added with a wry grin.

Up to five hundred refugees jammed the mission at times. The Japanese asked Mae to send them away. When she refused, they sealed the compound, allowing no one to either leave or enter.

Just before the city fell, several business men asked Mae to store their supplies of wheat in the deep cellars beneath the mission, knowing the Japanese would seize them when they took control. "If you need grain," they said, "help yourself." The carrots that Mae had stored earlier and the wheat sustained them during the time they could not leave the mission to hunt supplies.

They ground the wheat by hand to make coarse flour. When they ran out of the shortening desperately needed to make bread from the crude flour, they prayed. Just before daybreak Kathryn answered a knock on the door. A small man dressed in black stood there; no one had seen him before or since that morning. "I have brought you three dressed pigs," he said. Though they could not understand how he got past the guards, they welcomed fresh meat and joyfully rendered lard for baking.

Just before Mae returned from furlough, the nucleus of a Red Army took over thirteen counties of Shansi Province with much bloodshed and suffering. They claimed to rob the rich to help the poor, but everything went to support the army. They became too powerful for the National Army to promise protection against them.

Now, fleeing deserters from the Chinese army joined the Red ranks and spread destruction from their strongholds in the mountains. In the beginning, the Japanese bought some of their supplies, thus seeming more orderly than the Communist terror that seized property, murdered and raped indiscrimminately. The Reds disguised themselves as villagers; they burnt bridges and destroyed railway lines, causing the death of untold innocents as the Japanese wiped out whole villages in reprisal.

Large numbers of refugees camped in the church which made services impossible. Five missionary personnel aided by national workers did the only thing possible—an intensive personal evangelism thrust. They witnessed to and prayed with each one, and had them memorize verses of Scriptures. The Japanese began rebuilding the empty shell of Taiyoh-town after a few months. Slowly, restrictions eased and the missions overburdened with forced guests began to disperse, cautiously learning how to live under occupation.

The first letter Mae could send out ended with these words;

Many times since the war started I have been at wit's end, but a Voice in my soul said, "God has a way." And He always has. "God is our refuge and strength, a very present help in trouble."

He never allowed fear to enter my heart for a moment, but joy just bubbled up. There is none like Jesus!

A Christian Japanese general stationed at Taiyoh occasionally came to the mission to enjoy a few moments of peace and quiet away from the harshness of war. He often assured Mae that she would not be sent to a concentration camp.

Revival fires swept the mission in the lull and the Holy

Ghost fell in every meeting.

Out of stationary, Mae wrote a letter on wrapping paper March 22, 1938. She told of a discussion with Pastor Li about the large number who had repented and been baptized: 416 in a month, 289 of that number men-business men, professionals and scholars.

"I am almost afraid," she said. "How shall we shepherd so many? My heart fails."

"Never let it worry you," Pastor Li answered. "We prayed and preached for years, and sowed good seed. It must grow. As we thin our grain, no doubt these will be tested and thinned. But remember, you did not go out in the hedges and ask—say nothing of compelling them to come. God got behind them with His whip (the Japanese) and drove them to where they had to listen to God's Word and repent or be lost. Don't forget the word Jesus gave you at wit's end corner; God has a way!"

Early the next morning the Lord wakened her with Isaiah 38:2. She got up and read, "Then Hezekiah turned his face toward the wall, and prayed unto the LORD."

"The Lord reminded me so sweetly," Mae said. "Hezekiah turned to the wall where he could see nothing and do nothing, but trust in God and reach for God alone. And the Lord said, 'I have heard. . .I have seen. . .I will!' So, as the Chinese say, 'I put my heart down and go on.' "

By the end of 1938, concern over Kathryn's health troubled Mae. When she found her hard-working helper coughing up blood, she got military passes from the Japanese to take her to a hospital. After three weeks the doctor said she had acute bronchitis and should either return to the United States or go to the coast for a rest.

A stay at the coast brought only slight improvement,

but Kathryn wanted to stay in China. She had to return to Taiyoh in a box car, suffered a relapse and lay delirious for three weeks. By this time the Japanese had brought in a doctor and a few nurses and the friendly general sent a nurse to care for Kathryn full time. The doctor discovered she had tuberculosis. Nothing remained but to go home in a ship's hospital. The doctor feared she would die on the way. She not only made it, but lived to return later to China. That's another story.

After a lengthy silence, word came that Stiegie still held the fort in Kwo Hsien, cheering Mae, though she missed the sweet fellowship they enjoyed before the invasion.

A letter written October 18, 1939, and published in the *Pentecostal Outlook* states.

Greetings from war-torn, bandit-ridden, water-soaked China. Eighteen days of continual rain has caused such floods and danger that even the oldest citizen cannot remember hearing of the equal before. The Chinese bury their dead on top of the ground and pile dirt on the coffins. The floods have washed the coffins out of their places to swirl in the dirty black waters rushing through the streets of the city. This has caused a fever epidemic in spite of all the Japanese, foreigners and Chinese could do.

The rain has washed away whole villages until nothing remains to show where they stood. Our large church and other buildings here at the head station, and several outstations, have taken many weeks of work and many dollars to repair, but we can see our way through at last.

Prices are very high and there will be much suffering. Please pray that many will find God in this time of distress. Twenty-six have received the Holy Ghost in a few days.

A year later, in 1940, Mae reported abundant crops; ample cabbage, carrots, onions, Kohlrabi and Chinese cabbage were laid in for winter use. Best of all, the Japanese showed a pleasant courtesy, often asking if they could do anything to help her. Ardley Reynold's return to California, after seven years of faithful service, was made more arduous and dangerous by the complications of war.

Brother Witherspoon received a letter from Mae in February 1941, telling of deep heart-hunger and the Spirit of the Lord searching hearts in her work.

She stated on a circular letter sent out on November 1, 1941:

The last of my foreign co-workers has returned to the U.S. Brother Hodges fulfilled the five years he promised and greatly blessed the work.

I became ill six months ago and have suffered frequent bouts, diagnosed by the Japanese doctor as heart trouble. Though weakened by a stroke and not fully recovered herself, Sister Stieglitz came to minister to me during a difficult time.

The Japanese froze our assets on the first of August, but allow us a small amount each month to purchase supplies. They are kind to us and have not restricted evangelistic meetings in the villages or here on the mission. They have drafted young men and even girls for military training, which affects our attendance.

I have Joy! Joy! Joy! in my heart and feel more than ever to stay here and occupy until He comes or makes a change. I have never considered leaving, by God's grace. Jesus knows the future. I am resting in Him without fear. The command "Be still and know that I am God." is still in effect.

Early in 1942 Mae noticed that courtesy had cooled and the friendly, Christian Japanese general had evidently been transferred. She did not know about Pearl Harbor and the start of the war until later. Her mail had reduced to a few personal letters from December, and she couldn't understand a gradual clamp-down of restrictions.

The Japanese told her she could still visit Chinese homes. But she found this a trap, for spies hurried to the houses she visited and brutally interrogated the saints afterward. By February they restricted her to two companions, a Swedish missionary lady and her Chinese Bible woman, and forbade her to have prayer with them.

Early on the morning of March 15, 1943, Japanese soldiers came and told her to pack her things. They, however, would check and decide what they would allow her to take. While she hurriedly gathered a few things together, more soldiers came on the orders of the Japanese officials and carried everything belonging to Mae and the mission to the yard. A large crowd gathered.

The officers came and chose the items they wanted from the heap of furniture, musical instruments, typewriters, folding organs, mimeograph machine, sewing machines, linens and dishes. They allowed her to take two trunks and three suitcases. When she left for the railway station just before dark, a truck drove out of the mission carrying the rest of her belongings to be sold at auction.

Two solemn rows of sad-eyed Chinese lined both sides

of the street from the mission on the north side of town to the station on the south. No one dared speak. Her two friends supported Mae on the long walk, shepherded by stern soldiers.

After a week's confinement at a seized Catholic Mission Station, they took her to an "assembly camp," as the Japanese called it, at Wei Hsien, a city at the base of the Shantung, Peninsula. The camp, which had been a large Presbyterian Mission, was now converted to top security with guards at the gates, electrified wire on the top of the walls and high pillboxes with guards.

Grace Chang, a naturalized Chinese-American repatriated on the *Gripsholm*, December 1, 1943, brought the first word of Mae after her internment. Excerpts from the lengthy letter she wrote Mae's daughter states;

Your mother was firm in her decision to remain in China until they put her out. She refused to apply for repatriation. The Japanese took over the mission and she wants to be there when the war is over. She is the only one who knows the details of the mission property. Though she lost everything but the contents of two trunks and her suitcases, the loss of this world's goods doesn't mean much to her.

She brought plenty of bedding and warm clothes, except her coat was too thin. However a missionary leaving gave her a lovely, fur Chinese garment, so she is fixed for winter. She had no bed but another missionary gave her an iron bedstead with springs.

Since our camp was for civilians, we did not have the harsh treatment meted out to war prisoners. We numbered 2,500, seventeen different nationalities, and only 250 came home on the boat. I was with your mother and twelve others in a classroom converted to a dormitory. On our depar- ture they transferred her to a small room with a room- mate, whom she knew and liked very much. Her room has a small coal stove.

Everyone in camp shares work, governed by the in- ternees and their committees and not the Japanese. The whole camp has been wonderfully organized and an amaz- ing amount of comfort has been wrought out of chaos. What a mess it was when we arrived! Now, small gardens grow in front of the little rooms, and everything possible has been done to make things comfortable. We had a Pentecostal prayer meeting every Friday night, and other services too. A spirit of cheerfulness and helpfulness prevailed in the camp most of the time.

One who had been a missionary found camp bearable, but it was very hard for business people taken out of a life of ease and plenty. The first month was the hardest for all of us. Those who could trust the Lord proved once more that "underneath are the everlasting arms." Those without confidence in God suffered physically and mentally.

American and British doctors cleaned and organized the hospital on the premises, with the help of interned nurses, and together they carefully watched over our health. Your mother spent eleven days in the hospital last summer with a touch of dysentery. She is well now and does not have to work as she is aged. She peels vegetables or some small task when she feels like doing something.

We all lost weight at first, but no longer. The food is plain. However, we got a little meat every day in stew or soup. The camp bakery gave us good bread to fill up on. For breakfast we had stale bread boiled in water to a mush and tea. Our cooks became miracle workers after the first month, finding new ways to make nicer meals.

We would buy eggs, fruit, peanuts and honey from the canteen and divide it evenly among us. Your mother didn't like sweets so she would trade her honey for peanuts. We fourteen would each contribute some of the ingredients for pancakes that we cooked on a little stove we made.

Your mother had enough money to sustain her for a year—only allowed to save a hundred dollars a month. She can get more from the U.S. through the Swiss Consul later. Everything considered, she is getting along well and has the desire of her heart to stay in China.

Mae spent two and a half years at Wei Hsien. Food became scarce and conditions had degenerated to intolerable when an American plane suddenly began to circle over the camp on August 17, 1945. The whole camp ran to an open space, waving flags and pieces of cloth. With no airstrip near, seven soldiers parachuted down to a poignant welcome. The Japanese backed off and the Americans took over. Joy filled the camp.

The plane called *Armored Angel* came first, dropped the soldiers and returned several times followed by an armada of planes. Small parachutes rained from the sky bearing food, medicine and needed supplies.

A letter from Mae October 22, 1945, states:

We were evacuated to Peking by airplane on October 15, 1945. The Navy will care for us for a month—we are fed army rations—very, very good. As soon as possible we are to go on our own. I had rheumatism for eight months, now recovered—well and strong. God never fails.

I cannot get to the interior yet, no transportation. Everything gone there except some bedding. I am anxious to return to my station, but good prospects to work for the Lord here—will find my corner in Peking until then.

Mae worked in every avenue of service to her Lord she could find while she waited for railway repairs that would allow her to return to Shansi province. However, civil war raged in North China.

She said of Peking:

Here are open doors in every place. From the Spirit-filled Pentecostals to the rich, modern and popular churches—everyone is busy in their own line and way. God's heart must ache because of things done and taught by those who claim to be called and go forth in His name. I do praise the Lord for those who still preach the cross, a Spirit-filled life, separation from the world and His soon coming.

A vicious Red army fought for control in the vacuum left by the Japanese retreat. They took Taiyoh in August, 1946, and Mae's Swedish missionary friend became a prisoner of the Communists for four months of cruelty. She survived with her endearing sweet spirit intact, but her account caused Mae to groan. "If ever China needed Christ Jesus the Lord, it is now."

Mae wrote in November 1946:

There is a great move toward God among the youth. Some of it seems real and I pray God may deepen and establish them in Him. I'm afraid if Jesus were here in person He would say to many leaders now what He said to

Peter: "Thou savorest not the things that be of God, but those that be of men."

May the Lord help us to humble ourselves in prayer, waiting on Him for the message of the hour—the anointing of the Spirit and trusting Him for the harvest—it will be sure!

Joy filled Mae to learn that Stiegie and Kathryn had sailed from the United States in October enroute to China. She anticipated working together again with co-workers and friends so dear to her heart. But about that time, the belligerent Red Army accelerated civil war on broadening fronts. Their cruel advances let Mae read correctly the handwriting on the wall: the Communists would take China. Reports of devastation and suffering humanity behind them crushed her loving heart beyond endurance. Weakness overwhelmed her and nothing remained but to return to the United States early in 1947.

Tender care, rest, nourishment and absence of peril and strain speedily restored Mae physically. Precious fellowship with the saints in America refreshed her spirit. Of her years under Japanese occupation and the concentration camp she said:

Oh how sweetly God watched over me and those who put their trust in Him. In these places we prove that everything He has promised us is sure—very real. The sweetness of daily companionship with Jesus, the knowledge of His purpose in permitting us to suffer with Him, outweighs every hardship, every disappointment and every pain.

Insistent invitations came from the churches and the seventy-one year old veteran answered calls hither and yon. She spoke with direct earnestness, keen perception, and always, threads of joy bound her message together. Over and over listeners heard the same request, "Pray that God will open the door to Shansi Province, again. I am ready to return."

Along the way she sent frequent letters to China, always longing for word from her dear ones there.

Brother David Gray remembers Mae saying, "Jesus seeks workers who are able to stand alone, drawing strength from hidden springs that no one can see. They can remain green while others dry up. Send your roots down deep and tap the hidden reservoirs of God."

She also taught him this favorite poem;

Isn't it strange that folks like you and me are builders of eternity,
And each is given a bag of tools,
A shapeless mass, and a book of rules
And each must make ere life has flown,
A stumbling block, or a stepping stone.
(Author unknown)

"Remember," she said, "tools are bodies and minds, shapeless mass is the life ahead, and the book of rules is the Bible."

The Bamboo Curtain closed against the rest of the world in 1949 with complete Communist control of China. A curtain of mercy is appropriate on the last days of a weary pilgrim with worn-out heart, worn-out body and hope deferred that gradually faded to no hope. Mae re-

169

turned to Michigan for the final chapter.

One thing is certain; the last word here and the first one before the throne had to be the same—the theme of her triumphant life—Joy! Joy! Joy!

Mae Iry on furlough, 1935.

Mae Iry in China.

Kathryn Hendricks, Mae Iry, & Virginia Weddle just before sailing to China August 9, 1936.

August, 1939, Taiyoh, North China, back row, lt. to rt. Ardley Reynolds, Frank Gray, Arthur Hodges, front row May Gray and Mae Iry.

Lt. to rt. Elizabeth Stieglitz, Arthur Hodges, Virginia Weddle, Mae Iry, Kathryn Hendricks and Ardley Reynolds, June 28, 1937.

Mae Iry, Kathryn Hendricks and Virginia Weddle on cart going to the villages.

8

THE STORY OF
Georgia Regenhardt

by Nona Freeman

An ordinary cottage prayer meeting at Corinth, Mississippi, in 1935, suddenly became extraordinary for Georgia Regenhardt. The Holy Ghost flooded every recess of her being with infinite sweetness. While she spoke fluently in a language unknown to her, a vision of dark, silent faces with pleading out-stretched hands surrounded her.

"I am called to Africa!" she whispered to herself in wonder. Excitement banished sleep that night as she retraced her life from its beginning on May 29, 1902, at Memphis, Tennessee. Only a faint memory remained of her father, Will T. Younger, who died when she was five years old and her sister Gazelle, was eight.

Georgia recalled the pleasant stay with her grand-parents, "Ma" and "Pop" Carothers near Adamsville, Tennessee, and playing with her Uncle Melvin, her own age. Then, her mother, Maud, married again and shoved her family into hardships and unhappiness. Books of exploration and travel at school became Georgia's refuge, transporting her from drudgery and trouble to adventure.

She regretted the end of her schooling between the seventh and eighth grade, but not her marriage at fifteen to Henry Regenhardt in May, 1917.

"We had love and hard work and little else," she thought. "Trying to make a home in the aftermath of World War I made us realize we needed God's help, and things improved slightly after we joined the Missionary Baptist church.

"Just when I had given up on a family, Kathadene came in 1923," Georgia mused. "Then Marie arrived in 1926 and William Conrad in 1928. How I love my little children.

"We had few material benefits, but I've tried to teach them everything I know and all I could find in books. I took them on long walks and pointed out the beauty of the world around us, learning from books on nature.

"I remember the community singing schools that taught us to sing by shaped notes. Without piano or organ, we tuned up with 'do, re, mi, do' and practiced at home. 'Kathadene, this line of notes is alto, you sing it while Marie sings the soprano notes.' It sounded beautiful to me.

"Because the church was too distant for walking and we had no means of transport, I had Sunday school with Bible picture cards and coloring books. I read the Bible to my children and we prayed together. Then two years ago in March, 1933, Henry got sick and five days later left me alone with our three young ones, ten, seven and five years old.

"Without money, insurance or security, I determined to keep us together and refused different offers to 'take one of the children.' I believe God directed kind friends and family to help me move from Tennessee to Corinth where Brother A. D. Gurley's tent meeting changed my life. I will never forget how light and clean I felt when he baptized me in the name of Jesus.

"Now God has called me to Africa. . . ." She stopped reminiscing and lifted her heart in prayer:

"O Lord, however long the road may be, help me prepare myself to go when the time comes."

Georgia worked in a factory to support her family and arose an hour or two earlier than necessary every day to study the Bible and pray. Determined faith brought her victoriously through the next obstacle, a serious lung disease. Without fanfare, she cherished her call as a guiding star shining secretly within, that promoted courage for every battle.

In the meanwhile she read and studied, taught Sunday school and promoted missions enthusiastically and helped wherever her pastor directed with cheerful willingness.

With the advent of Pentecostal Bible Institute at Tupelo, Mississippi, in 1945, Georgia became a student and dorm mother. Eighteen-year-old Will considered himself grown; her two daughters had married and Georgia's ten-year-old dream turned into a possibility.

175

The Foreign Missions Board appointed her to Liberia, West Africa on March 27, 1946, before school ended. The ailing L. E. Haney family needed someone to take care of Maheh mission, Liberia, West Africa while they came home on furlough. As rapidly as the last few pieces of a jigsaw puzzle fall into place, God's timing moved Georgia toward Africa.

Georgia ate Christmas dinner in Brooklyn, New York, with Pastor Rubin's family and they took her to the Pan American office at 8:00 p.m. where Mother Holmes, veteran missionary returning to Liberia, waited for her. Witnessing her friend's grieved farewells to her children when the limousine came to take them to La Gaurdia Airport at 9:00 p.m. reminded Georgia of the sorrowful parting with her own children earlier.

The Constellation took off at 11:00 p.m. with thirteen passengers and twenty crew members. They reached Moncton, New Brunswick, at 2:00 a.m. and walked half a block on ice to a station. A steward cooked eggs and bacon and made coffee for both the passengers and the crew.

They returned to the heatless plane knifed by freezing wind. Just as they wrapped up in blankets against the cold, a mechanical fault requiring repairs necessitated going back to the station. Shivering in a suit and light-weight coat, Georgia envied the mechanics and said to Mother Holmes, "I wish we had fur-lined Eskimo suits with fur-lined hoods like they have."

Repairs took three hours, and three more hours passed after take-off before Georgia's feet which were huddled under blankets got warm. Her watch showed 2:30 in the afternoon when they landed for an hour at Santa

Maria in the Azores Island under a dark, star-studded sky. She set her watch forward to the correct time and bought five richly embroidered handkerchiefs for a dollar each.

"I'm so thankful we're together," Georgia told Mother Holmes, "since you've gone through all of this before." She struggled to understand the English spoken by the Portuguese when they reached Lisbon, Portugal, at 3:00 a.m. for a twelve hour stay. They welcomed time for rest at a splendid hotel, took an interesting walk and had lunch with four people who were also enroute to Liberia; a man and his wife returning to their job with Firestone, and two men going for road construction. Georgia rejoiced to learn a road would soon be built near Maheh Station.

After a short stop at Dakar, Senegal, they took off on the last leg of the journey. On the way, flight attendants showed passengers the cockpit by turns. They reached Robert's Field in Liberia at 1:00 p.m., December 28, 1946.

Mother Holmes and Georgia rode the bus forty miles to Monrovia and a humble, very old, three-story house rented by Mother Holmes for her headquarters in town. Her daughter had a beauty shop there and served as hostess. Georgia wrote first impressions to her family:

The ocean comes right up to the town and gives us a nice breeze. There are a few nice houses though most of them are old and delapidated. Some are made from zinc roofing, walls and all. No screens, everyone has his own mosquito net. I bought one and a pure white helmet yesterday.

This place is so scattered, I got a blistered heel walking to all the offices, attending to business and permits.

177

I wish you could see the scene around me. The trees are banana, coconut, grapefruit and orange. Some of the small children are well-dressed, but many are naked. They call food, "chop." It's mostly "soup" (stew of some kind) over rice, not refined or even husked good.

I've just had "chop" and the beef soup had a strange odor, but don't get the wrong idea—this is my Africa. I think Liberia is the most beautiful country I've ever seen. It only needs to be developed and opened up. I'm also sure I'm going to miss you all.

Georgia rode a motor launch three hours down the St. Paul River on December 30 with other passengers. An hour's walk brought them to a Lutheran Mission, which was still another twelve hours' walk from Maheh. She looked, listened and learned, while waiting for the carriers Brother Haney struggled to find. Safe drinking water must be boiled for twenty minutes and filtered. Quinine or a substitute is essential to prevent malaria. The Firestone Rubber Company near Robert's Field will be an alternate source of supplies, and raw palm oil over rice plays havoc with an American stomach! Miss Zeigler, a nurse at the U.S. Public Health Clinic on the mission, told her the native-born Liberians are easier to work with than the American-Liberians and their descendants.

The two groups of four carriers designated to hammock or carry one person could not be found. Instead, Brother Haney sent four workmen he considered to be reliable. Hiding her trepidation behind a smile, Georgia crossed the river in a motorboat and started down the trail carried by four strange men. She could not understand one word of their pidgin English. Most of her luggage remained at the mission to be brought to Maheh later.

Shoulder-high saw grass turned to snarled greenery overhead which blotted out the sun and made somber going on a slippery path that was treacherous with convoluted roots and fallen limbs. She walked for short intervals whenever she thought she could make it to rest the carriers, and wrinkled her nose at the constant sweet-rotten smell of decaying vegetation. Twice the Headman carried her over swift rushing streams, and led her across several precarious footlogs.

When night made its usual rapid descent, on the travelers beside a river shrouded in jungle blackness, Georgia felt rather than heard the near-rebellion of her carriers. In Mississippi and again in New York, the Lord gave her a promise, "The eternal God is thy refuge, and underneath are the everlasting arms. . . ." (Deuteronomy 33:27). In a time of consternation He renewed the promise with assurance, and minutes later a voice called out of the darkness, "Hello! Hello!" An educated lawyer and government official's wife from Monrovia had come to their rubber plantation in the "bush" (local word for jungle) for a few days' rest. She had been a friend to the Haneys and welcomed the new missionary to a glistening white, mosquito-net covered bed for a needed night of rest after her strenuous day on the trail. Best of all, Georgia could understand her. The lunch and boiled water Miss Zeigler gave her had lasted for the day.

The carriers chanted in a happier tone when they started out the next morning and jogging turned to dancing as they neared Maheh. Georgia had learned firsthand the difficult and painful manner of transport through the

179

bush. It's no wonder Georgia thought she had traveled ninety miles from Monrovia, though it was less than half that distance.

"I don't mind having a hard mud floor; I will put linoleum on it anyway," she told Brother Haney about her house under construction. "I hate to think of these poor men carrying ninety pound bags of cement on their heads."

Even while the Haneys gave Georgia a royal welcome, she could not help but dread the awesome responsibility ahead when they left on furlough in March and she would find herself in charge of the mission. Maheh had neatly scraped paths, extensive orchards and gardens, with smooth lawn around the main buildings. Of the fourteen buildings, only three, the combination school-chapel and two residences, had metal roofs. The rest utilized mud and palm thatch construction. All had partitions (and ceilings, if ceiled) of bamboo mats. Tropical deterioration on these edifices required continual repair and replacement, demanding a corp of workmen.

Nineteen boys and five girls, from seventeen or eighteen years down to eight months, had to be housed, fed, trained, schooled, disciplined, and hopefully brought to a saving knowledge of Jesus Christ. Joyous testimonies of thankfulness from the children for the new missionary's arrival won Georgia's heart and sweetened her contemplation of the demanding task ahead.

On January 6, 1947, Sister Haney took Georgia on a two hour walk to neighboring Beajah Mission, headed by the Otis Petty family. She met Pauline Gruse, who returned with them to Maheh on her way to Monrovia.

In an excerpt from a letter to her family dated January 12, 1947 Georgia stated:

*"Sister Gruse has decided to come over and work with
me while the Haneys are away. Sweet lady and well recommended. I will certainly need her.*

*While we were at the Petty's, a whole delegation of rel-
atives and town and district officials came to ask if we
would take a five-day-old baby girl whose mother died at
birth. They knew the baby would die otherwise, for nine
out of ten babies born here do not live. We could not give
an answer until we talked to Brother Haney, who left the
decision up to Sister Gruse and me.*

*Early the next morning a whole congregation of the
family and officials came to Maheh with the father bringing the naked baby wrapped in a ragged scrap of blanket.
Since Brother Haney was sick, Sister Haney and I took
them to the chapel. She typed an agreement and explained
we would try to raise the child to serve Jesus and we
wanted them to know more about Jesus, too. Those who
could not sign their names made their mark on the paper.*

*We gave the baby an oil bath, dressed her and tried
to feed her, though she could only take a few drops at a
time. This makes twenty-five children on the mission.*

*Brother and Sister Haney are going to try for an air-
plane while they are on furlough, and he has started
building a runway. The new road is still a rumor. They
are opening an iron ore mine nearby and talk of a railroad
—no telling how long it will be before it is built. It's so
hard to get materials to the mission. Think of it! With a
plane we could get to Monrovia in fifteen minutes.*

*Brother Haney can make almost anything and almost
out of nothing. I must tell you about our shower bath. It*

is a five foot square house with a palm thatch roof, concrete floor and ample drain. A half drum sits high on a scaffold at the back of the building. The boys fill the drum every day, the sun warms the water and a pipe with a spray on the end brings it inside—such a blessing!

Nine letters from Georgia's children in one mail package cushioned a disappointment. The doctor had ordered ill Pauline Gruse home. Hope revived with a fervent letter from Gladys Robinson wanting to come immediately.

Joannah, the new baby, thrived and became a comfort to Georgia, struggling to learn how the mission operated, and the native customs. The children's menu had rice for a staple with varying sorts of soup (stew) over it—country beans, monkey, fish or birds. Yams, cassava, eddoes, pumpkin and greens, with tropical fruits, completed their diet. Everyone had a job. The boys cut grass and bush, brought water, ran errands, tended gardens, cooked and did a share of the washing. The girls took care of babies, did housework, helped with washing and cooking. She made a mental note to work towards using only girls for cooking and household tasks. The older ones received a small remuneration for the work they did. Each child became responsible for his or her own laundry at a certain age. Excerpt from a letter to her children written in February 1947:

We are getting a 500 acre grant of land for the mission so the natives cannot crowd us by cutting the bush and planting farms too close. We will need the timber for

*building, the land for hunting and farming. I have big air
castles and do not know how many will fall to the ground.
I am new, and will have some disappointments before I
settle down to the usual run. It is something to keep me
interested and if I hitch my wagon to a star, I will probably accomplish more than if it isn't hitched to anything.*

*Put my picture on the cedar chest. When any of you
need to be corrected about something, just look at me there
and know I mean for you to behave. You should hear me
bragging on my family. I hope you live up to it.*

Every day brought its own adventure. The boys that
fished, killed a five foot snake one day and Brother Haney
killed two monkeys for "chop." Georgia wrote home for
knee-length boots to help her elude blood—thirsty mosquitoes and black gnats. The weird sound of drums beating in the nearby village of Maheh disturbed her especially
when she learned its connection with death. The natives
would have a frenzied session of singing or chanting and
dancing a week after a death, then live in fear of the dead
person's spirit until they could have another "play" to
"cross them over" a year later.

Georgia looked forward to every church service. The
young men shook their tambourines emphatically; everyone sang with fervor, listened with hunger and prayed
earnestly. They refreshed her spirit.

She would live in the Haneys' house in their absence.
But, thinking of the need later, Brother Haney worked
frantically to complete her house and the "airport,"
though he kept moving by determination alone. Azmona,
the headman, confided in Georgia that the workmen
would not cooperate, waiting for the Haneys to leave and

the new missionary to take over, with hopes of less work and more pay!

When the Haneys packed their personal belongings, Georgia realized how many gaps had to be filled. She bought thirty hens, a homemade chest of drawers and some linens from Sister Gruse, and wrote her family for help on smaller items: cotton or lisle hose, hairpins, hair combs, safety pins, straight pins, air mail stationary and toilet soap. "Send as you can," she said, "and some eats would be welcome; dried fruit, dried beans, candy and peanuts."

Brother Haney turned the mission over to Georgia on the first of March and would leave as soon as carriers could be found. Her boxes shipped by Brother Rubin from New York arrived opportunely containing a twelve-gauge shotgun, kitchen-ware and food. Her steamer trunk still tarried somewhere along the way.

Instructions from Missionary Secretary Director Wynn Stairs the second week of March sent shock waves through both missions. Since both of the Pettys' health had failed, they were told to close Beajah, turn everything over to Maheh and come home. The same mail however, brought good news; Gladys Robinson was appointed to Liberia.

Brother Stairs did not specifically mention the children of their mission. The Pettys asked if Georgia could take them, and offered to stay with her to help until May, hoping Gladys could be there by then.

Dreading the responsibility of twenty-five children, Georgia wondered how she could possibly manage twenty-two more. But allow them to be abandoned? Unthinkable! Undergirded by prayer and God's Word, she found courage to say, "I'll do my best," and walked to Beajah on March 15 to give the Pettys her answer. They made plans to split the move to ease adjustments on both sides.

While Georgia wondered how far her $60.00 a month allotment would go, she dipped into a diminished reserve to buy the rest of the Haneys' food and a few other things. Banjo Lansanah made "sweet mouth" (flowery speech) at their farewell service on the sixteenth of March. He was District Overseer and Joannah's father. All of the enormous crowd who came expressed their gratitude to the Haneys, who left the following day for Monrovia.

Letter addressed to "Dearest Everybody" on March 21, 1947:

Here I am, a lone missionary in the wilds of Africa—so busy I can hardly eat or sleep. I not only have the work the Haneys did, but am cleaning up and making room for the Pettys, with continual interruptions. The only thing, my mind is so busy, it doesn't allow me to sleep much. When I get everything straightened and going good, I will relax more.

When Brother Haney got to Waterside, he took part of my things out of the steamer truck and nailed them up in wooden boxes and sent them back by the men who carried for them. I hope to send four men down for the trunk tomorrow. They are so afraid of anything big, whether it's heavy or not. It scares me when I think of trying to get my refrigerator here. And I have a letter that it and the rest of my freight will arrive soon.

I don't know how I'll pay for everything but depend on my verse, "My God shall supply all your needs according to His riches in glory." He has never failed.

185

The teacher came Tuesday and seems very nice. She brought a boy to look after her very spoiled two-year-old. She is only allowed to teach twenty-five pupils at a time, so will have to have morning and afternoon school when Beajah gets here. A note just came from Sister Petty with the carriers who brought a load of their things. She, the girls and little ones will move in tomorrow. That will be fine; I'll have some help.

It's raining, so the girls who went to bathe in the river are back in the kitchen combing each other's hair. Some are looking at old magazines; they love the pictures. Sister Petty sent over a babybed; we've penned crawling Timothy in it to keep him out of trouble. I think he's talking Gola, I can't understand him. Joannah, with a clean dress and full stomach, is lying contentedly on a mat. The teacher's three-year-old girl is playing around with the others, and the pet chicken that wouldn't follow his mama is cheeping away. I've had to stop and spank five of the children already. Does this sound like a picture of "The Old Woman Who Lived in a Shoe?"

Be good,
Mama

Out of the difficulties of getting twenty-three children to school, a routine evolved with Georgia blowing signals on a horn.

5:00 A.M.—Rise and pray.
5:30 A.M.—Do assigned tasks.
7:00 A.M.—Bathe and dress for school.
7:30 A.M.—School starts.
10:30 A.M.—Lower grades dismissed.

11:30 A.M.—School ends, breakfast, study period.
2:00 P.M.—Work and play.
5:30 P.M.—Chop.
6:30 P.M.—One hour of Bible study.
8:00 P.M.—Bedtime.

Inspiration to tackle many projects rose with Georgia in the early morning and evaporated by noon. A sense of duty kept her plodding on. Red letter days came with the return of the messengers sent to Monrovia, if they found mail in Box 44. Sometimes they came back empty-handed. The expense of the trips spaced them a week or more apart.

By the end of March Brother Petty completed the move from Beajah with his boys crowding the boys' dorm and the Pettys settled in Georgia's newly finished house. It took a while longer to get a smooth routine in motion. In the split school sessions, it worked best to have the older children go in the morning and the lower grades in the afternoon.

With the arrival of her trunk, bed and a few boxes, Georgia arranged the country-made furniture and put her rose spread on the bed to make a homelike bedroom. All of her freight, except the refrigerator, came up tediously piece by piece. More than half of the canned fruit and vegetables sent from Corinth and many other things were either broken or spoiled. Being unpacked, rearranged and repacked three times did not help. The high cost and aggravation of transport inspired many daydreams of having a missionary pilot with a plane.

The Pettys helped where they could until the middle of April when Sister Petty developed a high fever. Then both Brother Petty and their daughter Lois Ann became ill. Hope dimmed that they would be able to stay until Gladys arrived, hopefully, in June.

"Palaver" in Liberian lingo means a discussion, often heated, always lengthy, to reach agreement on a matter ranging from trivial to earth-shaking. When the carpenter, who did much of the work on Georgia's house under contract to Brother Haney returned, they had a big "palaver" before he agreed to make the finishing touches at a price she could afford to pay. Another "palaver" ended in a firm "No" with a boy who had run away from the Haneys and wanted to return.

The long awaited refrigerator reached Monrovia, and May 3, Georgia made her first trip back to the capital since her arrival in December. She made it in one day; four men carried her halfway to Suehn Mission, another four the last half.

Reverend Falconcer, Superintendent of the Baptist Mission to Liberia and stationed at Suehn, had visited Maheh looking for timber before the Haneys left. Georgia and Sister Haney had prepared dinner for him. He now offered to send his truck to Millsburg for the refrigerator and bring it to Suehn, thus saving a day's walk. After a good meal with the Falconers, Georgia crossed the river in a canoe and got a ride in the Public Health Services pick-up, reaching Monrovia at 10:00 p.m.

On May 12, 1947 Georgia wrote:

Yesterday I would have said I wouldn't take another baby for anything. The mother, father, a civilized lady and Brother Major (who used to work with Brother Haney) came bringing the baby. The mother had seven children and all of them died because her milk isn't good and they cannot give the baby the right food and care. It was so cute and hungry. I said, "I don't see how I can take her, but I'll feed her." They left. I have named the baby Ruth Eason.

Was I ever glad to get back from Monrovia. The refrigerator is at Suehn, six or seven hours away. I stayed Friday night and until noon Saturday, but only had twenty-two men and three of them would not even try. Three of Brother Falconer's headmen agreed to get men and deliver it to Maheh for $20.00. I left the money with him, but a messenger brought word today that they could not find enough men. They will try again later. It is a monster, and I wish it were smaller, but when it gets here and I enjoy cold water and ice cream, I'll forget about all the trouble.

Sister Petty has been deathly sick again. They will try to get as far as Suehn tomorrow, and on to Monrovia, hoping to get to the States soon. They are dear people; it's been nice having them here, but I'm glad for them to go—she desperately needs relief.

Before May ended Georgia declared Africa to be a wonderful place for developing patience. She got a bad case of poison ivy, the date Gladys Robinson gave for her arrival came and went without Gladys, the new baby kept her up night after night with an infection and all she had of the refrigerator was palaver and more palaver. Her deepest longings centered around revival. "If God will only give us revival," she said, "I can bear all the rest." One of the hardest things to bear was the lack of letters. mail was often slow.

Georgia's family grew. Jason, a dependable, budding

189

preacher brought a brother and sister and begged her to let them stay. A well-to-do man from Bomi Hills brought his two children with a promise to supply their clothes. Her charges now numbered fifty-two and the missionary secretary wrote her to cut back. The $100.00 a month to operate the mission did not increase with the addition of Beajah. Letters said, "Pray that mission funds will come in, or there will be nothing to send."

Other overshadowing griefs had to be faced every day, including the influence of superstition and evil in the initiation rites for boys and girls from the Devil Bush Society and the Heart Men, who watched their chance to collect human hearts for witchcraft.

Georgia put small boys in a swamp area to cut bush—mostly grass, weeds and sprouts—to be piled and burned later. She planned to plant corn in the three or four acres of cleaned ground. Even before the seed nestled in the earth she counted the benefits of the corn and mused, "I'm still hitching my wagon to a star."

In the midst of minor palavers about her flashlight borrowed without permission, an unexpected student romance and the big boys missing prayer meeting to sneak behind the wash kitchen to boil a pot of monkey meat, winds of the revival Georgia longed for began softly. The young man who ran away from the Haneys came to a service and received a glorious filling of the Holy Ghost.

Mother Holmes of Zordee Mission maintained her friendship with Georgia, a mutual blessing. She wrote Georgia the last of June that she would remain in Monrovia until Gladys came and would help her get to Maheh. The pressure cooker shipped by Brother Rubin reached Maheh then, but the stove sent at the same time got lost.

190

On July 2, 1947, Georgia penned:

Last Sunday morning I preached on the Holy Ghost and gave the people a chance to seek the Lord. Azmona, Sammie Gessie, old, hard Bandy Boy, Beah and Moses Washington, all my workmen and Samuel Cole, my wash man, were struck by the power of God and shaken out of their seats onto the dirt floor. They didn't know what it meant, but all of them said their souls felt good and they want to walk the God Way.

The men tried again that week to bring the refrigerator and failed.

Georgia had a difficult, wearisome trip to Monrovia on the seventeenth of July. The motor launch got stuck in the mud and stalled about 8:30 A.M., a short distance from Monrovia. Pelting rain compelled tightly closed curtains. The stuffiness, loud talk, and laughter gave her a headache. Jason, attentive as a son, helped her into a canoe after 2:00 P.M. and they hurried to the Post Office for a disappointment—Gladys still delayed in America. Her most significant errand turned out to be an interview with Colonel Poindexter, a highly qualified Public Health official. She requested that he come to Maheh and examine her clan.

She wrote Gladys before she left town that she could neither stay longer nor return later. She hoped Mother Holmes would be there, but she would send boys every week until she came.

On the twenty-sixth of July, Liberia's Declaration of Independence celebration, her charges had "Big Chop" and no work while Georgia wrestled with a sick baby,

Ruth. The festivities had barely ended when she learned of friction and bad feelings. The Maheh crowd told the ones from Beajah that Mother Regenhardt said they caused all the palavers and people in America only sent money for Maheh and not for them. It took a big palaver to straighten them all out.

Besides, her heart ached over news of divisions and scisms in the church at home. "Why will the church squabble," she cried, "when there are millions in darkness, going out into eternity every tick of the clock and most of them going to hell!" It took a long session on her knees to restore her equanimity.

Baby Ruth had the boils, Georgia didn't, but she lost her appetite and stared disconsolately toward rolling Maheh River. "I just can't eat alone," she sighed. "I've looked for Robbie so long, and the boy didn't even bring a letter from her when he returned yesterday—I wonder if she will ever come." After a bit she resisted discouragement: "Oh well, I'll send helpers down again next week—maybe!"

August the sixteenth one of the boys she sent to Monrovia came up the hill shouting, "Mother Robinson is in Monrovia!" Georgia quickly made plans and sent Gladys a note. Mother Holmes had given up, but the new teacher replacing the sick one could guide Gladys to Arlington. Georgia would arrange for carriers to meet Gladys there.

As Gladys alternated between walking and being carried, the rainy season gave its drippy offerings intermittently. Fifteen minutes from the mission a bridge collapsed and dumped her in the river. The new missionary arrived dripping wet and bedraggled.

"Oh, Robbie, you are here!" Georgia's tears of joy

flowed.

"I have made it, Reggie! Soaking wet, but I am here!" Gladys replied.

Gladys adopted Ruth and quickly won all hearts. Georgia especially appreciated the fifty pounds of flour she brought. She had been out of flour for two months. Gladys bought half of the hens and assumed half of the grocery debt to the Pettys.

They had just started Bible study the next week when a message came that Colonel Poindexter would be there on Sunday. They hurried to prepare sleeping rooms at the new house. Two Liberian technicians came first, and the ladies brought out their choicest delicacies: cream of tomato soup, Spam, Ritz crackers, peanut butter, cookies and banana pudding. The men barely touched it, preferring rice. A good laugh broke the ice for all, and the ladies served them rice and bitter balls for breakfast the next morning, saving their imported goodies for the American Colonel, who came a week later.

The team completed the examinations of sixty-one mission people with technical efficiency, besides the missionaries and many villagers. Most of those on the mission had worms of some kind. They found twenty-eight cases of hookworm, five with malaria, four with yaws and many with skin infections. The doctor gave Georgia a medical record of each of her charges, and she felt relieved to find them in fair shape and herself doing well. He left ample medicine for all the diseases and any predictable reoccurrence.

The revival continued; three mission girls and the new teacher received the Holy Ghost in the next service. The ladies dreaded going into the swift Maheh River to baptize, but the river conveniently flooded and it got deep enough on the mission ground near the river to immerse twenty-five: the teacher, five workmen, thirteen mission students and six villagers.

The last Sunday in September Gladys preached powerfully on "Pentecost Has Come Again." It truly had, for ten received the Holy Ghost including the heathen mothers and family of several of the students. Gladys had been serving morning duty to relieve Georgia, but by Monday a serious attack of malaria laid her low. Georgia and her helpers nursed her tenderly and prayed until they weathered that storm.

Gladys had barely regained her strength when another kind of setback invaded the mission. The revival did not coast to a standstill, it cut off. Georgia led everyone in prayer and fasting. There had to be a reason. It turned out to be reasons that led to a marathon palaver. Both ladies shuddered at the very word *palaver* for months afterward. It started with accusations, then conviction came and confessions of wrong doing to chill the heart went on and on. The ladies asked one young man to leave the mission permanently, but genuine contrition and repentance saved the day.

They felt a different atmosphere the next Sunday that built up into renewed revival, after some of the offenders made public confessions. Then began a great evangelistic outreach that had blessed and wide-spread results. The ladies took turns choosing a team of workers to accompany them on a charge with the gospel to villages beyond their normal range to those who had never heard.

In between, the mission continued with the usual assortment of sore fingers or toes, bruises, cuts, stings, headaches, diarrhea, fever and boils, besides various acts of naughtiness, spats and disagreements. Rice became scarce and expensive. Georgia planted rubber trees for extra income and pushed the big boys to plant more cassava and rice. She welcomed the school's closing on October 25 to be rid of the teacher's humbug (bother) about school needs she could not supply.

Packages and letters from Box 44 brought joy. Georgia wept happy tears over a picture of the monument her children placed on their father's grave. Gladys got her share of the missives. However, not all of them brought good news. One letter said Georgia's allotment was sent to another missionary by mistake and gave the sad news that the Haneys would not be returning to Liberia. Cherished hopes of an airplane died that day.

Georgia and Gladys climbed the Scenic Hill one day by a steep, tricky path hacked by railroad surveyors. While they enjoyed the scenery and the breath-taking view from the top, Georgia sprained again an often-sprained ankle. It bothered her so much that she consulted a doctor on a mid-November trip to Monrovia. She could only follow half of his prescription: "Keep the ankle bandaged and stay off your feet!"

She hit the jackpot on packages at the Post Office including the .410 shotgun sent from the Corinth church. Shopping for the mission went to the limit of buying ability before Georgia started to Maheh. Floods, broken vehicles and misunderstanding combined to make the trip home both tedious and painful. Another effort to bring up the refrigerator failed in December.

Between their village circuits, the ladies wondered about Christmas with shreds of uneasiness. "Robbie, I don't know how in the world we can have the Christmas spirit," Georgia remarked, "when it feels so much like July!"

Georgia began services in the village of Mannah early in December, hoping to win Joannah's father, a Moslem. Before the end of the month he repented and acknowledged Jesus as Lord of his life. Christmas brought the ladies to the brink of a chasm of homesickness when the mission children decorated their children's pictures with flowers and serenaded them with old, familiar carols.

A swarm of people, many of them Moslems, came unplanned on Christmas day and wanted church. Both ladies preached and a great number responded to the altar call with tears of repentance. Afterward they distributed the rest of the small gifts sent by the Haneys, and went late to the kithen for a cold, dried-out Christmas dinner, rejoicing over the diversion. Then they had to call a palaver to mete out punishment for the mission children who fidgeted restlessly during church, annoyed by the delay of their special chop.

The new year of 1948, earnestly prayed in by the ladies, would bring changes for both of them that neither foresaw.

They brought the deathly sick baby of Jack's uncle to the mission and tried to save it. Many of the villagers, whispering that the witch would eat the baby, watched in horror as they removed the witch charms tied around its arms, neck and waist. When death came, in spite of their prayers and loving care, they felt defeated, though they had opportunity to preach to an immense crowd before the burial.

"Robbie, can you believe that what we considered to

be failure would be God's way to stir the village as never before?'' Georgia asked in amazement after the Sunday service. ''What a crowd we had today!''

''And how fervently they sought God!'' Gladys answered. ''You know, Reggie, I think they felt our love and are begining to believe that we really do care.''

The long-lost kitchen stove reached Maheh the second week of January, though two more attempts to bring the refrigerator failed. Best news of all came from a surveyor; the new road in building for the Bomi Hill Mine had reached Clay, a five-hour walk away, and would come nearer. They asked God to give them a pick-up.

Handicapped with easily blistered heels and the swollen, ever-painful ankle, Georgia settled for villages near at hand and encouraged Gladys to continue evangelizing the regions beyond. Letters from Brother Stairs urged them to find good homes for as many children as possible so their outreach would not be hindered. Georgia felt heart-sore—the only homes she had found were heathen homes where fear and superstition reigned, though she understood his reasons.

Georgia's zeal to reach in all four directions moved her to forget handicaps and plan an extensive three-day trip to unreached places. ''I hope we can do something here that will count for God and eternity,'' she wrote her children.

Returning, the ladies rejoiced together over hungry hearts touched by the Word of God. Bomi Hill tugged on Gladys' mind continually. She said, ''Attracted by the chance of work when the mine is in full swing, people are pouring into that little village. Reggie, I can hardly wait to get back. It's like a wild west frontier town—an African version—sin and vice are pouring in, too. Only the gospel can stem the tide."

Georgia shivered with a sudden premonition but did not answer.

In a letter dated February, 1948, Georgia wrote:

Listen to this! They say trucks will actually be driving from Monrovia to Bomi Hills within three months. It can't come too quick for us. We've asked for a pick-up truck.

The District Commissioner sent a letter for the third time that he would supply sixty men to bring up my refrigerator. Promises are wonderful, but I hope something happens this time.

I'm so thankful you have nice, comfortable homes, children. When all of you were in school and we had such a hard time, I encouraged myself by looking forward to this happening and kept you in school, though others said I should take you out and put you in the mill.

The response in the new village is so good. It's a privilege to go, though I do get weary.

The new teacher had barely assumed her duties in March when the Inspector of Education came with only four days warning. He dispelled Georgia's anxiety by friendly interest and gave the school his wholehearted approval.

Red Letter Day! After almost a year of frustrating struggles, the refrigerator reached Mahah on March 27. Iced tea, Jello and ice cream became realities at last, best of all cold water.

April brought sadness, too, the kind that includes thankfulness. Gladys decided to establish a mission at Bomi Hill. The time she spent there had progressively increased through February and March until Georgia almost managed the mission alone, again. She would acutely miss her friend, yet rejoiced over the prospect of another light against encroaching darkness. She hadn't much time to grieve. Whooping cough had invaded Maheh and sunny-dispositioned Joanna had a severe case of it.

Georgia wrote an account of a trek through the bush with the gospel in April:

I left Momo in charge of the mission and the teacher in charge of the girls, praying that everything would be all right while we were gone. Three boys and one girl accompanied me, carrying bedding, food, clothes, lanterns and a gallon of boiled water. Smaller boys had dipped water out of the boat for us and we crossed the river near the mission.

The trail wound through bush for twenty minutes then across an old cassava field grown up in saw grass. Try as one may to escape, it's impossible to avoid burning, red streaks on arms, legs and face from its long, serated-edge blades. Next, we faced a dreaded blockade; a tree had fallen across a deep ditch, with big limbs, brush and more trees piled on and across it and immense saw grass bordered the whole conglomeration.

We traveled easier after we got past that obstacle to a creek with a "big stick" (foot log). I tripped easily across that to a high bank. Tree roots and washed out holes helped me keep my footing while I climbed. Better going on the old Holland Syndicate Road, now taken over by thick clumps of grass. Twenty minutes walking after the turn off brought us to a river with a narrow monkey bridge that appeared on the point of collapse. We prayed our swaying way across.

When we crossed the new road, we paused to thank God for it, on through a small village and to a shallow stream where a helper led me over from chunk to chunk. We lost the trail on a "farm" where the trees and brush had been cut to plant rice, everything lay before us in tangled confusion. The oldest boy zig-zagged ahead of us trying to find a way through. I'm glad I didn't know then that three more farms lay ahead!

We paused for lunch on the other side and a brief rest. On again; I removed my shoes and waded through two rivers, crossed more farms, a treacherous swamp and came to a place of large reeds. Fallen ones carpeted the ground smoothly providing some relief for weary feet. The trail we followed led up and down hill, etched out by multitudes of feet and torrential rains for many decades exposing booby traps of stones and snarled roots.

Finally we reached our target village and I rested in a "kitchen" (thatch roofed shed with one foot high walls) while my helpers cleaned the hut assigned to us. Bright-eyed urchins clad only with strings of witch medicine around their waists surrounded me saying shyly "Makay!" (Hello!).

After a quick wash and a short rest, I watched the women beat out the rice they brought from their "farms" in a hollowed block of wood with a pole—they call it a "pencil." They cooked their only meal of the day—rice and soup—in open pots. When everyone had eaten all they could hold, the chief called then to the palaver kitchen for "zodo"

*(prayer). We hung up our lanterns, took the tambourines
and began singing in Gala.*

*The Spirit moved and a sweet anointing responded to
the heart-hunger of my listeners. Some understood, others
seemed doubtful; all but the Moslems knelt and prayed with
sincerity. We had prayer with the people again and encouraged them to truly follow Jesus before we left the next
morning for another service in another village.*

*We promised to return to both places as soon as pos-
sible and headed back to the mission. To our weary eyes
it appeared the most restful and beautiful place in the
world. But, I know the hungry hearts of the villages will
speedily make us anxious to go again.*

Before Gladys moved to a small, native hut at Bomi
Hill early in May, she took responsibility of the mission
to give Georgia a carefree week in Monrovia. Five young-
sters with whooping cough made the nights a series of
wearisome interruptions. Georgia returned with good
news: Pauline Gruse planned to return to Liberia in August. Help, maybe?

News from America in August: Will recovered quickly
from an appendectomy and married Clara Fae. Now, her
family numbered six.

Early in September, Georgia rode in a pick-up for the
first time on the new road, on her way to Monrovia. No
charge, though passengers were limited to mine workers,
missionaries and government officials. The *Pentecostal
Herald* published a combined report from the two ladies
that month saying that they reached twelve towns a week
with the gospel.

At Bomi Hill Gladys wrestled with "mud and stick"

building operations for six months. Settled at last in her new home, she invited Georgia for a visit. They wondered when they would hear from Pauline Gruse; August had come and gone without a word. They shared their grief over the failure of some promising mission students they had hoped would develop into gospel workers.

Maheh lost its "sunshine" the first week of December when Joannah died. They could not believe diptheria caused her death until Ruth got it too. Georgia appreciated her friend as she shared her sorrow and helped with sick-care, only returning to Bomi for the weekend services. Loved by all, Joannah's passing brought a shadow over the festivities, but staggering services and celebrations allowed the ladies to participate in Christmas at both missions. Double activities kept them busy enough to allay the keenest pangs of homesickness.

The record-player sent by a California church proved to be Georgia's most popular gift. She could hear again the beloved voices of her children and the good singing records they sent. Best of all, Pauline Gruse returned to Africa just after Christmas.

"Georgia, you need a vacation and a medical check-up," Pauline said. "I'll man the mission while you go to Monrovia for a couple of weeks."

It turned out to be five weeks instead of two, because Georgia needed two ten-day treatments, with a rest interval in-between, for intestinal parasites. She wrote her mother that her furlough should begin in eleven months, and added, "I am richer than most people, for I have two countries and two groups of loved ones and friends, besides the glories of my heavenly home!"

Maheh became a three-week long haven for Gladys,

brought to an extreme state of exhaustion by overwork and the pressures of building.

"Well, it seems I've come to the kingdom for such a time as this," Pauline remarked, pleasantly. "Let me take Gladys home where she can rest in her own room and I'll take responsibility for the mission to speed her recovery."

Alone again! Not quite as overwhelming with her friends only two to three hours walk away, at Bomi Hill mission. May brought Georgia dysentery and fever up to 103⁰ for three days. The teacher came down with malaria at the same time and complicated the situation. Thankfully they made it through without having to call for help.

When Georgia recovered she saw a hitherto unseen sight on a two-village preaching tour; a mother feeding her small infant Liberian style. The mother gripped its body tightly with her arms. While one hand pressed a steady stream of thick mush into the baby's mouth, the fingers of her other hand poked it down the gagging infant's throat. When she paused, the baby wailed and vomited. Without mercy, the forced feeding began again. Georgia could not resist interrupting this mealtime to give a lesson on child-care with the help of an interpreter.

Always, it seemed that both the good things and the sad happenings came hand in hand to the mission. Gladys brought home the new pick-up for the use of both missions in the middle of August, and the same week two young people left in disgrace, returning to the old superstitious customs. They had been the missionary's most faithful and dependable helpers at one time.

For many years, the school had doubled as chapel. With furlough only a few months away, Georgia pressed for completion of a new mud church on the mission. August brought the exciting news that Kathadene would make her Grandma and the disappointment that the mine would not allow them to drive to Monrovia on the new road until the end of the rainy season.

Georgia booked passage home on a boat in November and at the same time applied to travel on a church plane that transported only missionaries, but she did not make it in November. Everything fell into place in December. Sister Gruse took over the mission setting Georgia free to go. She fell into the loving arms of her family for the best Christmas ever.

Brother A. D. Gurley officially welcomed Georgia, January 8, 1950, with a homecoming service in Corinth, Mississippi attended by family, friends and officials of the United Pentecostal Church. Soon afterward she enrolled in the Pentecostal Bible Institute for the second semester.

Georgia's beckoning star made her a flaming beacon of missionary vision and directed her back to Liberia soon after graduating from Pentecostal Bible Institute in 1951. She sailed out of New Orleans on May 16, on the *Del Oro* with a warm farewell from the Johnny Thomas family. She reached Monrovia on June 6, well rested and somewhat bored.

Georgia returned with new vigor for the old routine, noting how slowly improvements developed in Liberia:

We can use the new road more often; in billows of red dust in the dry season and negotiating from mudhole to mudhole when the rains pour down.

The Petty family are at Bomi while Gladys is on furlough—exchanging visits with them brightens my whole

204

week.

I've had three invasions by driver ants since my return; we mix kerosene and water to rout them—burns like fire when they sting.

My family is smaller—have twenty one boarding students and three day students, only two little ones. I want to concentrate on evangelizing the villages this term.

New missionaries came; Gene Bailey was followed a little later by the Hubert Parks family. Georgia taught Bible lessons and applied Band-Aids, grieving over a persistent mental picture of her mother's hands bruised in picking cotton according to her letters. More sadness when Gladys had to leave the field because of suspected cancer, only three months after her return from furlough. Word of her death came in December, 1953.

Georgia found solace for the hurts in her with rigid attention to duty and continual reaching toward her goals. Her first term crawled, tediously long and slow; the second one seemed to flit by. Only deep exhaustion from three years exposure to the tropics made her know leaving time had come.

After a short whirl of visiting homeland churches, Georgia entered the Pentecostal Bible Institute and graduated with a Bachelor in Theology degree in the spring of 1955. The gentle tug of that star persisted until she returned to Maheh in 1956.

Slightly improved roads and having a car made her third term somewhat easier. But a changing world spread its influence, even to the jungles in limited touches, bringing a slow, subtle restructuring of the mission concept. Georgia and Missionary Valda Russell agreed that all of the changes did not prove beneficial. However, they determined to be faithful and touch as many lives as God would enable them.

Georgia's mother became seriously ill in October 1959. Georgia wrote her sister:

I wish I could turn loose here and come home. How glad I would be to help care for Mama. To think I'm so far away when she wants me with her. I'm praying constantly for God to spare her life until I return.

The same day your letter came, I received one from the Missionary Board asking me to stay another year. I do not want to miss God's will even though I would love to be there. The Lord loves us and knows how much we can bear. Let us love and trust Him.

And to her mother she penned:

You asked when I would be coming home to stay, Mama. When the Lord is ready, I'm ready to come. I've been asked to stay another year, but if it is God's will for me to come sooner, He can make it so. Let us trust Him fully and be obedient to His will. God is great and greatly to be praised. Blessed be His Name!

Georgia remained at her post for the extra year before she returned to her longing family in 1960. She became Instructor and Dean of Women at Pentecostal Bible Institute that fall, a position she held until 1970. For 1971 and 1972 she filled the post of librarian at the college.

Service aptly describes Georgia's life—service to God and man. She entered the hospital on July 21, 1976 at

8:00 a.m. Six hours later, with a gentle lossening of earth's hold and an exquisite glow, her star ushered her into the presence of the King.

Georgia Regenhardt.

Georgia with baby Ruby Martin.

Georgia with babies Timothy and Sherry.

Georgia and various children from Maheh and Bomi Hills.

School children with Georgia Regenhardt.

209

Georgia Regenhardt at Maheh.

Georgia Regenhardt as Dean of Women at Pentecostal Bible Institute.

9

THE STORY OF
Gladys Robinson

by Nona Freeman and Marie Ross Wallace

Farmers and relatives crowded the one-room school where the dark-haired lady spoke each evening with evangelistic fervor. Dim light filtering from unshaded windows revealed many horse-drawn wagons outside and a few cars. This was the summer of 1944. As World War II still raged, gas was rationed, tires and spare parts were scarce and few cars were operating.

Gladys Robinson, scripturally correct, was working on her "Jerusalem," sponsored by Raymond Yonts and backed by teenaged daughter Carmen, and a faithful friend. Gladys' mission was to take the whole gospel to her birthplace, the rural community of Ozark, Illinois.

Gladys Elizabeth Cox, the youngest of Betty Elizabeth and John Allan Cox's four children, was born May 17,

1907, at the home of her grandmother near Ozark, Illinois. She was a pretty little girl with bright blue eyes and curly, dark brown hair.

Her parents bought a 120 acre farm three and a half miles from Ozark the year before Gladys started to school. The nearest school was Reagan, a one-room grade school. For eight years, Gladys walked a mile and a half daily with her brother, Orlan, and sisters, Audie and Bertha to attend this school. Near tragedy struck her entire family, as it did most of the nation, when the flu epidemic broke out in 1918, but fortunately they were spared.

Gladys enjoyed helping her family in the garden each spring and summer. Later she helped can the fruits and vegetables. In winter months, she followed her dad and brother as they ran their traps.

The Spirit's tug on her heart came at an early age. With tears of repentance she joined the Baptist church, influenced by her maternal grandfather, a Baptist minister. "When Grandfather Brown came to visit, he told Bible stories and sang hymns," Gladys remembered.

In 1924, life took on a rosy glow when, at seventeen, Gladys married her childhood sweetheart, Garrie Everett Ross, but dulled to hurting gray when her mother died of cancer that first year. The clouds fled when Marie Evelyn was born in 1925. Before the birth of her only son Allen Loree, in 1927, however, trouble came again when her marriage failed. Gladys then moved in with her widowed father near Cambria, Illinois.

Wedding bells and another hope for happiness came with Laban Carter Campbell in 1928. Gladys and Carter purchased a home in Hurst, Illinois, and attended the First Christian Church there. With the addition of Carmen Elizabeth to the family in 1930 brought joy. But when Carmen was only five years old, Carter Campbell died, and Gladys' world again caved in on her.

A cousin, Anna Young, came from Mayfield, Kentucky to keep house and care for the children while Gladys worked as a waitress in a hotel dining room to support her family. Her father, John Cox, kept them in fresh vegetables, fruit, meat, dairy products, and eggs that came from his farm.

In 1939, Gladys married a widower, Leo Robinson, with three children. Jackie, his son, was Carmen's age. The girls, Barbara and Sue, were younger. Although her family, was now twice as large, Gladys' loving heart embraced them all.

In July, 1940, someone invited Leo and Gladys to a tent meeting in Glendale, Illinois. The preacher was Raymond Yonts, father of the present Home Missions Director of the United Pentecostal Church, Reverend Jack Yonts. She listened entranced as the powerful message driven by God's Spirit pinpointed her life of heartache, sin and vain search for happiness.

"He's talking to me! Just to me!" she thought.

An unbearable longing for peace and pardon engulfed her. She was not conscious of running to the altar, but when she found herself there, deep-racking sobs came from the depths of a soul that seemed beyond comfort. Suddenly, a soft edge of peace touched her and slowly spread its benign flow over the once tortured heart. Forgiven! The assurance was overwhelming. Tears fell again, but those were different, more like the benediction of a gentle rain.

Those around her urged, "Press on! Reach for the infilling of the Spirit." She wanted only to bask in the glow of forgiveness and savor that amazing calm in her inner being. The voices were insistent, "Praise the Lord! He wants to give you the Holy Ghost!" She began to worship and was blessed. Someone leaned over and said, "You have stammering lips; that is the Holy Ghost!"

She returned home with a question in her mind about the Holy Ghost and early the next morning diligently searched the Scriptures on the subject. About the time she was fully convinced that the evidence of the Holy Ghost was a full language given by God and unknown to the recipient, Brother and Sister Yonts arrived to pray with her.

They went to a wooded area for prayer to eliminate possible distractions. On a carpet of grass under a beautiful tree, Gladys was born of the Spirit with clear utterance of an unknown tongue and was given a commissioning burden that would direct her for the rest of her life. She saw a dazzling light at the top of a large oak tree, in the center of the radiance she saw briefly the head and shoulders of Jesus. That vision faded and in its place were mud huts with palm thatch roofs, scantily-clad black women and naked babies. The women reached for her out of dire need. The scene changed and she saw herself ministering to them and praying for their dusky little ones. She knew then that one day she could go to the land of mud huts, but she confided only in her pastor, no one else. Then Brother Yonts baptized Gladys in Jesus' name.

At this time Leo made a start for the Lord then changed his mind. Later he amicably bowed out of Gladys' life. Having no desire to either walk the new road with her or to hinder her in anyway, he went to live with his widowed mother.

A year later when Missionary Peter Jensen spoke at the church in Carterville, Illinois, he paused and said, "Someone in this church will be a missionary to Africa."

Gladys whispered, "I hope it isn't me." But in her heart she *knew*.

Gladys and the family moved to Nashville, Tennessee, in June, 1942. The West Nashville Pentecostal Church at that time was worshiping in a tent. Gladys, who became an active member of the church, told Pastor James Wells Wallace of her call to the mission field. She taught the Berean Class of young ladies, conducted Junior Church, and did much personal work in the hospitals and T.B. Sanitariums in that area. In 1943 Gladys' oldest child left the nest when Marie married Pastor J. W. Wallace's youngest son Glenn.

In the summer of 1945 Gladys returned to Ozark, Illinois, and conducted a revival. A number of people were converted and filled with the Holy Ghost. Gladys established the United Pentecostal Church in that town and pastored there until God provided a way for her and her daughter Carmen to attend Apostolic College in Tulsa, Oklahoma, in 1946. The Missionary Board had already endorsed Gladys as an outgoing missionary to Africa.

Gladys, hunched over the wheel of a flatbed Model T, hair bound in a bandana, suitcases and necessary paraphernalia tied down, swept past every obstacle on an evanglistic foray that touched several churches. She was not oblivious of the chagrin and discomfort of seventeen-year-old daughter Carmen and her dear friend, but she moved on with the rigid determination to do God's will that characterized her life. That purpose ultimately compelled her to admit her call to Africa. Incredulous friends hooted, "Africa? You're so afraid of worms, bugs and spiders! What about snakes? Plenty of them over there! You'll never make it!"

Gladys liked little jokes and pranks and could laugh heartily, but this time she was definitely serious. Before long she was preparing to go to Africa. So the Bible school in Tulsa, Oklahoma, church officials and Mary and C. P. Williams, the school directors, recognized a genuine mission call and the singular anointing that rested on her.

On July 31, 1947, her face set towards Liberia, West Africa, Gladys boarded a train at Jackson, Tennessee, leaving all. The Rubin family helped when there were technical delays in New York. Finally on Friday, August 8, all was clear and her plane left for Dakar, Senegal. She had hoped to receive news of being a grandmother for the first time before leaving the States. Allen's wife, Verla, was expecting. She would like to know whether it was a boy or girl. Oh! to be there with them.

Stranded at Dakar for five days with uncertain hopes of leaving, it was easy to grieve over the dear family left behind. "I must keep my mind on Jesus and leave my children in His hands. I'll trust Him for a glad reunion someday in His will! But oh I'm glad He understands a mother's love and longing tears."

At last! After a terrifying, low flight over dense jungles and rivers, Gladys landed at Roberts Field, Liberia. There was a strange let-down feeling as she sat alone on a bench in front of the airport surrounded by her suitcases, wondering if anyone even knew she had arrived. Her cable did reach the friends prearranged to take her to Monrovia, and a truck came for her a few hours later.

There were frequent introductory stops along the forty-mile journey to Monrovia, Liberia's capital. But Monrovia was still at least two days' bush and river travel from Maheh Mission where Gladys would be working with Georgia Regenhardt. While she was wondering how to get word to Reggie, two boys from the mission, Kenny and John came.

Fleet-footed John started back at once with the exciting news: "Mother Robinson has arrived!" While waiting for helpers for the trip, Mother Robinson got acquainted with the sights, sounds and smells of Monrovia. She learned particularly the intensity of tropical rain and Liberian red tape. She bought a white, cork-lined sun helmet, met the new teacher who was to travel with her, and tried to wait patiently.

Jason and Alfred arrived from the mission at 8:00 p.m. Monday night, August 18. They were weary and hungry, having traveled two days and all night, leaving their rice at Waterside, and Alfred hurting his toe on the way. Jason explained, "We hurry to get you!"

The boat was due to leave at 2:00, Tuesday afternoon. Since Alfred got lost in town, Gladys sent Jason to find him. Alfred returned, so Kenny went to hunt Jason. The teacher and the two missing boys came almost breathless and the boat left at 2:30.

Wedged among the seventy-five people on board, she watched through the rain, banks of the river with avid interest. Swamps, palm and banana trees, and mud huts, occasionally one with a metal roof, captured her attention.

When they reached Waterside at 4:00 p.m., carriers and mission boys were waiting for her there and the trek through the jungle began. Because there were not enough

217

carriers, some groceries and luggage had to wait for the next trip. Hammocks were provided, but Gladys walked for nearly an hour, slipping and sliding in the mud. Then, reluctantly, she and the teacher got into the hammocks. Jigging, trotting, singing and bouncing, they arrived at Arlington to spend the night. She was thrilled to find a teacher and group of children there from Zordee, the Holmes' mission. That made unpalatable surroundings easier to endure.

Early Wednesday morning she headed down the trail that progressively degenerated from an old roadbed to a path, gloomy and rough. Vine and tree limbs intertwined overhead; grass was almost head high. She was carried over two streams; they negotiated one river with a raft. The Po River, very swift due to heavy rain, was crossed in a canoe.

They paused for a glimpse of village life, and then trudged on uphill through vegetation so thick the path looked like a tunnel. With weird ferns standing four or five feet tall and huge trees having fallen across the trail the procession strung out for a mile or so. When bone weary Gladys submitted to the bouncing of the hammock for short intervals.

Rain fell for most of the day; when it stopped they walked in steam. Gladys was carried across the third creek into another village in a clearing and then into dense jungle again. "Many monkeys live here," she noted as she admired one in a tree. Carriers behind her yelled, "Look out!" She had walked into a wide black column of marching driver ants. She suffered several fiery stinging bites before they were knocked off her legs.

Just after dark, Jason announced, "Only fifteen min-

218

utes to the Mission!'' In front of them stood another long narrow bridge; the river underneath was full and swift. Gladys refused a helping hand, no longer afraid of these precarious structures—besides, the journey's end was near. Then suddenly with a loud crash, the middle section collapsed, dumping five of them in the turbulent water. She grabbed her sun helmet as it floated by and hung on to her purse. Eventually, two of the boys recovered from shock and pulled her across the wreckage onto the bank. Jason took off with his flashlight and she stumbled along behind him wishing for a chance to clean up.

Fifty-two mission children standing beneath lanterns in the rain welcomed the soaking-wet missionary whose shoes were filled with sand, hose torn, dress muddy, and wet hair falling down. Suddenly the children began to sing. Over and over the beautiful words rang out:

> *We're marching to Zion,*
> *Beautiful, beautiful Zion,*
> *We're marching upward to Zion*
> *That beautiful city of God.*

After twenty days how happy Gladys was to finally arrive and how good the spotless mission house looked! Linoleum floors, clean white sheets and mosquito nets on the beds. After a welcomed bath and a delicious chicken with palm butter supper, Georgia and Gladys talked very late. They had so many things to share.

The mission complex was large and beautifully laid out. Beajah Mission had recently been combined with Maheh because of insufficient workers and funds. Their charges at Maheh now were four babies between four and sixteen months, fifty children of assorted ages, and seven grown young men, the hope for future evangelism.

Georgia arranged a teaching session with the young men the day after Gladys arrived. At the start of the meeting, all eyes suddenly focused on the rafters where a large snake laid coiled. As one of the boys poked it with a pole, it swung out striking and the two missionary ladies edged towards the door. The snake was soon knocked down and when the battle was over, service continued with blessing!

Several fruitful services in the next few days were mixed with more encounters with snakes, big black wooly worms and poisionous spiders.

About 8:00 p.m. on the tenth day after Gladys' arrival, boys returned from Monrovia bringing five letters from home!

The new teacher, three of the mission girls and several of the workmen were filled with the Holy Ghost in a thrilling service. Baptism was planned in the Maheh River which winds on two sides of the mission, but the river, swollen by rains, came out for the occasion. Twenty-five candidates were baptized on the lawn several yards from the river's normal banks. The next day the waters receded, and grass glistened in the sun. But as the bridge over the valley to the boy's dorm washed away, they had to swim back and forth, morning and night.

During her sixth week at Maheh, Gladys awoke Sunday morning feeling ill. She spent the day in bed, but determined not to be defeated, she went to church that night and preached a fiery sermon. Ten people were filled with the Holy Ghost, but malaria is not easily routed.

After several cables for prayer, aching days and lots of tender care, she was able to get back in harness.

Palaver is a convenient Liberian word that covers every discussion from minor arguments to murder trials. The next crisis on the mission was a spiritual palaver of such dimension the missionaries could only cry for grace and wisdom. Ernest had a palaver; someone took his eddoes (edible root). Trying to uncover that culprit, many misdemeanors and culprits were revealed. After a grievious time of contrition, confession and some rebellion, with due punishment meted out and one offender dismissed, peace and revival returned to the mission.

Gladys and Georgia took six of the boys and climbed a high scenic hill where mine laborers had cut a narrow path to an observation point on the top. Extreme exertion to get there was rewarded by a breathtaking view. They saw red-roofed Maheh, neat and lovely, deserted Beajah on the other side of thick jungles, and miles to the north, Bomi Hills where iron ore was mined. Gladys felt a strange tug on her heart as she looked toward the unique hill.

When necessity took Georgia on a trek to Monrovia, Gladys was left alone with the children. A week later the hammock carriers returned from the prearranged meeting place without Georgia. Gladys sent them back and afraid the eight boys waiting to carry loads would also return, she divided the small stock of remaining rice and sent two more boys with food and instructions to wait until Georgia came. They were out of soap and money, and only two small cans of Carnation milk were left for the four babies. An older mission girl came: "Mudder, the rice, it is finish."

"If so, I'm leaving," answered the missionary.

But, of course, she stayed and borrowed from their tithes to buy rice, the staple food for West Africans. Then they made a great discovery. The garden they had given up as hopeless had green beans and okra ready to eat.

When Georgia returned a few days later, she brought bad news; no checks from the Mission Department. The $60.00 monthly allotment that each received was sent only as funds were available, and thus it came eratically. But there was also good news: a Sunday school in Nashville, Tennessee, sent an offering that bought food and supplies! Sometimes Box 44, Monrovia, yielded letters from her children. Oh happy day! One such letter told of the birth of her granddaughter, Rita Joy. She longed to see and hold her close. Photographs helped to ease the pain. She was a beautiful baby and healthy. Oh this trip, however there were none, so she clung to the hope of perhaps "next trip!"

A steadfast determination to reach out to the villages took Gladys to Weehama. Though the people were Moslems, they listened respectfully to the gospel, and in the second service the whole village responded to the altar call. A large crowd walked halfway home with her and begged her to return to teach them more about the "God-way."

Next, she took nine of the mission young people with her to Kowadee, a very large village. The trip was strenuous, involving over an hour's canoe ride up the river and then a two-hour walk through rice fields, bush and jungle. The town was dominated by a beautiful Mohammedan temple in the center. Nevertheless, the chief welcomed her graciously, led his people in kneeling for prayer at the close of the service, and extended a warm invitation for her to come back regularly. Tears streamed down her face as she saw how hungry they were for the gospel. She promised to come every Saturday.

On the next visit to Kowadee, they held a service at Bugbay on the way. They wanted them to stay longer. "Can't you come to see us one day when you don't have to hurry on?" The man who asked that question was formerly involved in witchcraft. She promised to have services with them every Saturday morning and stay as long as possible.

Just before Christmas she was deeply disappointed that no one came from Maheh Village for the Sunday night service. Someone explained that the Devil Bush Society had opened and no females were allowed out after sundown. After prayer she took Jason with her to Maheh Village and confronted the head of the Society.

"We have left our families and come eight thousand miles to help your people. Now because of your activities the people are afraid to come to church on Sunday nights. I ask that you make it possible for them to come so they can worship God." The astonished man agreed. She thanked God and him and returned rejoicing.

Along with letters, packages from home were highlights for the missionaries, and because of the packages, they were able to bring Christmas happiness to the mission children and the villagers who attended services regularly. But Christmas spirit was the one thing the missionaries were not able to conjure up in the tropical heat so far from all their loved ones.

There were repeated sad scenes when Georgia and Gladys refused to accept pitifully frail babies. The Mission Board's orders were strictly, "No more children." The ladies agreed with the verdict, but it was still heart-rending to send the babies away to die. Finally, Gladys had to settle the matter in her own mind: "These little souls will go to Jesus, but many thousands have reached the age of accountability and need to be reached with the gospel so that they can be saved. I must use my strength to help them."

In 1948, the U.S. Steel Corporation of America made plans for a mining camp at Bomi Hills for the mining of iron ore. This was one of the villages in which the gospel had been carried by these missionaries. Gladys wrote Brother Stairs, Secretary (Director) of Foreign Missions, for permission to establish a day school and church at this location where representatives of many tribes would obtain employment and make their homes. Brother Stairs was so impressed with the opportunities offered at Bomi Hills that he felt to personally sponsor this endeavor until such time as missionary funds were available to take care of another mission. Gladys then obtained permission from the Liberian government to move to the village.

Early in 1948, she planned a trip up-country to Bomi Hills and Bolah, taking four mission young people with her but, to her disappointment the carriers did not come. As she felt unable to walk all the way, she went to Maheh Village on January 20 hoping to get carriers. Again she met frustrations, they had just been vaccinated and couldn't go. Walking defeated back toward the mission, the thought came, "A day's walk won't hurt my body any more than leaving my loved ones hurt my heart." She made her decision and waited on the trail while Jack and Ernest went to the mission for their luggage and the rest of the group. She spent the waiting time talking to Jesus.

When they went through Bomi Hills a man gave them a white chicken and said he was praying for someone to come for regular services. He shared good news that road-building was planned from Bomi Hills to Monrovia. Gladys rejoiced, she had often prayed for roads to use while reaching the people.

They arrived at Bolah about 5:30 p.m. After plenty of rough walking on the way. Service soon started and lasted until 10:30. The people left reluctantly, requesting a sunrise meeting before they went to the fields the next day. After that service the hungry-hearted people didn't want to leave either, and the acting chief requested they return every week for service. Gladys said, "I cannot refuse, for this cause I came to Liberia."

Two other villages near Kowadee requested services, making four places on the circuit in that area. As Bomi Hills, Bolah and Bopola were the opposite direction, the workers had to split up. Georgia had services at Mannah, near Maheh, for several years. Then following Gladys' example, she too branched out in wider evangelistic efforts. And God gave the increase.

But among these sincere and hungry, there were often schemers of evil designs. A woman came begging Gladys to visit her village. Going, cost considerable effort and a whole day's walk. On arrival the chief said, "It's too late for service now, have it tomorrow morning."

When Gladys walked into the hut given her for the night, she felt a strange uneasiness. There was a very low platform for a bed and an odd gaping hole low in the opposite wall. She prayed more than usual before turning on her stomach to sleep. In the night she was wakened suddenly by something extremely heavy and cold lying across the middle of her back. Her heart pounded with fear, but she tried to lie very still while her whole soul cried silently to the Lord for help. Slowly, the heavy object slid off an she heard dragging movement on the mud floor as it left the room.

When she emerged from the hut the next morning there was instant consternation. She soon understood why. This village on a river bank worshiped a huge crocodile and she was brought by guile for a sacrifice to their "god." It didn't work! The woman who was used in the scheme fell at Gladys' feet asking forgiveness. Gladys sternly demanded all the people must come together so she could talk to them. She pointed out the powerlessness of their "god" and told them in ringing tones how Jesus, the Almighty One, delivered her and wanted to save them. And good came out of evil when salvation came to that remote village.

In April Gladys completed her plans to move to Bomi Hills and open a day school for children of the area. She realized the golden opportunity for sowing the Word for many tribes would converge on the newly opened mining camp. Brother Wynn Stairs personally promised $30.00 a month for a teacher's salary and books.

Georgia finally received a small kerosene refrigerator, but while Gladys thoroughly enjoyed its benefits, her heart had already moved to Bomi. The pending move required several trips to Monrovia, working on papers for a twelve and one-half acre land grant. The new road was completed to Klay, so she could ride that far on a mine company truck; then it was only a seven-hour walk to Maheh.

The grant was conditional on her doing the surveying. The mission boys twisted bark into "rope" to measure the land by the yard. Two of the boys cut a trail wide and high enough to pass through thick saw grass. Gladys followed, unwinding the "rope." At one stage Robert was supposed to tie the "rope," while J. D. took the other end down the trial. Gladys, in the middle, pulled with all her might and wondered why the rope didn't tighten. They walked and walked in the oppressive tropical heat. Finally she yelled back at Robert and found he was bringing the end along with him!

Seven or eight men using cutlasses (long knives) spent several weeks cutting vines and undergrowth. Then, over the whole area they cut the trees that later had to be chopped in smaller pieces to burn with the brush. After that, they cleaned again and burned what didn't burn before. The next step was digging out rampant vine roots and stumps.

Gladys knew nothing about building with mud, sticks and mats, but she had to learn. Not one day could the workmen be left alone. They were fond of squabbling but not so anxious to work. She was continually either making peace or encouraging them to keep moving.

Of course, the two essential buildings, residence and chapel-school, were begun before the land clearing was completed. In May, Lajetta Smith, a school teacher, and Nancy, a mission girl from Maheh, moved with Gladys to a small mud hut near the building site. About the same time Gladys received word that her allotment had been cut and there should be urgent prayer for an increase of funds.

Lajetta started school early in June in the town "kitchen," a thatched open-sided structure with a mud floor used primarily for "palavers." ABC's could be heard over the whole village.

Another allotment reduction came in June and building became strictly a faith project. Workmen received $5.00 a month and Gladys endeavored to supply their clothes, thanks to packages from family and friends in America. The most expensive building material was cement for the floors. The walls were made of bamboo sticks brought from the jungle and tied in position with rattan, native rope growing in the bush that had to be split. These were daubed with mud made from ant hills. The finishing touch was rubbing the walls with white clay from the river bed on the outside, and basket-woven mats lined the mud walls inside and made the ceiling.

When they learned that the Ottis Pettys' return was uncertain, Gladys borrowed windows and doors, a stove and a large cupboard from the unused house at Beajah. There were continual interruptions and delays, such as waiting for what was left of the allotment to arrive and time off to spend a day at Maheh sewing on the children's clothes.

Gladys held two services a day besides open air meetings at the mine compound on the weekends, yet she continually thought of the villages. She wrote her daughter Marie, "I'll be so glad when this building palaver is finished so I can do missionary work again. It takes different kinds of work to spread the gospel, and though building at Bomi Hills is a direct blessing from God, yet evangelism is sorely needed."

The leaky hut was their abode for five months. Rats in the roof thatch knocked trash and dust down in their faces and kept them awake at night with their noise.

Without the umbrella and raincoats they would have been soaked in the frequent rains.

The chapel-school building was completed the last week of August and occupied with thanksgiving. Unfortunately a two-headed snake appeared in the loose palm leaf thatching over the large back porch. When the second one stuck his head out, the thatch was removed and replaced by cord thatch, a more compact effect made by twisting or plaiting the palm leaves.

Welcome news arrived. Virgil Hughes, a Bible school student in San Antonio who had taken over the sponsorship of the school, raised $175.00 on the building project at his home church in Parkersburg, West Virginia. Brother C. P. Williams of Tulsa also raised money to buy Gladys a kerosene refrigerator.

On September 24, Gladys moved into the bedroom of her new home. The lack of cement for floors held up the use of the rest of the house for awhile, but, finally, she had a home again. The furnishings were simple. Marie and Carmen sent curtains, couch cover, shelf paper, oil cloth and odds and ends. Gladys found linoleum and grass rugs at the Monrovia market. Posts, bannisters, doors and shutters were painted light blue. Bright red hibiscus bloomed by the door. Fruit trees were planted and all paths were edged with shrubs. The garden effort was quickly and vociferously devoured by prolific bugs in the new ground, but she would keep trying.

News flash! Pauline Gruse was returning soon to Liberia.

Georgia and Gladys had heavy responsibilities but thoroughly enjoyed fellowshiping together when there was opportunity.

They comforted each other in early December when diptheria took one toddler at Maheh Mission and threatened another. But everything cleared by Christmas. Gladys celebrated with the mission family at Maheh on Christmas Eve and the next day hurried to Bomi Hills for the Christmas service there.

On December 26 word came that Sister Gruse was waiting in Monrovia. For the first time Gladys got on a truck in front of her door and rode forty miles to Monrovia—no walking! There was an instant rapport with Pauline, whom she escorted to Maheh to help Georgia.

Gladys' long-awaited refrigerator came in January. A crew of six (one drunk, one naked, etc.) held it upright on a top-heavy canoe across the St. Paul River. She watched in trepidation from the bank as the boat rocked violently. She looked away in fear of seeing it sink, then went behind the bushes and cried to the Lord for help. God answered!

Good news came in February, 1944. Brother Stairs wrote that a truck was on the way for the work in Liberia. Bad news, however, was not far behind. Pauline and Georgia, knowing Gladys was ill insisted that she have a medical check-up. The doctor's verdict of March 1 stated, "No malaria or parasites, but the lady's so overworked, a total collapse can only be avoided by complete rest."

"How can I rest?" she asked. "I can turn the mission over to Joseph—he's trustworthy—and the teacher can handle the school, but I'm haunted day and night by the villages. People are begging for the gospel and dying daily. It seems so heartless to stretch out and relax in the face of such need; I don't understand why no one volunteers to come to help."

Gladys reluctantly agreed to rest at Maheh for two weeks that stretched into three. When she insisted on returning to Bomi Hills, Pauline went with her, realizing Gladys was not physically able to cope. There was no improvement in May. By June she considered giving up but decided against it, though the continual weakness was hard to understand.

The new truck came in July. It was a tremendous blessing, and gradually, the worn-out missionary gained strength. By August she resumed giving Bible lessons, and in October, she was able to return to village services.

News also came that her youngest daughter, Carmen, married Norman Harper in July. Part of the price a missionary pays is being absent and far away on such tender occasions.

Early December, 1949 Georgia left for an overdue furlough and Pauline took charge of Maheh. Gladys' third Christmas in Africa was spent alone with her helpers on the mission. Both ladies had their hands too full to even get together for Christmas dinner.

1950! The year started with some outstanding victories. The chief at Bugbay and nine others were baptized, even though elders of the village spent the night inquiring of the dead and trying to block the services. Robert, the workman, was taken forcibly by the Devil Bush Society; his release, in answer to prayer, was a day of rejoicing.

The new church building, which was started several weeks before Christmas, progressed slowly with hopes of completion by Easter. Three buildings on the mission were not properly thatched, so they had to be reworked, making the thatch much thicker. Gladys decided that building on the mission was a task without an end.

Gladys rejoiced over the steady growth of believers in the Bomi Hills church, but her greatest happiness was the many souls gleaned on the village trips. She could endure privation and hardships cheerfully, but she sorrowed deeply over the failure of a worker sent to minister to the villages.

The church was not finished by Easter and April handed her another bout with malaria. "Small-small" she said.

Amazing news came in early June. It was a letter written by Marie when Carmen's baby daughter was three hours old! Two weeks later she learned that her new grandbaby's name was Suzanne!

In the middle of June, Pauline came over on a Sunday. The ladies planned to leave for Monrovia early Monday morning. About 5:00 p.m., a "strong breeze," as the natives called it, hit. The school house, the temporary church and the teacher's house were all flattened. The metal roof on Gladys' residence probably saved it. All the thatch roofs were spoiled and a tree fell across the toilet and the chicken house. The new church roof of palm leaf cords was badly damaged, but school for sixty students opened after a three-day holiday with all hands busy repairing damages.

In July, the third letter from Brother Stairs about furlough arrived. The Board was looking for a replacement so she could come home. Her term was completed and she felt it.

The big news of August was that Brother Petty's health had improved so they would return to Liberia after the October conference. Jesus said, "Occupy till I come," so work continued on the new school and the first Christian wedding was held with flair on the mission.

Though her allotment had returned to $60.00 for several months, the next letter from Brother Stairs in October was discouraging. Three new missionaries recently went to other fields, but fares were not available for the Pettys to come or for Gladys to return.

On October 22, she wrote her children: "I still don't know anything about my homecoming. I'll send a cable when to meet me."

A letter from the Pettys, dated November 2, said they were ready, packed and waiting for passage on a boat.

On November 22, it dawned on her that she would probably not leave before Christmas. She dreaded the palaver, all the hands stretched out wanting gifts, and began praying for boxes to come. God heard! Some packages arrived that saved the day and she survived Christmas.

The slowly passing days held much building, roofing and reroofing. White clay was laboriously dug from the swamp and all the walls freshly rubbed. The truck made shorter work of the hauling problem but longer hours for the missionary. However, when the Petty family arrived on January 8, 1951, the mission fairly gleamed. Gladys was relieved and glad that her replacement had arrived. In the next few days friendship ripened into respect and love for the Pettys. Now she could leave with a light heart, knowing her beloved mission was in capable hands.

She boarded the Farrell Lines' *African Sun* on January 22, 1951, at Monrovia. Two days later during a boarding delay, she sent her daughters a letter that in twelve to fourteen days she expected to land at New York. Three and a half years after leaving from that city for

Africa, she returned and counted minutes until she finally reached Nashville, Tennessee, and a tearfully joyous reunion with her children and many dear friends.

The deputation whirl swept her away too soon—camp meetings, mission rallies, churches and conferences. Everyone eager to hear the experiences she told with unique verve and anointing. Refusing the heroine's role, she played down times of danger often beginning, "This happened to a lady I know. . . ." All the while, she was gathering equipment and supplies for her return.

The alchemy of dedication that moves a missionary to say goodbye to beloved children and the privilege of cuddling a grandbaby took Gladys back to Liberia in 1952. Accompanied by Jean Bailey on March 18 she returned to Bomi Hills to an uproarish welcome, in which some laughed, some cried, while others wailed.

By April she was settled into familiar routines, as though furlough had not happened. There were 108 students now, and large crowds packed the mission church for every service. She was grateful for new teaching aids enthusiastically received. The batter of merciless elements still made continual repair supervision necessary. And the insistent challenge of the villages nibbled on her heart.

One Friday, Jean went with her to Bugbay. The service was beautiful, but six and a half hours of walking round trip wearied both of them unreasonably. Gladys said she had never climbed over and walked so many tree trunks on one trip before. Tenderfoot Jean was in bed afterward with blistered feet and sore muscles.

Gladys was sure she would soon "get back in shape" and continued making village trips though each one left her miserably exhausted. She joked about her lame leg until it became too painful to be a laughing matter. Sheer determination kept her going through June, but in early July the missionary family insisted she should see the Dutch doctor at the mine hospital. Examination disclosed a tumor, and he recommended she return home for surgery. When her reluctance to go was evident, he said bluntly, "Mrs. Robinson, I suspect malignancy."

Determined to stay she called for prayer and fasting. When there was no improvement, however, mission officials insisted on an immediate return. She went, leaving her heart and most of her personal possessions behind, sure that she would soon go back to Africa.

The doctor's suspicion was confirmed by surgery that revealed the fatal extent of the cancer invading her body.

Leo returned, repentant, to stand by her in a dark hour. They had never divorced. He was a constant friend and helper and made plans to go with her to Africa when the sickness was over. She refused to return to the hospital. The old determined spirit asserted, "I'll not leave my family with hospital bills to pay when I'm gone, if Jesus does not see fit to heal me."

Those who loved her stood helplessly by as she suffered and retreated into remoteness overshadowed by man's last enemy to be conquered.

When E. L. Freeman, on furlough, visited her in November 1953, she spoke wistfully of the miracle that would let her return to Bomi Hills. There could have been one. There have been many such miracles, but the frail candle that flamed so brilliantly and with such compassion in gross darkness was flickering down to the end of the wick in God's will.

A month later, December 10, 1953, one moment inexorable pain traced its haggard etching on her face, and in the next, a valiant spirit took wings. In that split second, a flash of sudden glory illumined with rare beauty the empty house of clay.

Goodbye Gladys, until morning—that morning without clouds!

Gladys Robinson, on July 1947 prior to leaving for Liberia, West Africa.

Traveling through the countryside, Gladys & Pauline Gruse and students.

Gladys Robinson's home in Africa.

Traveling to Bougbar.

The church in Ozark, Illinois that Gladys Robinson started.

Banana harvest, Nov. 2, 1947, Gladys Robinson and Georgia Regenhardt.

10

THE STORY OF

Nina Ryan Russell

by Ralph Vincent Reynolds

As we travel through life we meet people who leave a great impression upon us. Some influence and change our lives greatly. One who left a lasting impression upon me was Nina Ryan Russell, Mother Russell, of Jamaica.

Mother Russell certainly was one of the most unforgettable characters I have ever known. It was a great privilege to have labored with her in the gospel for over five years. During that time the Russell family and ours shared living quarters at 68 Wildman Street, Kingston. We lived almost as one family, and the relationship was very happy and congenial, blessed by the Lord.

Mother Russell was wholly dedicated and completely given to the will of God in her life. She was fearless, yet humble. She was unselfish and generous, always ready to share with others, and constantly giving of herself to minister to the needs of those around her. Consequently, I have hesitated in telling the story of Mother Russell, for I know that I never could do justice to the memory of this wonderful Mother in Israel.

Mother Russell was born Nina Louise Ryan, on Christmas Day, 1888, in Liberty Valley, Brown's Town, St. Ann, Jamaica. She was the sixth of seven children born to godly parents, David and Margaret Malone Ryan. David Ryan was Irish while his wife, Margaret Malone Ryan, was Spanish.

The family settled in Brown's Town and the children were brought up in a strict Christian manner and in the fear of the Lord. Each morning and evening the family met for devotions in their home. Each child was drilled in the reading and knowledge of the Bible. On Sundays and at the mid-week services, all the children attended the Methodist church with their parents.

At the age of sixteen Nina Ryan was converted under the ministry of Reverend Myer and Reverend Johnson, two English ministers of the Methodist church. They were conducting special revival meetings and large crowds attended. They were spiritual men and given to much prayer. Just before each meeting started Reverend Johnson would ask all the people who came through curiosity to leave and make room for those who wanted to be saved. Many of the elite who were present would leave. As fast as they left others would come and take their place.

In those early years following her conversion Nina Ryan had two dreams and a vision which left a deep impression upon her life. This is shown in an account given by her step-daughter, Mrs. Dr. Pryce (formerly Nina Russell), as she remembered Mother Russell describing them:

After her conversion she dreamed that she saw a well-dressed man coming towards her with his fingers decked with rings, and a big grin upon his face. He kept moving his fingers to attract her. He kept looking back, and when he got very close to her, he looked back for the last time. Then he ran away and she realized that he was the devil. She then saw Jesus with His hands raised. A wonderful peace came over her and she awoke from her dream.

In another dream she was at home and saw two ladies standing at the gate. They beckoned to her and she went to find out what they wanted. She noticed that their shoulders were stooped. They inquired for the lady of the house. She told her mother that two ladies were there to see her. They asked her mother if she was the lady of the home, and her mother, smiling, said, "I am the captain of the ship." They told her to come along with them and if there were others in the house, they were to come also. They were taken to the sea and both ladies stood very close to the water. They flicked their wings and with a loud voice proclaimed, "This is the resurrection morning." Immediately the sea receded and formed a great wall as far as her eyes could see. The dead were raised.

She saw a friend and had not known that she had died from drowning. She spoke to her and her reply was, "This is the resurrection morning."

A band of music started to play on the top of the sea wall, and the angels announced the twelve tribes of Israel. She recognized Moses, Abraham, Joshua, and all the other patriarchs. Israel came first and the others came after.

241

For months she could still hear the music, and when she was telling us she could still hear it all over again. Never on earth had she heard music like that. They were singing the song of Moses and the Lamb.

One day she had a vision of the rapture. It was the most beautiful sight to behold. As far as her eyes could see all the saints were going up in unison. Their garments appeared as if a great shimmering light. She got to her feet and started to praise the Lord.

These dreams and visions left a great impression upon Mother Russell. From those early days in her life until the moment the Lord took her home to higher service, her heart and mind were set upon wholly serving the Lord. She gave herself completely to the Lord's work.

By 1914 Nina's brother, Horace Ryan, was in United States in business. At this time she helped him by purchasing goods for export to the United States. While she was assisting her brother, the Lord spoke to her. She went to Brown's Town, St. Ann, and again God spoke to her. God told her to go in the town, kneel in the middle of the square and pray. All she took with her was a sweater, which she threw over her shoulders. She prayed for some time, and when she stood there was a large gathering of people. She began to speak to them. They seemed very hungry for God. When the invitation was given, crowds came forward to be prayed for.

Having no place to house the people she had a thatched booth made and held services there. She wrote home to her sister, Mrs. Annie Scoltock, telling her of the revival and inviting her to come.

Prior to this a missionary by the name of Mrs. Nina

Stapleton had come to Jamaica from Chicago. She brought the Pentecostal message to Jamaica and held meetings in Kingston. She wrote to Brother Arthur Watson, a Pentecostal English man living in Montreal, and invited him to come to Jamaica. Brother Watson wrote to a friend in Ontario, Canada, Brother Lathwell, and told him of the invitation. Brother Lathwell paid Brother Watson's fare to Jamaica. Another Canadian, Brother William Bodie Smith, accompanied Brother Watson to Jamaica.

Upon the invitation of her sister, Sister Scoltock, along with Brother Watson, went to Brown's Town. Accompanying them was Elder Lee, a Jamaican and a former Baptist minister. Eventually Elder Lee became the pastor of the church that was established in Brown's Town and the presiding elder of the Pentecostal Assemblies of the World churches in Jamaica.

Nina had not yet received the Holy Ghost, but during the revival that followed in Brown's Town, many believers were filled with the Holy Spirit. The Anglican and Baptist churches were almost emptied, and the ministers got very upset. The police were sent to stop the meetings.

One night the police officers came to stop the meeting. The power of God was being mightily manifested. A police corporal pushed his way in and asked in a loud, gruff voice, "Who is in charge of this meeting?"

Brother Watson replied in a quiet meek voice, "The Holy Ghost is in charge of this meeting."

The power of God struck the officer. He took his baton and beat a hasty retreat. He could not arrest the Holy Ghost.

Nina learned a lesson the hard way in an incident which took place during this revival. A young man was

243

under the power of God and she attempted to quiet him. His foot caught her in her stomach. She heard God say, "Don't try to steady the Ark." She became very fearful and felt that she would die. She left the meeting and went home. She prayed and told the Lord she was sorry for what she had done.

The outcome of these meetings brought people from seventeen districts to attend the services. Men and women were slain under the power of God and had to be carried home on boards. At nights one could hear praying and singing in their homes. Many were afraid that they were going to die, for they had never seen the operation of the Holy Spirit before.

In those early days in Brown's Town, Nina showed the same spirit of compassion and generosity that she had all her life and was so remarkably revealed in her later years of ministry when she was known to all as Mother Russell. For example the people were suffering from drought and had to carry water long distances. She ministered to them not only spiritually, but materially. Many young people came forward and gave themselves to the Lord. Some of them had no shoes and came to church barefoot. Nina had no source of help except her own funds and those of her sister, Annie Scoltock. To keep things going and to pay for a place to have meetings, she sold the old home and this helped her out financially for a time.

Another sister of Nina Ryan, Eupemia, had married a Jamaican by the name of James C. Russell. The Russells had a family of eight children—five sons, and three daughters. The three daughters were Valda, Maggie, and Nina. Later when the church started at Wildman street in Kingston these three girls helped Mother Russell faithfully and each made a great contribution to the new church.

After we arrived in Jamaica in 1947, Valda Russell was my secretary. She also held an excellent position in one of the large offices in the city. Later she attended Bible college in Tupelo, Mississippi and received a missionary appointment to Liberia, where she ministered for five terms, or a total of twenty years. The youngest daughter, Nina, was Mother Russell's right hand helper. Much credit must be given to her for the great contribution she gave in the early days of the Wildman Street church. Later she married Dr. C. Pryce and still resides in Kingston.

As their family was growing up, the James Russells decided to sell their businesses in Montego Bay and Black River. In order that their children might finish high school and college, they moved to Kingston and bought a home on Clovelley Road. They then offered their large living room for gospel services.

Sister Nina Ryan, along with Brother Watson and Brother Smith, joined in these meetings. They gathered some people together and launched out for street services. Sister Ryan was in correspondence with Brother Andrew Urshan in New York, who mailed her some of his tracts on the deity of Jesus and speaking in tongues.

In July, 1920, Nina Ryan was baptized with the Holy Spirit. She experienced the Pentecostal blessing in her own home at Penrith Road in Kingston. This caused much excitement, for it was the first time anyone in the home had witnessed such an occurrence. Her eldest sister, Mary, suggested that they should send for the family doctor. When Nina and Mary's mother, Mrs. David Ryan, saw what was happening, she said there was no need for the doctor. Years before she had seen people fall under the power of God in revival in the Baptist church. She recognized that this was the power of God as spoken of in the Bible.

Later, the Lord called Sister Euphemia Russell home. She left behind her grieving husband, James, and eight motherless children. Because some of the children were quite small, the Ryan family at Penrith Road wanted the entire family to be there with them. Some years after his wife's death, Brother Russell proposed to Nina Ryan. She accepted and they were married on November 28, 1928 in Kingston. She was now the stepmother of her dead sister's children, and she helped her former brother-in-law raise his family. She became known to hundreds as Mother Russell.

Her new role as wife and mother did not interfere with her calling and ministry. They continued holding prayer meetings in the home, and the crowd began to grow. Their home was in a residential area and opposition arose from the neighbors because of the clapping and shouting. Since a complaint was made at the city hall, it was necessary to look for a place of worship. Mother Russell was able to get the use of a public place in the east end of the city. The seekers would stand around long tables, and many received the Holy Ghost.

Mother Russell and Sister Nina (Pryce) kept looking for a property that they could use for a church. After a long search they located the property later known as the headquarters church. It was a two story house located at 68 Wildman Street. Each floor had a large veranda running across the front and down the side. It had at one time been used as Father Divine's "Heaven" in Jamaica, but when Mother Russell rented it, the building was a dwelling. Brother and Sister Russell, Sister Nina, and another prayer warrior, Sister Loretta Blyer, moved into the building. Some rough benches were made, along with a little pulpit and a small table for the song books.

Services were held every night except on Saturdays. Once a week they would get the Rockfort Gardens where a lovely service was held every Friday. It was quite a distance to the Gardens and the saints would ride the tram-cars. Some times it would take two tram-cars to bring the people home after the meeting. Riding on the trams the saints would sing and shout the praises of God. This created much interest, and the attendance at Wildman Street grew.

Soon there was a large group of converts who desired to be baptized in Jesus' name. Mother Russell wrote Andrew Urshan in New York, requesting him to come to Jamaica and baptize the converts, most of whom had already been baptized with the Holy Ghost. Brother Urshan was unable to come but referred Mother Russell to Reverend William T. Witherspoon in Columbus, Ohio. Brother Witherspoon, accompanied by his wife, arrived in Kingston in 1934. He ministered to the church at Wildman Street and then conducted some baptismal services at sunrise in Kingston harbor. In the first service Brother Witherspoon baptized sixty-two believers. Mother Russell herself was baptized by Brother Witherspoon at this time at Sirgany Beach in 1934.

Until the time of his death Brother Witherspoon was a great friend of the Jamaican church and made three visits to the island. He encouraged by helping to set the church in order, by his wise counselling, and also by his liberal financial support. From this point the new church in Jamaica, with Mother Russell as pastor, was affiliated with the Pentecostal Assemblies of Jesus Christ of which Brother Witherspoon was chairman.

For ten years the property at 68 Wildman Street was rented. Since the crowds continued to grow, the landlord gave permission for the walls to be pushed out until the entire downstairs was used for church services. In 1944 this property was purchased by the local church.

The first business meeting for the purpose of purchasing the property took place on July 17, 1944, with sixty-five present. Mother Russell's husband, Brother J. C. Russell was the chairman. The church decided to purchase the property, to be held by five trustees, for 1550 pounds. A mortgage for 1200 pounds was secured from the Victoria Mutual Building Society. Another 150 pounds were raised by pledges.

In a later meeting the five trustees were announced. They were: W. T. Witherspoon of Columbus, Ohio, J. C. Russell, Mrs. J. C. Russell, W. O. Stewart, and Ivan Russell.

Brother Witherspoon donated the sum of $500.00 or 123 pounds, nine shillings, one penny. This offering certainly encouraged Mother Russell and her struggling assembly in their great step of faith.

The assembly took possession of the property on March 29, 1945. On April 30, 1945, a business meeting took place with sixty-five members present. As one reads the recorded minutes of this meeting, he is impressed with the spirit of joy and victory is evident. Here is an excerpt from those minutes:

It was then moved by Brother Russell, seconded by Brother P. Codner, and unanimously resolved that Sister Russell take the chair.

Sister Russell on rising said that she was glad to be present and to see so many out. She said that we had assembled to give gratitude to God for having helped us in a wonderful way to purchase our Church property. She could look back on the years past when they first came into the building, and in taking a retrospective view of the many difficulties, days of hardships, days of sorrow and days of joy experienced, she could certainly say that surely the Lord had been with us and had never failed us. The fact that we have purchased the property will go down in the history of the church as great proof of the love of God and of His protection during the many years that have passed. She went on to say that, although we had been able to purchase the property on terms through the Building Society there would be additional monthly expenses attached to the upkeep of the church which would have to be met and emphasized the point that if all the members united together and contributed their share in helping to shoulder the burden we would be able to meet these expenses with the help of the Lord—Minutes, Apostolic Gospel Church, April 30, 1945.

Following Mother Russell's appeal, the sum of eight pounds one shilling was pledged to be paid monthly by the saints. At the close of the meeting Brother Russell announced a special thanksgiving service and a special musical evening. The minutes of this meeting concluded with his statement "A very pleasant spirit pervade the gathering and everyone felt it was good to be there." It certainly was a great time of victory for Mother Russell and the saints at Wildman Street.

For some time Mother Russell had been suffering from poor health. It seemed that Mother Russell had expended herself in the preaching of the gospel. She never spared herself and apparently never thought of her own welfare. She simply gave until she was fully exhausted. To make matters worse Brother Russell became ill and passed away in June, 1946. Losing her faithful companion who had been such an encouragement to her was a crippling blow. At this point the Reynolds family entered the picture and became a part of Mother Russell's story.

In May, 1946 Brother Wynn T. Stairs sat in my living room in Lansdowne, Ontario, Canada. He began to talk about the need of a missionary in Jamaica. He said that Brother Russell was on his death bed and that Mother Russell was not well. Then he looked across the room at me and asked, "Will you go?"

I did not hesitate, for I was ready and simply answered, "We will go." We immediately began to make preparation. I resigned the school where I was teaching and the two churches I was pastoring. On February 9, 1947 the Reynolds family arrived in Kingston, Jamaica.

The wonderful spirit of this great woman was soon revealed to me as we corresponded with her concerning our going to Jamaica. The very first letter that I received from Mother Russell, dated October 16, 1946, reveals the spirit of love and hospitality which was extended to the new missionary family from the very beginning.

Dear Bro. & Sis. Reynolds,

   Greetings in the Precious Name Jesus.

   We are in receipt of your good letter of 10th October and was very pleased to have heard from you. We had a fine letter from Bishop Stairs informing us of your appointment as missionaries to Jamaica—which appointment was made at the Conference held at St. Louis, and appreciated much the kind manner in which he spoke of you both and of your willingness to come over and help us. We feel this is the Will of God as much prayer has been made for sometime that someone would be moved upon to come as much can be done at this time to further the good cause of the gospel of Christ.

   We thank you very much for snapshot enclosed of self and family, we are delighted with the family especially the kids—the little girl is cute. We regret to hear that Sister Reynolds is ailing and pray she will soon be better. Our family is a very large one—the majority are married and settled in their own homes.

   Jamaica is a beautiful little Island in the Caribbean Sea—it is surrounded by beautiful mountains. The population is about 2 million and is a mixed one. A good many American and Canadian families have settled here. There are churches of almost every denomination here.

   We find much pleasure in supplying information asked for—statement is enclosed. If you would like to have any further information please do not hesitate to ask as we would be glad to assist in whatever way we can.

   We note you are planning to be with us around the end of the year and would appreciate your letting us know the exact date as we would like to have this published and also make the necessary arrangements to secure a larger

*building where meetings could be held. Could you send us
a larger picture so that it could appear in the Newspaper
when you arrive?*

*We are praying for your coming trip accompanied by
Bishop Stairs and trusting to hear from you again,*

> *We remain,*
> > *With United Christian love from all,*
> > > *Yours in Christ,*
> > > > *Sister J. C. Russell*
> > > > *& Saints*

Mother Russell knew how to show true Christian
hospitality and to make strangers feel right at home. With
this spirit the Reynolds family was welcomed to Jamaica.
We arrived late one Sunday evening. The saints had refused to go home after church until they had seen the missionaries. Mother Russell met us at the church and escorted us to the platform. The entire congregation was
singing with all their hearts,

"Welcome, welcome all of you;

Glad you are with us."

She then escorted us upstairs where we sat down to
a Jamaican feast of fried chicken.

For over five years the Russell family and the Reynolds family lived as one family with complete harmony.
My wife and I and our three oldest children lived on one
side of the living quarters while Mother Russell, Sister
Nina, and Sister Blyer lived on the other side. It did not
take long for the Canadian family to be inspired by the
dedicated spirit and example of these three consecrated
sisters.

Mother Russell was one of the most charitable people we have ever met. She was always giving of her means to others. One day a young couple was getting married. They had very little and no furniture to set up housekeeping. Mother Russell gave them her own mahogany bedroom suite. She went back to sleeping on an ordinary bed while the young couple were able to enjoy the beautiful suite. This is only an example of her generosity. Her giving to the needy never ceased. It was a ministry of helping and sharing that continued daily.

Mother Russell was quite fearless. A few feet north of the headquarters building was an Adventist church where a large Jamaican man pastored. He had no use for the Pentecostals, and on Sunday evenings he often came to the door and preached to our overflow crowd. Mother Russell was known to walk the upper veranda and rebuke him saying, "In the name of Jesus, I rebuke you, you uncircumcised Philistine!"

Jamaica lies in an earthquake zone. Many times while we would be talking, a sharp shock would rattle the doors and windows. Upon more than one occasion, Mother Russell leaped to her feet when an earthquake would strike and rebuked it in the name of Jesus. "In the name of Jesus, I rebuke you!" she would speak to the earthquake in a commanding voice. "This building is built upon the name of Jesus. It cannot fall!"

Mother Russell was certainly a noble character. Just what it cost her personally to turn the church over to me, one will never know. She had raised the church up with her own prayers, fastings, and tears. To turn it over to a foreigner must have been very difficult to her, not only to step aside, but to have to live on the same premises and be an onlooker to everything that was happening. One day she was the pastor in charge; the next day she was on the sidelines as an observer. Only a person of noble character could have done it.

No doubt Mother Russell saw many mistakes as I struggled to lead the Jamaican church on to victory and revival. However, she solidly supported and encouraged me in every way possible. I shall never know just what this must have cost her in her own personal feelings. However, I do know that she never wavered in her prayers for my wife and me, and upon many occasions in the heat of the battle I could feel the strength of Mother Russell supporting me.

Physically, Mother Russell was a weakened woman, broken in health. Although we prayed for her many times and understood in part just how frail she was, we did not realize just how close her end was. On March 16, 1952, we returned home to Canada. One month later in April, 1952, Mother Russell was called home by her Lord. We would never have left the island if we had known that within a month Mother Russell would pass on to her reward.

When Mother Russell passed away crowds attended her funeral. They lined the streets on the way to the cemetery to pay respect to the memory of this great woman of God who had ministered among them.

For the last five months that I was in Jamaica during the first term, I had no automobile. I traveled in the city on a bicycle and in the country on the country buses. As a result I talked to many strangers who did not attend the church. To my amazement almost all of them knew or had heard of Mother Russell. They were not acquainted with me nor had attended the church, but they had heard of Mother Russell. A good report concernng this mother in Israel had traveled far and wide.

That the church in Jamaica is still growing and flourishing pays tribute to her memory. The wonderful church at Wildman Street, under the leadership of Pastor Sammy Stewart, is a living memorial to the prayers and ministry of this dedicated handmaiden of the Lord. We should also pay tribute to Sister Pryce (Nina Russell) who labored at the side of Mother Russell in those early days. We humbly thank the Lord for the contributions of the late Brother W. T. Witherspoon and others who helped in the founding of the United Pentecostal Church of Jamaica.

One of the great blessings of my own life has been the privilege of being closely associated for a few years with this twentieth century prophetess. The impression she left upon me has been lasting. No doubt everyone who came under the influence of her ministry would also testify that they were never the same again.

The frail temple in which Mother Russell dwelt lies in the grave, but Mother Russell is not dead. The influence of her life lives on and will continue to do so until that glorious resurrection morning about which she dreamed as a young girl. At that time hundreds will thank her for the true message of salvation that she brought to them.

1947, Reynolds, Stairs and Mother Russell with saints.

1949, Conference at Kingston Jamaica, Brother Morgan, Mother Russell & Reynolds in center.

1940, Lt. to rt. Sister Keane, Bro. J. C. Russell, Sis. Witherspoon, Bro. Witherspoon, Sis. J. C. Russell, Bro. Stewart.

1950, Mother Russell breaking sod for new tabernacle.

Sister Valda Russell.

The Reynolds family, outgoing missionaries to Jamaica.

11

THE STORY OF

Ellis and Marjorie Scism

by Audrene Scism

On a beautiful morning in Oakland, California on September 19, 1932, two lives were joined in holy matrimony. This union of two special people would influence others even on the other side of the world from where this modest ceremony took place.

Marjorie Moyer had come to Oakland to join the Missionary Training Home. It was connected with a big downtown mission run by Brother Harry Morse. He was especially happy to have young people come to his training home who felt a call for foreign missionary service and Marjorie had a call to India. Their room was limited, students were carefully chosen. Ellis Scism, a young man from Salem, Oregon, came a year later. Interestingly, he also had a call to India. What a joy for everyone when, at the end of their training, Marjorie and Ellis decided to blend their lives and call.

After the wedding they wanted to leave for India preferably to go with friends who had also been at the training home and were planning to leave shortly. However, Brother Morse felt that Ellis and Marjorie needed more experience at home. They were able to join these friends for a missionary tour in the fall of 1933 that took them through Arkansas, New Mexico, Colorado, Wyoming, Idaho and back to California to the training home. These were depression days, but God kept His hand on them and they had their first taste of missionary deputation.

Back in Oakland, Harry Ellis Scism was born in March of 1934. Everyone at the home was delighted. Brother and Sister Morse considered themselves the grandparents, but no one was happier than Harry's mother and father.

When Harry was seven months old, Marjorie and Ellis decided they should move out into the work of God to prepare themselves for their call. After visiting Ellis' family in Salem, Oregon, they went on to Rupert, Idaho, to help Brother and Sister Haskel Yadon in their church all the while praying that God would open the door.

They soon heard of a group of people in Clarkston, Washington, who had been baptized in Jesus' name and filled with the Holy Spirit in special meetings held by Brother Oscar Vouga. They had even built a church building on some leased land. After Brother Vouga left, however, division came among them. Some dropped out and others moved away, but there were a few faithful ones left. So, it was to this little group Ellis and Marjorie went.

Times were very difficult for everyone during the depression, and the little church and the pastor's family struggled bravely. Yet, even in those difficult days, God gave special answers to prayer from time to time. The young couple knew that His hand was on them all the time.

After a year and a half they got a call to go to Tieton, Washington. They felt that God wanted them to move on, but they did not want to leave the church in Clarkston. The structure was in such a bad state of disrepair, however, that it had to be closed. Then they felt at peace to move on.

The Scism's new home was two rooms in the back of the church and two bedrooms upstairs off the auditorium. They were very happy. Brother Scism was in district work by this time, and Sister Scism took charge of the services during his absence. During this time in Tieton, Ferne Lenore was born in September, 1935. The church people loved the children very much. Brother and Sister Scism began to train them at an early age to be obedient and respectful.

In 1938, the church in Twin Falls, Idaho needed a pastor, and Brother and Sister Scism were accepted. That began a busy, wonderful six and a half years filled with jail services, street services, Saturday children's church, and ladies prayer meetings, as well as all of the regular church services. While in Twin Falls, Sister Scism had the opportunity to start services in the nursing home. She took a group of young people with her, along with Harry and Ferne, who also helped with the singing.

One day while in prayer for the little city of Rupert, Idaho, which was without a pastor, the Lord spoke to Sister Scism asking her if she would be willing to go there with her husband. The Lord had been speaking to Brother Scism also, so they made arrangements to leave Twin Falls and take the church in Rupert.

In addition to pastoring the church, Brother Scism was now the District Superintendent of the Northwest District, which included Montana, Wyoming, Idaho, Washington, Oregon, British Columbia and Alaska. He travelled much, so Sister Scism shouldered many responsibilities of the church. She loved to teach, preach, play her guitar, cook meals, and take care of her family considering it was all part of her work for the Lord. While the Scisms were in Rupert, Harry met the little girl who would one day become his wife.

After pastoring in Rupert, Idaho for a year and a half, the district conference voted to have Brother Scism full-time in the district work, so he had to give up the Rupert church. They moved back to Oregon City, Oregon so Sister Scism could be with her mother while Brother Scism travelled. It was a change in their lives, but prepared them for a ministry that was to come.

In the spring of 1948, Brother Stairs wrote to Brother and Sister Scism asking them how long it would take for them to be ready to leave for India. After waiting for nearly fourteen years, it came as a shock. At the next district conference Brother Scism resigned, and Brother J. A. Johnson was elected to take his place. In January, 1949 they located a ship, made reservations and began preparations. They had mixed emotions, since Brother Scism's father was getting old as was Sister Scism's mother. The Scisms intended to make India their home and were not planning to return. What a joy it was to finally answer the call of God that had been on their hearts for many years. The door had opened at last.

There was very little time for deputational work. They sold their first new car and bought an old jeep, thinking it would be more suitable for travel in India. A few churches were able to help them, and God made a way. They loaded their belongings on the ship in Portland, Oregon.

The Scism family set sail from Portland on the China Mail on January 31, 1949. Since this was a freighter, it could accomodate only about twelve passengers. They went to Seattle and stayed there until the second of February, when they set out on the high seas.

It was a severe winter and the ocean was rough. Most of the passengers were seasick. The ship made two stops in Japan, one in Hong Kong, and four in the Philippines. Cargo was unloaded, then they proceeded to Java and Singapore. From Singapore they sailed into the Indian Ocean and travelled south until they reached the Madras harbor on the evening of March 26. The next day the unloading began. It took several days to get everything through customs.

From Madras they travelled to Kodaikanal in the mountains, rented a house and enrolled Harry and Ferne in a missionary boarding school. Brother Scism had been sick on the trip over but now at Kodai the pain became more intense and he needed to see a doctor. The Christian missionaries in India usually came to the hills during the hottest season, took their children out of boarding school and kept them at home for awhile until the rainy (monsoon) season began. Then they would leave their children in the boarding school in Kodaikanal and return to their mission stations on the plains. Most of the doctors had left Kodaikanal by this time, but one doctor was still there, so arrangements were made for Brother Scism to have an appendectomy.

It is rather cold in the hills, so the nurse put wool socks on Brother Scism's feet and a hot water bottle under his heels to help keep him warm while under anethesia. As he was coming out from under the effects of the anethesia he complained of pain in his heels. Sister Scism called for the nurse, but she told her, "Oh, don't pay any attention. They always say strange things when they come out of anethesia. Wait till the doctor comes." But Sister Scism kept insisting that they look at his heels. Finally, the nurse agreed and when they removed the socks they found third-degree burns due to the very hot water bottle that had been placed there. The surgery healed in due time, but the heels caused trouble over months and months of trying one thing and then another. Finally Brother Scism had to travel 550 miles to Vellore Mission Hospital for live skin grafting which was performed by Dr. Paul Brand, one of the authors of *Fearfully and Wonderfully Made*.

In the meantime, Brother and Sister Scism moved to Travancore, a very densely populated area along the southwestern coast. They moved to the town of Adur and rented a house which was located between two schools. The Indian children were naturally very curious about the newcomers to their village and would stop on their way to and from school to look in the windows. The house was small and Harry's cot was on a closed-in veranda. Since school in India operates in shifts, and the first shift starts early in the morning, Harry would be awakened by giggling and look up to see a window full of faces. It did not do much good to go inside because there were eyes looking in all the windows. Eventually, the children got more used to having the newcomers there and were not quite so curious.

One day not long after the Scisms had moved to Adur, a Hindu man came carrying a baby whose feet had been badly burned by a hot teakettle that had been removed from the stove and placed on the floor nearby. Sister Scism applied some burn salve and bandages and took care of him as best she could. She told the man that her God could heal the child and then prayed that God would heal him, knowing the child would kick off the bandages before long. Soon, others began to come. One little baby had fallen from a wall and seemed to have a concussion. She was able to wake him up enough to eat some mashed banana. In a few days, with much prayer, he was on the road to recovery. Many of the children had "itch," which is caused by a parasite that burrows under the skin and lays eggs and continues to cause scars, itching and inflamation. Sister Scism lovingly cared for all who came, even those with smelly, ulcerous sores. No one left without a sincere prayer that not only would they be healed physically but that they would be healed of their sins and have their hearts and lives cleansed, and that they would find something to live for.

After skin grafting on his heels Brother Scism was still unable to wear shoes for awhile. On his trip into Northeast India he wore Indian sandles. Brother Scism had heard of a revival among the tribal people that lived in Northeast India, so he planned a long trip into this area. The long trip included a train ride from India's southwestern coast to the city of Calcutta in the northeast, a flight across Bangladesh (which was then East Pakistan), and a journey across the steep mountainsides by jeep. The road was too narrow for more than one-way traffic, so gates were erected along the way and traffic would proceed in one direction for a certain number of hours after which the direction would be reversed. It resulted in some long waits at the gates.

Brother Scism finally reached Aizawl and met some wonderful people who had been experiencing an outstanding revival. They were hungry for God. Brother Scism began to explain to them the work and power of God, explained to them their need to be baptized in Jesus' name and to understand the Oneness of God. Like the Bereans of New Testament times, they searched the Scripture, saw that it was true and with great joy followed the Lord. The new church began to grow tremendously under the kind and wise guidance of Brother Scism. Besides his annual visits he kept in touch constantly through correspondence.

In the meantime, the Scisms were very busy with the work in Kerala. Convention time was especially busy. Special revival services were held under a thatched roof in the open air. In many places everything they needed personally had to be taken, including camp cots, folding tables and chairs, bedding, clothing, food, matches and lamps. The Scisms would usually leave Mission Bungalow in Adur on Wednesday or Thursday drive to the area where the convention was to be held, have services through Sunday night, pack up, come home to get everything washed, get fresh bread, get a new supply of food, pack everything again and leave for the next place. This went on every week throughout the convention time. During this time Ferne and Harry were home from boarding school and could participate, which greatly helped their parents. All in all, it was a busy, productive and happy time.

Furlough time came in 1955 after six and a half years on the field. Brother and Sister Jimmy Burns, missionaries to Ceylon, came to look after the work while the Scisms were gone. During this furlough, Harry met his childhood sweetheart again and plans were made for their wedding. Both Harry and Ferne had planned to stay in the United States, but God dealt with both of them to return to India with their parents. So after a busy, but refreshing year filled with deputational travel and with the joy of visiting family and friends and after the marriage of Harry and Audrene, they returned, eager to be active in the harvest field of India.

Brother Scism had long been feeling the need for a Bible school, and in 1957 that dream became a reality with the help of concerned friends in America. The Bible school was started in an office building on the property that had been purchased in Adur. A rented house nearby provided a dormitory. Now young men from different areas, even from the tribal area far away in the mountains of Northeast India came. They could go back into their areas and other places some of which were greatly restricted to foreigners. In later years, a Bible school building and dormitories were built on the mission compound.

In April, 1958 God blessed Brother and Sister Scism with a little grandson, Stanley Keith. He was a real joy. But Harry and Audrene felt a burden for north India, so when Stanley was ten months old, they packed most of their belongings in their jeep station wagon and started out for the language school in Mussoorie in the foothills of the Himalayas. There they studied Hindi in preparation for opening a new work in the northern area. In

267

March, 1961 the Lord again blessed the Scism family with a new little member, this time a granddaughter named Loretta Jane. By this time, Harry and Audrene, having finished language school, were starting to open a new work in the city of Bhopal, Madya Pradesh.

Missionary life and work has its glad times and sad times, difficult times and productive times, lonely and happy times. The Scisms experienced all of these. It was a sad day when Sister Scism told her mother "goodbye" feeling in her heart that she would never see her again. It was a sad day, too later in that term when she received the news that her mother had passed away. There were times of sickness when, but for the help of a little girl, who was hired to sit with Sister Scism after surgery and who called for help just in time, she, too, would have passed away. There were times of sickness for Brother Scism also, with a none too successful ulcer operation and other health problems. It was a sad day, indeed when they told Ferne "goodbye" as she had to leave India in 1965, having contracted tropical Sprue. However, it was a glad day when the Shalms who were already good friends and had worked with another oneness organization, returned in India to work with the United Pentecostal Church. Hands were strengthened. What a joy it was to see numbers added to the church daily and yearly and to see so many graduating from the Bible school, ready to go out into the harvest. What a joy it was to see Indian leadership develop and become mature and strong.

Not many visitors came to India during the sixties. It was a real pleasure to have Brother and Sister Adams, their daughter, Sandra, and friend, Diola Satterwhite (now Diola Willoughby), visit them in 1966. After spending some time in the Tamil area with the Shalms and then in Kerala with the Scisms, Brother Adams planned to accompany Brother Scism on part of his annual trip into Northeast India.

In February, 1966, Brother Scism and Brother Adams made the long trip to Lahkipur. From there Brother Adams planned to return to Delhi to join the rest of his party for their onward journey, while Brother Scism would go on into the mountain region of Northeast India. When Brother Adams returned, he mentioned that Brother Scism was not feeling well at all, and he did not like to see him go so far away in that condition. Another very difficult problem was that a lot of trouble was brewing in this area at the time. There was much political unrest, and the area was on the brink of erupting into a full-scale rebellion.

As Brother Scism and Brother Hnuna, a Northeast Indian pastor, reached the place where they were to start up the one-way road to Aizawl they found a tree cut in such a way that it had fallen across the road. Their bus could not proceed up the mountain. Brother Hnuna said he must go up anyway by foot as his family was in Aizawl. Brother Scism, had to turn around and go back. The rebels had done this and the army was called out to fight the rebels.

Many people suffered during this rebellion. Many churches and whole villages were burned. Some pastors were put in jail. Brother Hnuna, as he was walking up the mountain accepted a ride that was offered to him by people in a jeep, not knowing that they were rebels. The jeep was stopped by the army and everyone aboard was arrested including Brother Hnuna. He was put in jail for

6 months, his house was burned, but even in jail he was able to witness for the Lord and win souls. He was told he could read his Bible, but he couldn't preach so because the jailor couldn't understand his language he kept his eye on the Bible and talked to the other prisoners about the Lord who did understand his language.

When Brother Scism returned back home from the long trip he was surprised to learn that the army had been sent out to search for him. They had received the report that he had already gone into the mountains of Northeast India before the trouble started. Brother Scism was not at all well when he returned and kept getting worse. On June 13th his temperature rose rapidly. It was discovered he had Thyphoid. The doctor in Kodai gave him strong anti-biotics, but it didn't seem to help. It looked like he wouldn't live. Another doctor friend who happened to be visiting Kodai came by to see him and remarked as he was leaving, "I've never seen a man look so much like a corpse and still be alive." Even in that very weakened condition he was concerned about the church in Northeast India going through such turmoil and political unrest. He called Harry to his side and in a weak voice asked him, "Have we heard anything from Acsom? Do we know how they are getting along? Is there anyway we could get some of their funds to them?" He grew weaker day by day. Sister Scism constantly waited on him and cared for him. She would sometimes change his sheets two and three times a night due to the high fever. In addition to thyphoid he also got phebitis and had to keep his leg elevated. Then pneumonia set in. It was now August. The doctor in Kodai felt he should go to the Swedish Medical Hospital in Tirapatur where he could get better care than they were able to give in Kodai. A bed was made in the back of the car and he was taken to the Swedish Hospital. After getting somewhat better for a little while he again took a turn for the worse. The Swedish doctor told Harry, "If you want your father to live, you'd better get him back to the United States." Arrangments were made. Brother Scism had lost much weight and was so weak that he could only walk slowly with the aid of two walking sticks. Harry took his parents to the nearest airport and flew with them to Bombay and helped them get on the plane for the homeward journey all the while feeling that he would probably never see his father here on earth again. His little mother was still doing more than her part carrying all the hand baggage as they left.

So bode two pioneers of India farewell to the land of their calling and to the people they loved so much.

Fourteen years passed from the time they first felt the call to India until they were able to go but after the next seventeen and a half years of living and working for the Lord in that land they left a church of 30,000 members.

After returning to the United States Sister Scism said one day. "God has been good to me. If I had my life to live over, I would want it to be just the same." She went to be with the Lord on August 5, 1983. Brother Scism after going through much more sickness, including a brain tumor and all the anxiety that preceeded and followed that operation not only lived but became very active in the work of the Lord again. He pastored a church, became foreign missions district director, edited a district paper and helped in many different ways.

Two hearts became one as Ellis and Marjorie Scism

joined together to answer the call of God on their lives. The result of those years spent answering that call is a church growing and continuing to spread in the land they so dearly loved. Many lives were transformed by the power of God. Wonderful healings and miracles took place as God moved among the people. Younger men became mature and were able to take on the responsibility of leadership. Bible schools and training centers were established and Indian missionaries sent out to new unreached areas.

God is truly so good. What a privilege it is to be laborers together with God, to hear the call of God, to answer that call, and be a part of the wonderful kingdom of God. To God be the glory.

Brother Ellis Scism with Brethren from Northeast India, 1950.

Ellis & Marjorie Scism on wedding day, Sept. 19, 1932.

Lt. to Rt. Ferne Scism, Bro. & Sis. Ellis Scism, Bro. & Sis. Harry Scism, 1956.

Ferne and Bro. & Sis. Scism, 1966, returning from India.

12

THE STORY OF

Fred K. Scott

by Fred K. Scott

The *Brazil Maru* gently nudged the dock as the hawsers were drawn tight. We had arrived at Montevideo, Uruguay. On deck and looking toward shore, my wife and I and our two younger children, Kathy and Timothy, were greeted with a large welcome banner and a group of people from the Uruguayan church and several missionaries who had gathered for a conference in Montevideo.

How did this all come about? I have marveled many times, while traveling through foreign countrysides or perhaps preaching in the jungle by a fireside, "How could a skinny, freckle-faced, redheaded boy ever land in such far away places?" Looking back, I know now that God had His hand on me at a very young age to serve Him wherever He called.

I was born on October 30, 1915 in Calgary, Alberta the third son of Walter and Evelyn Scott. A few months later a sister, Helen, was born to ĥe followed by another sister, Alice, and then my youngest brother, Colin. My older brothers are Allan and Lawrence.

I had a very precious mother and a kind and understanding father but something went wrong in my young life. Before the age of six I was a very emotionally disturbed child. Perhaps it was because I was in the middle of this family of six children and I needed more love and attention than a very busy mother could give but God heard the prayers of a mother and father for their son.

When I was nine years old an elderly English brother asked for a Sunday school class for boys, ages nine through twelve. I was the only one, but he told the pastor he wanted me. The first Sunday, after we prayed, he took a penny and held it up as he told me that the first thing we would do was take up a missionary offering. This money would help to tell some little boy in some far away place about Jesus. At that moment the seed was planted in my heart that would later produce a missionary. Before long we had a class of about twelve boys. He impressed upon us that we were responsible for bringing other boys and we did.

In the summer of 1927 our family migrated to Salem, Oregon.

When I was fourteen, we were in a house prayer meeting on a stormy, Oregon winter night. As the people were putting on their coats to leave, we were all singing, "I will go where you want me to go, dear Lord." Suddenly the power of the Lord struck me to the floor and God called me to preach His Word. I thought I would just have to leave and start preaching, so I ran from God for the next three years. God, who sees the heart, knew that I really loved Him and wooed me back to renew the call. I was only too willing to say, "Yes."

The same year we moved to Salem, the Joseph Smith family moved back to Salem from Idaho. Brother Smith was a minister. They had four children, and one of them was a pretty, redheaded girl a couple of years younger than I. At that age I was not the least bit interested but at seventeen I fell in love with this young lady, Vida Smith.

The next three years are something to remember. She is a redhead and so am I. This is not to say that all redheads have hot tempers, but we both had our share. We went together, fought and broke up several times. Finally, on August 17, 1935 we were married. Some people in the church gave our marriage six months to last, but fifty years later we are still in love. God was so good to give me such a precious wife.

Our next big step in following God's call took place in the fall of 1939. I had served in many capacities in the local church and had been an assistant pastor for two years. Sister Augusta Lundquist from St. Paul, Minnesota was visiting in Salem. She asked me when I was coming to Apostolic Bible Institute to Bible School. I told her I would that fall if God would provide. He did, and we left for St. Paul. We now had a three-year-old son, Kenneth. I completed one year at Apostolic Bible Institute, and consider it one of the most profitable years of my life.

The next summer, A.B.I. President S. G. Norris thought I was ready to become a pastor, and there was a real need for a pastor in Cochrane, Wisconsin. After visiting them for a month I permitted them to vote on me. I was unanimously accepted and started my years of pastoring in the United States.

Before going to Cochrane, I was ordained in Clinton-ville, Wisconsin as a minister of the Pentecostal Assemblies of Jesus Christ. The same day that I left for Cochrane, I put my wife and little boy on the train to Salem to visit home for awhile. It turned out to be several weeks as she had to work to earn her way back.

During these weeks I got to know the people whom I had come to pastor. They were very kind to me and invited me to their homes for dinner. They brought me cooked chickens and dressed chickens, as well as many other foods. They also brought live chickens. The garage was full of them when my wife arrived home.

We have pastored several places and we loved them all, but Cochrane was our first love. We pastored there two different times. During our first pastorate there, our first daughter, Patricia, was born and during the second our son, Jerry, was born. God performed many healings while we were there. For example, Sister Malles was raised from the dead and her healing was a great witness in the area.

In the fall of 1942 God called me to Portland, Oregon to open up a work. Although this was during World War II with all its hardships, yet God helped us to establish the first Oneness church in this great city. From here God later called me back to be pastor in Cochrane a second time.

Later we pastored in Marshfield and Clintonville, Wisconsin. We saw miracles of healing in both of these churches. Our second daughter Kathy, was born while we were in Marshfield, and our youngest son, Tim, while we were in Clintonville.

Kathy is a miracle girl. God healed her of a brain tumor just before she was a year old. According to the doctor she had no chance of ever being normal and only one chance in a thousand of living. She is now a missionary in Argentina with her husband Darry Crossley and their three children. Timothy is assistant pastor at Pocatello, Idaho.

We also pastored in Salem, North Bend and Cottage Grove, Oregon. While we were pastoring in Salem, the Lord called me to be a missionary to South America. At the close of a power-packed service God spoke to me. I told Him I would go, but He would have to do something for our daughter, Pat. While we were in Clintonville she was struck with a very rare disease of the spinal cord that left her a paraplegic. I knew we could not take her to the foreign field. God told me He had provided for her so I left it all in His hands.

Four years later, while pastoring at North Bend, the call became so heavy that I could not wait any longer. God had provided for Pat. Rodney Buffington had fallen in love with her and, even though he knew her problems and what it would mean he told me he loved her and felt that caring for her was God's work for him. God reminded me of His promise of provision. They are married and have two children and love the Lord. Rodney is presently very active in Neighborhood United Pentecostal Church of Portland, pastored by Brother George Sponsler.

I had sought the Lord sincerely, and at last all my questions were answered. At that time I was forty-nine years old and felt I might be too old to go. Brother Ed-

279

win Judd encouraged me, so we applied and received our appointment at the New Orleans General Conference in 1966. Then we started deputation and the work to get our visas.

January 15, 1968 finally came and we were on our way, shipping out of Long Beach, California aboard the *Brazil Maru*, a Japanese vessel. We discovered that they served fish three times a day. Later, however, we learned that we did not have to eat fish for breakfast nor the other meals if we did not want to.

Leaving our eighteen-year-old son Jerry was difficult but we arranged for him to live in an apartment with another boy. Saying goodbye to Pat was still harder. We left her that morning, in front of her house in her wheelchair. Although she seemed defenseless her strong faith in God was a source of strength to me.

We spent the last week in the U.S.A. with the Harvey Davises, who are truly kind and lovely people.

Our trip took thirty-five days and we enjoyed every minute of it. We sailed from Long Beach, California to Cristobal, Panama to the Netherlands Antilles to La Guiara, Venezuela to Rio de Janeiro, Brazil and then to Santos, Brazil. The Samuel Bakers met us there and took us across the mountains to Sao Paulo, introducing us to missionary life.

While in Sao Paulo, the Bakers took us out to a little, country church where the pastor insisted we come to his house for lunch. There we tried their strong coffee, served in a little demitasse cup. One of these cups of coffee would make three strong cups of our style of coffee. Sister Scott could not drink it, but I did. Later she learned to love it.

After a mad dash across the mountains back to Santos, we journeyed to Buenos Aires, Argentina where we met the John Klemins and the John Hattabaughs. We spent five days in Buenos Aires and loved that beautiful city with its friendly people. It was there however, that about $2,000 worth of our goods were stolen. We found this out after we got to Montevideo, Uruguay and unloaded our things. We were reimbursed by the insurance for about $1,200.00, but there were many things such as family photos that could not be replaced.

At last we disembarked and were ready for our foreign mission work. All of the missionary families were staying with the Battles. The small chapel next door became a dorm. The ladies prepared stacks of food and we had a good time of fellowship.

The conference was quite a new experience for us. We knew no spanish and the sound was strange. There was nothing strange, however, about the moving of the Holy Spirit. A tent was erected over the cement slab that would later be the church.

The Elga Battles were great people to be with. Brother Battle helped me to get acquainted with the Uruguayan ways of doing things, and translated my preaching and teaching. I was with him almost every day as we went to government offices and worked on the church building.

After a few weeks we took a trip around Uruguay, camping out at nights. There were no churches in the interior at that time.

The first three years in Uruguay were very trying. We learned the language while taking charge of the work as the Battles had returned to the States. The many hours spent in government offices for one thing or another cannot be counted.

Here is an example of the frustration of dealing with governmental red tape: After the church building was completed, I filed with the Department of Taxation as a church so we would be tax exempt. Nine months later, after spending at least six hours a week in one office or another, I was told the President and the Secretary of State had signed the form, and it was now on the way back down. Finally, it was time for us to return on furlough, so I tried to explain to the officials that the registration needed to be done before I left. The official told me not to worry, that everything was fine and that the man who was taking my place could handle it. When he tried to do so, the officals told him that the Department of Law had turned down the request. We were right back at the beginning again.

Learning Spanish was not easy for Sister Scott and me. I was fifty-one when I began learning the language. Our daughter, Kathy, was my interpreter after the Battles left. She was a great interpreter, but she finally suggested that I try on my own as she would be returning to the States in a few months. Those first feeble efforts were very trying, but she was always there if I got stuck.

God helped us to see some victories while in Uruguay. The Stanley Bakers and the Darrell Geisslers worked with us. The Geisslers continued on and did a good work there.

Our first real break occurred after our furlough when the D. L. Spears Evangelistic team came. We saw a great move of God and several received the Holy Ghost. This laid the foundation for an upcoming crusade in which 148 received the Holy Ghost. Because of a well-planned follow up, we were able to contact ninety percent of these people. As a result, we opened new churches and had great growth in the existing churches.

During the crusade there were many healings, and one man spoke in perfect German when he received the Holy Ghost. One man went through the prayer line without receiving his answer. As I took him aside the Lord revealed to me his problem. He was on drugs, demon-possessed and immoral. As I prayed with him, he was delivered. A few days later,while driving through a barrio where we had a church the pastor in the car with me pointed out a fine looking, well-dressed man with a little girl holding each hand. It was the same man. Since the crusade he had been baptized and had received the Holy Ghost.

After an extended furlough because of illness, we flew to Paraguay. I became superintendent over both Uruguay and Paraguay. Paraguay is a very beautiful country, but quite primitive. The capital city, Asuncion, has a population of about 300,000. There are two other cities of about 25,000. The rest of the villages are very small. Sixty-five percent of the people live in the jungle and not in towns.

The Donald Bryants were there when we arrived. They went there independently, and laid a good foundation. The missionaries in southern South America encouraged them to come into the United Pentecostal Church and they did so while still on the field. Upon arriving in the United States for furlough, they met the Foreign Missions Board and were appointed back to Paraguay. They are still there and doing a good work.

Before the Bryants returned home, we bought property on which to build a church. Our first building was twenty-eight feet by forty feet. We started services in it before it had a roof and floor. When it rained we could not have services for the tropical rain storms are severe. When we had a portion of the roof on, we would get under that part. With no windows and lots of wind, we were hit from every side by "showers of blessings."

This church grew, and the building has been enlarged several times and a Bible school attached to it. While the building was being dedicated, several young men threw bombs at us. They had manufactured home-made bombs of black powder; which were balls about ¾ inches in diameter. We still had no windows, but the Lord protected us and no bombs entered the building. I counted 198 holes in the outside finish, some over four inches across. We were never molested again.

Many people have come to know the Lord in this church. The first woman that Brother Bryant baptized was an elderly grandmother who had been a Catholic all her life. Several times I noticed her praying at the altar, making very strange noises groaning as if she had a bad stomach ache. One Saturday we had a youth rally and several churches came. During this time I noticed her doing the same thing. I called some of the ministers over to pray for her. As they started to pray for her, they turned to me and said, "She isn't ill but is speaking in tongues." One of these men had grown up among the Lenguas, a very remote Indian tribe. He said it was almost impossible to learn to speak the Lenguas' language as it consisted of many guttural sounds, but he could understand everything she was saying.

The second church we opened was in the Chaco. This is the western part of the country and is very much like the Old West, including cowboys with guns on their belts, great herds of cattle and even Indians. Getting to the little village of Villa Hayes required crossing the river by ferry and driving over a dirt road for several miles. We either had to catch the last ferry at 8:30 p.m. or stay overnight, which meant sleeping outside with the mosquitoes.

For our first baptismal service we had to walk about three miles. We came to a beautiful pond. There was only one problem. Several boys, ranging in age from ten to seventeen, were swimming in the nude, which is a common custom in Paraguay. When I baptized the first candidate, a rather heavyset woman, one of the boys did a belly flop as close as he could making it appear that the big splash came from the woman.

At this point I stopped and preached a little message from the water, not scolding nor condemning, but just telling the old, old story again. From then on the people were very respectful. A group of the young men followed us back to the church and stayed for the service. The local pastor talked to them most of the night and several of them were baptized. One of them became a preacher.

A group of trinitarian Pentecostals in southern Paraguay had received one of our Truth Series tracts about repentance. They came looking for an explanation as we were the only church that preached repentance in Paraguay. The other churches only preached mentally accepting the Lord Savior. This contact resulted in the opening of a new work.

The precious people of this church were persecuted by the people of the other church. When Brother Bryant and I went down to explain the way more perfectly, two of the men came to warn us that the colonel in charge of the area had forbidden them to have any more services and had taken away their I.D. cards. This was the equivalent of a house arrest.

We informed them that we had orders from our Captain that we could have a service. They were thrilled, and soon runners were going through the sugar cane fields to inform the people of the meeting. That night at the close of the service thirteen held up their hands to be baptized. The persecution continued, however, resulting in four of the men being put in prison. The other church had told the authorities that these people were Communists. After several months they were proved innocent and were released.

There is now a good, strong church in this place. They built their first building at a great sacrifice and have had to enlarge it at least twice. Because of my bad health, we were forced to come home after three years.

Some things in life we do not understand, and I did not understand the next three years. I became pastor of a church in Cottage Grove, Oregon. We found some very precious people there and they are still very close to us.

This time was probably one of the hardest in my ministry. The church was small, and I had to work. Working a secular job was not new for me but what made it difficult was the lack of growth in numbers. The church grew in the Spirit, however, and became a good, well-founded church. Today it has a new church building and is a growing church.

I worked a full shift at a local meat plant, boning meat. This was very hard work for a man my age. Most boners are burnt out by the age of thirty-five. Many times I said, "Why, Lord? Can this be Your will for me?" And yet, I knew I was there in the will of the Lord. God was just getting me ready for our next assignment.

One day a letter came from Brother Paul Leaman, who was then the Regional Field supervisor of the Latin America Caribbean Region, asking us to go to Central America as replacement missionaries. My wife said, "We will have to pray about it." I said, "No, I have already done my praying and this is God's will for us." We applied, and in less than three months we were on our way, driving a Sheaves for Christ pickup to El Salvador to replace the Wynn Drost family while they were home on furlough.

To tell the story of El Salvador would fill a book. Brother Wynn Drost did such a wonderful job of organizing the work and preparing the people for our coming, that there was not even a ripple because of the change. Brother Luis Giron, the vice president of the United Pentecostal Church of El Salvador, and I worked well together.

Once a month, we traveled together with the district secretary for a mini-conference in each of the five sections. We covered three one day, and two the next. At each place I conducted a Bible study and Brother Giron took care of any business. The pastor's tithes were brought in and also the tithes from the churches as each one tithed to the central fund. Also the Youth Department and Ladies Auxiliary gave a percentage to the general fund.

Our first shock was going to a Ladies Auxiliary Conference. Over one thousand people crowded into a place big enough to seat five hundred. These people worshiped, sang and preached all day long, standing on their feet most of the time. There was no place to sit and not much room to stand. About twenty received the Holy Ghost.

I was pastor of Brother Drost's church while he was home. I told the people, "Let's give the Drosts a gift of a fifty percent increase when they return." We had over a one hundred percent increase in seven months. People repented, were baptized and received the Holy Ghost in almost every service.

During one Sunday evening service a rather heavyset woman came to the altar. After she had repented, some of the women as was their custom, began to show her from the Bible her need to be baptized and receive the Holy Ghost. The woman wanted to be baptized. When her feet touched the bottom of the tank, she began to speak in other tongues. She shouted so enthusiastically that I could not hold her up any longer. As she went down I just had time to say, "In Jesus' name." When I fished her out of the water and brought her up, she was still speaking in other tongues!

One Sunday evening at the beginning of the service, there was a lot of noise at the back of the church. A man and two women were dragging in a woman who was kicking, fighting and biting. I advised the young man who was leading songs to keep the people singing. Brother Santiago, my assistant, and two other men went back with me. The woman was demon possessed, but in a very short time she was delivered. At the close of the service she and the husband came to the altar and were baptized along with several others. She came possessed of the devil, and left filled with the Holy Ghost!

The next evening, Brother Santiago and I went to their humble home in a very poor barrio to have a Bible study. The little two-room houses were built in long rows and just had a board wall in between. Between the rows ran an open sewer where little, naked children were playing.

We started a service, and Brother Santiago was teaching when people began to fill the place. The man of the house opened up the flap door that served for a window. There were several hundred people gathered out front. I said, "Preach, Brother Santiago." And preach he did:

While he was preaching, some men brought in a woman who was completely dumb. The people of the community knew what God had done for the demon-possessed woman and these men said, "If God could heal this demon-possessed woman, He can also heal this dumb one." While we were praying for her, she raised her hands and began to praise the Lord. The first words she spoke in her life were praises to the Lord.

Brother Santiago continued to preach and five families were saved through this service. Brother and Sister Wynn Drost came back to El Salvador for the annual District conference. This was an exciting time. Brother Paul Leaman, the missionaries from the other Central American countries and many of their people also attended. The people from throughout the country of El Salvador crowded in. They slept on the grounds and did their cooking there. Some of the church groups cooked and sold food to help pay their way and to raise money for their ladies groups. We had up to 1,900 in the services.

How these people worshiped! During the day the national preachers did the preaching, each country having their time. It was exciting to hear the ones from Honduras. I had a special feeling about this country before we left the States. Reverend Raymond Beesley was the evening speaker and his preaching blessed our souls. The worship and the enthusiasm of the people that make such a sacrifice to be in these meetings is remarkable. Since that time, the district conference has increased by over 700 percent.

Many people were filled with the Holy Ghost during the conference. One boy, a deaf mute about twelve, from the central church, received the Holy Ghost and spoke in other tongues. About a year later he was completely healed. Several were baptized in Jesus' Name.

For three days during the conference, the water and electricity were cut off by terrorists. There was no bread and no way to cook. One of the dear sisters from the church came walking about two miles with five gallons of water on her head. Following her was one of the young ladies carrying a big stack of homemade tortillas. God blesses such people as this. They were always so kind and ready to do what they could, asking so little in return.

Costa Rica was our next field of labor. Sister Scott flew down and I took the pickup by ship because of the war in Nicaragua. It took eleven days to get passage. I was on the ship for two nights and part of three days. There was no water for the restrooms, and I slept on the deck. The last night it rained and there was no shelter. I had foresight enough to take drinking water and food enough for several days. I disembarked on a bank in northern Costa Rica and could hear bombing about twelve miles away.

After disembarking, I drove south through the beautiful countryside. The homes and yards were well kept and clean. Costa Rica is a little paradise. In contrast to El Salvador where the weather was just hot and hotter,

Costa Rico's climate is mild. Also, Costa Rica's larger cities are quite modern and the educational level is quite high.

I met my dear wife at the home of Ralph and Donna Holland where she had been a guest. Quite a number of churches were opened up throughout the country while the Hollands were there. Their biggest problem was lack of qualified men for such rapid growth, but they did their best with what they had.

Before the Hollands left for home, I made a trip with them to visit the churches in the interior. To get to the church of Penuela, we had to ride horseback for almost two hours. Although I had not ridden a horse since I was a boy, I did not have a single sore spot. The poor horse was so small that at times I felt that I should get off and carry her.

Sister Scott could only go with me on trips when we could go by pickup. She was able to visit several of the churches, and it was always a pleasure to have her along. One time, accompanied by another pastor and his wife, we went to visit a church that we thought we could drive to even though we had to ford a river. When we got to the river, it was a rushing torrent, but we waded it. I thought it would be a ten-minute walk but instead it was forty-five minutes, walking in pouring rain and fording two more creeks ...all up-hill. When we arrived at the church we were soaked. The pastor' wife took the two women and found clothes for them.

The people thought we would not come because of the bad storm and started service at 4 p.m. they were just closing when we arrived. Nothing would do but that I should preach. I opened up my Bible case to find it half full of water. When I got through preaching I was standing in a big puddle of water.

After lunch we started on our way back through the rain and dark. I got pneumonia from the trip, but my wife only got big bruises on her arm where I had held on to her tightly so she would not fall.

The end of our time in Costa Rica came all too soon, and we were on our way to Honduras. For some reason, from the beginning, I had especially looked forward to Honduras. I was not disappointed.

We left San Jose, Costa Rica on May 6, 1980 and crossed over into Nicaragua. The Communist government was in power at this time; however, we were treated well by the officials. The oppression and the poverty was unbelievable. Before the Sandinistas took over, Nicaragua was a prosperous country. But now, the shelves were empty of staples and there was fear everywhere. It was a pleasure to cross the border into Honduras.

Honduras is a very beautiful place, it is quite mountainous and covered with pine and hardwood trees. The hardwoods grow mostly along the coastal areas. There are many beautiful flowering trees and vines such as the bougainvillea. The main highways are good, but leaving them is another story.

We drove to Tegucigalpa, the capital of Honduras and met the Danny Schreckhise family at the airport as we had pre-arranged. They lived up on a mountain several miles from the church in a large, cabin-like house that had big cracks in the floor and also in the wall. One night, when I was getting out of bed, instead of just stepping on the floor, I looked first and saw a six-inch, black scorpion. It scurried down through a crack. The Schreckhises later rented another house and we moved into it. We really enjoyed living up in the cool mountain with all the delicious tropical fruit.

Two days after our arrival, we received word that one of the pastors had been missing for eleven days and was presumed dead. According to the report he had left for his father's house, an eight-hour walk over a very dangerous mountain path. The people of this area were very brutal.

Brother Schreckhise and I left as soon as we could. After a three-and-a-half-hour drive, mostly over impassable roads, we arrived at the young pastor's home only to find him sitting there very unconcerned. He did not know he was supposed to be missing. A few minutes later his parents came walking in with pieces of clothing that they thought were his. What a relief! The problem was a telegram that had been sent ten weeks earlier but had just arrived a few days ago.

After a short visit we started back across the same route by jeep, taking the parents with us. We visited at their home for a while for a rest and a bath. After a meal we went about ten kilometers farther to the house of Pastor Isabel, who was the leading pastor in this area. He had baptized sixty-five percent of the people of his village-and had several other branch works.

That evening we went to one of his branch works, which was back the same direction we came but by a different route. We had to leave the jeep at the bottom of the mountain and walk up a very slippery path. On the way back down, crossing the creek by a log, I slipped off three times. Finally I decided that as long as I was wet, I would just walk through the creek.

The next adventure was a visit to a little village near the Nicaraguan border, which was on a high mountain, at least 2,000 feet in elevation. We had a little church group up there and the mother of Brother Benigo, who was to be my assistant pastor, lived there. We arrived at the little village at the foot of the mountain and were expecting to be met by horses. They did not arrive, however, so we started up the steep climb by foot, carrying our gear for spending the night. In about an hour and a half we made it halfway, but I could go no farther. I told Brother Schreckhise just to leave me here and pick me up on the way down. But Brother Schreckhise said he could not make it either. He sent Brother Benigo up the mountain to bring back horses. I guess my sixty-four years of age was catching up with me, but we finally made it.

Several months later Brother Benigo and I made another visit. We had sure footed horses waiting this time. Even by horseback it was a very rough ride.

Besides the cooking area there was only one room in the house where everyone slept. That night the room was filled with wall-to-wall people sleeping on the floor, although I had a bed to myself. Some time after midnight I felt something brush against my foot. I thought it might be a chicken, so I reached down to push it away and encountered hair. Thinking it must be a rat I gave it a swat, only to hear a little whimper. Grabbing my flashlight I found one of the little boys about two years old had gone potty by the bed, just missing my shoe by about an inch. I got him back in bed with his mother and then turned to the wall, put my nose to a good-sized crack and went back to sleep. In the morning, after coffee and tortillas, we made our way back down the mountain.

Sister Scott went with me on several trips to Campo Olivo, where we had a church in the middle of a banana plantation. We always had a service on the plantation and sometimes in a branch work nearby. The young, struggling work was growing quite well. Before we left for home, revival broke in his church as well as in most of the churches.

After service at Campo Olivo we would drive to San Pedro Sula, a large industrial city and an important part of the Gulf of Mexico, and spend the night in a lovely hotel there. Then we visited the San Pedro church. They had no building at the time, just some poles in the ground with a makeshift roof, on a dirt street where the dust blew in rotten fruit and stones. We had some Spirit-filled services there. There is now a good strong work in San Pedro Sula and a new church building.

Brother and Sister Schreckhise and Brother and Sister Larry Hickman from Arkansas came to Honduras for the District Conference. God moved in our midst during the conference and eight were filled with the Holy Ghost and six were baptized. This was the springboard for revival fires to sweep Honduras. Within four days, fourteen received the Holy Ghost in two of our interior churches. For the remaining time of our stay many new souls were added to the church. The church in Honduras is growing and reaching many new areas.

From January 1 until we left the middle of May, 1981, forty-three were baptized and forty-one were filled with the Holy Ghost in the Tegucigalpa church. It seemed almost every service people were repenting, being baptized or receiving the Holy Ghost. People were being saved so fast that I had very little time to teach them. I told Brother

Schreckhise when he returned that I was turning a bunch of babies over to him. Before service the people always came down to the altar to pray. Quite often sinners would come with them and repent and it was not unusual for them to receive the Holy Ghost.

During one Wednesday service, a woman came to the altar. Not long afterward I baptized her on a Sunday night, and she received the Holy Ghost. Her thirteen-year-old also received the Holy Ghost. In the next service it was another of her children, then her seventeen-year-old son, then another one.

Her husband had not been to service although some of our workers had visited him. He said he was a Catholic and that was good enough for him. But when his seventeen-year-old son was baptized, he came to watch. He did not sit with his family, but the Lord let me know that he was Pedro, the woman's husband. I went back and greeted him, surprising him by calling him by his name. He told me he was a Catholic, but he liked what he felt. The next Sunday service I baptized him and he was filled with the Spirit.

Also, God healed a baby girl who was born with a solid skull and had no chance of living beyond a few months. A young woman, who came to church an infidel, received the Holy Ghost, praising the Lord in English.

New works were opened, revival fires burned, broken lives and homes were restored. On and on the story goes in each of these countries. God has been so good to let us have a little part in gathering the grain.

The Schreckhise family returned to the field in May, 1981, and we returned to the United States. We arrived home in Portland, Oregon on June 1, 1981. This ended another interesting and exciting chapter in our lives for the Lord. I only wish we had more years to spend on the mission field.

Our time at home has not been spent idly. We have been quite busy filling in for pastors, preaching revivals and doing what we can. We enjoyed two and a half months in Alaska—in the middle of the winter—in revival services in several churches.

We are now located in Hood River, assisting Reverend Raymond Sirstad and leading in the Spanish ministry. In 1985, we reached a mile post in our lives, our Golden Wedding Anniversary. God has been so good to us and we have had a happy life together. Our pastor, Brother Sirstad, and our children decided to send us to Argentina to visit our daughter, Kathy Crossley and her family there.

In closing I can only say "I wish I had more than one life to give to the work of the Lord. And I would want that other life to be on the mission field."

Fred and Vida Scott, 1982.

Highway travel Honduras style.

Bro. Scott on horseback arriving at Coralitas. Service was held in this house.

A very weary missionary.

Bro. Fred Scott preaching in the water after the belly flop.

We were baptizing this woman when the boy did a belly flop.

Bro. Fred Scott climbing a mountain trail with Bro. Benigro.

13

THE STORY OF
Daniel and Alice Sheets

by Elaine Gibson

Do we pray for China's millions?
Do we feel the awful need?
Are we praying for the workers
Who have gone to plant the seed?
Days are passing, Christ is coming,
Time for work will soon be gone,
Whatso'er thou doest, do quickly,
Souls are passing to their doom.

This poem written by Alice Kugler Sheets expresses the very heartbeat of this courageous, self-sacrificing missionary.

Long before Alice Kugler heard of the outpouring of

the Holy Ghost, God touched her heart about the foreign mission fields. She told her cousin the night she repented of her sins at a Methodist evangelistic service, "You need not be surprised if I go across the ocean some day." This prophetic statement was made at the age of twelve.

Born on January 24, 1883 in Abilene, Texas, Alice Sarah Kugler was of Dutch and German descent. She arrived fifth in a family of eight children. Although her mother was a Mennonite and her father a Lutheran, there were no churches nearby of either of these two denominations. Therefore, they allowed the children to attend the Methodist services that were held at the Central Buckeye school house. The Lord had His hand on her life even at this young age.

Alice continued to serve God and work for Him through out her junior high and high school years. Later, after receiving her teaching certificate, she began teaching in a Holiness school in Iowa. At the same time she opened a Sunday school and taught the primary class.

Years later she received testimonies from some of these students who dated their Christian walk back to her Sunday school class. Sister Alice left behind these words of encouragement, "If you are a Sunday school teacher, you are sowing seed, and in the end there will be a harvest. Our labors are not in vain if done unto the Lord."

Once again the Lord dealt with her about the foreign field during a holiness tent meeting held in western Nebraska in 1910. He had not even revealed to her, as yet, where she would be going, but still she fought it. Sister Alice wrestled with the Lord in hours of prayer. At the end of a week without food or sleep, she finally submitted to God and said yes to His call.

At the close of the tent meeting she received a letter announcing a Pentecostal camp meeting in Topeka, Kansas. With only five cents in her purse, she could not have returned home, much less afford to attend the camp meeting. Sister Alice only knew to pray for this need. Over the previous three months she had read every verse of Scripture that she could find on the subject of the Holy Ghost and desperately wanted to receive it.

A good Baptist man approached her the next day with some good news. He said, "You don't have enough money to leave here, do you?" After she questioned how he could possibly know that, he told her, "Well, the Lord told me to give you all that you need."

God had not only answered her prayer for finances, but had also confirmed that it was His will for her to attend the camp meeting.

At midnight on the third night of services, God miraculously filled Alice Kugler with the Holy Ghost. For three days her English was gone; she could only speak in her heavenly language, speaking in three different tongues. They were all interpreted by people in attendance who knew the languages. One of these interpreters— the gentleman who interpreted her German messages— turned out to be none other than her future husband, Daniel Keefer Sheets.

The Lord finally revealed her destination overseas— China—at this wonderful camp meeting, but four more years passed before He allowed her to begin her journey. She spent these four years in evangelistic and obstetrical training.

One of the presbyters who ordained her tried to stop her from going. He reminded Sister Kugler that she was just a young girl and World War I had already broken out in Europe.

She answered, "Yes, I know, brother, but God said, 'Go ye,' and I must obey." The story of a truly dedicated soldier of Christ could never have been written on the pages of time if Sister Alice had listened to this well-meant plea.

In September, 1914, she joined thirteen Pentecostal missionaries in Seattle, Washington to set sail for China. They made a short stop in Japan and had the opportunity to attend their first foreign service in Yokohama.

A wonderful welcome awaited the fourteen Pentecostals in Hong Kong. But, since, the people in China had already seen so many missionaries come and go, so they quickly asked the newcomers if they were only globetrotters or if they had come to stay. Alice Kugler was quick to rise and say, "I have come to stay!" It saddened her to discover that so much money was wasted in this manner when it could have been put to much better use in opening new works.

Following a month's stay in Hong Kong, Sister Alice moved inland to a mission station in a chief village. Here, in addition to the mission, they operated a girls' school next door.

They prayed almost night and day for a revival and God began to move in their midst. His Spirit fell like rain during the song service and two rows of girls fell to the floor. At four o'clock the next morning the service ended with fourteen new souls filled to overflowing with the Holy Ghost.

God's power came down in another service; some people were dancing in the Spirit while others saw visions.

Several people spoke in tongues in English and they all gave the same message, "Jesus is soon coming; the angels are surrounding me." In the midst of everything one sister, who had been told by Sister Alice to drink in the Holy Ghost like drinking tea, proceeded to swallow three times and started speaking in a heavenly language.

One day the head fell off a large idol nearby and the Pentecostal missionaries were blamed for it. The Chinese posted a note on the door of their mission building saying the missionaries would be killed and the building burned. All of the workers prayed throughout the night. God protected, and nothing happened.

Sister Sheets looked back years later on this first term as some of the best and most wonderful times of her life.

After a short furlough Kwongsi Province became her main home for the next five years beginning in 1921. She loved this province located six hundred miles inland, near the French Indochina border.

The group she worked with consisted of a native minister, a Bible woman, and one other lady missionary. The four of them immediately secured a building upon their arrival and began holding revival services. Large crowds attended with many hungry souls seeking God. At the end of one month thirty people had been baptized.

Jesus dealt with Sister Kugler about moving further inland to preach His Word. She and an eighteen-year-old girl friend proceeded to move out by faith. In the first little city in which they stopped, twenty-seven persons were baptized in Jesus' name after only one month's hard labor.

The next stop was a village thirty miles further inland where the Chinese natives had never seen a white face. After preaching the gospel in the local school house, the two missionaries asked the congregation of approximately 250 if they believed what they had heard about Jesus. Everyone, including the mayor of the town, stood and waved their hands to heaven, saying, "We all believe, we all believe."

For six months prior to this Sister Alice had been suffering from an illness she had caught in a terrible storm. She had improved gradually, but was still very weak when she decided to leave on this mission journey. Not only did she have a landslide victory for the Lord, but He also completely healed her body. Her testimony gives God the glory: "I have always found that it pays to obey Him."

Later they traveled several hundred miles further inland to Lungchow. In this town about forty miles from French Indochina, they located two two-story houses that they could use for the work of God. Because these houses had been vandalized by rebel soldiers during the last war and were in terrible shape, the missionaries were able to rent them both for the equivalent of eighty dollars for an entire year.

For nearly two years they worked on repairs while they ran the mission. During this period of time the anti-foreign war broke out. Sister Alice and her helpers continued to work for six months with armed guards marching both before them and after them each time that they went to the mission hall. Cries of "Kill the foreigners [white people]! butcher them! get rid of the devils!" could be heard in the streets. Finally, they were forced to leave, but some English missionaries decided to stay and take over the use of the buildings.

Since it was apparent that the doors of China were

rapidly closing to the gospel, Sister Kugler decided on her voyage to America that she would remain at home. Little did she know of God's plans for her future when she reached this decision.

Back in her home church, Alice became reacquainted with Daniel Sheets, whom she had known since childhood. A few months later on September 25, 1926 they were united in holy matrimony in Topeka, Kansas. The wedding ceremony lasted for six hours and turned into a Holy Ghost service. God's power fell like rain with prayer, praise, and even healings taking place.

Two years later God led the Sheetses to Phoenix, Arizona. They began their first service in an old sawdust barn with a total of six people in attendance. The forces of evil fought in every way possible—throwing stones, putting snakes in through knotholes in the sides of the building, and cutting off the lights. But God was greater than any of Satan's powers, and the revival closed with one hundred baptized in Jesus' name and eighty filled with the Holy Ghost. The Sheetses pastored the Sunshine Mission until the time came for their return to China.

Sailing from Seattle, Washington on May 5, 1934, the Sheetses headed for Hong Kong, South China to begin nearly ten years of missionary work together. They assisted with the work in Hong Kong for several months while Brother Sheets attended language school.

In addition to assisting the work in Hong Kong, Sister Alice began traveling around to various stations where she had worked in the past. She was appalled by the great falling away of the Chinese saints that had taken place in just a few years. In place after place she found only a handful of Christians remaining. Most of these had no real burden of prayer. She had to spend her time stirring up the fires of prayer in their souls.

God led the Sheetses to Lui Shui, a town of about 5,000 within a district of ninety villages, in April, 1935. The town was thirty miles from Canton by boat and one hundred thirty miles inland from Hong Kong.

The Lord spoke to the missionaries who were closing this mission and told them to contact Brother and Sister Sheets about taking it over. This couple had been working there for two and one-half years with only four converts to show for their labors.

Sister Alice knew that for over twenty years mission halls had been opened and closed there with very little results. No one had to tell her that no harder field could be found in the Kwongtung Province. But God specializes in the impossible!

The Sheetses preached amidst the throwing of stones, ripe fruit, cannon firecrackers, flashlight batteries, and cane butts. They opened a Sunday school and began holding morning and evening services. By prevailing through prayer, it was not long before the rapidly increasing church needed a building of its own.

On October 30, 1940 the new debt-free building was dedicated to the Lord's service. It had taken only three months to build the church and another two months to complete the mission home. All of this was accomplished during war, amid bombs, anti-aircraft guns, Japanese soldiers and robbers.

Three more bright spots during these terrible war years in Lui Shui were the three Chinese children that the Sheetses adopted. An old opium smoker brought the first little girl. He claimed that he wanted money to buy her some milk. But since Sister Sheets knew that the baby would never see the milk, she would only feed the baby instead of handing over any money. For two days he brought the baby to be fed, then he just never bothered to return to pick it up. The Sheetses became instant parents of a tiny baby in November, 1938.

Sally Ann, as they named her, brought much joy and sunshine into their lives over the next few years. Little Sally really loved the Lord Jesus. By the time she was four she knew the Lord's Prayer and could sing many songs in both English and Chinese. Sister Sheets wrote, "It was Sally Ann who helped us through the fiery trials while we were imprisoned in our new home. God saw our need and supplied it. Our lives have been made fuller and richer in Him by this experience."

Mary came into their lives at the age of four. She had been adopted by an old beggar woman who was saved at the mission. Mary's parents had given her to this beggar because the child was missing a finger on one hand and one toe from each foot. This was considered unlucky.

This sunny-faced little girl became a living witness of the power of prayer after God healed her broken leg. Sister Sheets felt that the hand of God was upon Mary's life; therefore, she prayed much about educating the girl. The answer to this prayer came when Sister Sheets' niece wrote requesting a foreign missions project that their Gleaners Band could begin. Their generosity paid off when a few years later, Mary could read, write, play and sing for the glory of God.

Moses's father was on the verge of death from Japanese abuse when he came to door of the Sheetses and begged them to take his son if he should die. A few days later Moses showed up and said, "Father is gone; here I am." Since they had no room in their small home, they sent Moses to an orphanage managed by Brother and Sister Lien.

Both Sally Ann, age four, and Mary joined him there later as the war worsened. Eventually, the Liens managed to move these three secretly along with six other orphans to Free China. God protected them on this trip that took them through Japanese-occupied territory and which lasted on several days. A Japanese gunboat met them as they crossed the river at the border. The Lord hid the refugees from view by placing a mist over them; thereby saving them from death.

Although Brother and Sister Sheets did not see any of their adopted children again before leaving China, they corresponded regularly with all three. Years later, they had the opportunity to see Moses once more when he journeyed to Prescott, Arizona to visit them.

God moved in many miraculous ways during their years in Kwongtung Province. One young man who was in the last stages of tuberculosis began attending the mission services. Soon he repented and was baptized in Jesus' name. He came out of the water completely healed.

An idol worshiping farmer called to them for prayer for his foot. It had been cut so deeply that the bones could be seen and it looked as if the man would never walk again. Brother and Sister Sheets told him that he would have to get rid of his idols, so he had the missionaries burn them. As soon as they had completed this task and rebuked the devils out of the house, his foot immediately began to heal.

Their Bible woman found a little girl who had been

left outside to die. The child had fallen into a large pot of boiling water and had scalded one leg up to the knee and the other even higher. After the rice shop owner who owned her had spent several hundred dollars on doctors and medicine to no avail, he threw her out to die while she screamed from her terrible wounds. At the mission they began to dress her wounds and offer prayer for her several times a day in Jesus' name. Ten days later she was able to return home with new flesh already grown on her bones.

So much suffering was taking place due to the cruel torturing during the war that the Sheetses renamed their prayer room, "God's Hospital." Whenever they opened the doors there would be as many as fifty waiting at one time for healing or to have their wounds attended.

Sister Alice had to depend on the Lord for deliverance from illness more than once while they were in Lui Shui. She suffered three serious attacks of malaria each lasting three months. They went to another missionary's house, and everyone present went to prayer to get the victory over this disease. She was instantly healed and never had another attack.

Another time she fell ill with the dreaded smallpox. Hundreds of people were dying as this epidemic raged. She was burning up with fever when she heard a voice from heaven which said, "Many are the afflictions of the righteous, but God delivereth them out of them all" (Psalm 34:19). She knew then that even though her suffering seemed more than she could bear God would bring her through alive. For many more days she lay in much pain with boils from head to toe, but the Lord was with her in this Gethsemane experience.

Another peril that Brother and Sister Sheets faced more than once on this tour was bands of robbers. The robbers ran in gangs of one thousand or more throughout the province. One day the Sheetses heard shots from a battle between one of these robber bands and a gambling band. Even though everyone was ordered to stay indoors, Brother Sheets went out and peered over the porch railing. A bullet just missed his face as he jumped back in alarm. He, the rest of the mission workers, and sixty school children remained on the floor for the next several hours until the battle ended. Many people who disobeyed the command to stay indoors were badly injured or killed.

On December 22, 1939, the Sheetses endured their worst experience with the robber bands. For days previous to this, they heard rumors that the robbers were coming and, unless a ransom was paid, the city would be robbed and burned. Sure enough, about six o'clock that evening they heard machine guns, pistols, and hand grenades. Sister Sheets looked out the window and saw the gambling bamboo shed not far from their mission, going up in flames.

Over the next few hours they hurriedly packed their belongings and hid what valuables they could. Finally, around midnight, the Sheetses door flew open; the robbers searched the house taking what money and valuables they discovered. Much of the money was safe, though, because Sister Sheets hid it on her body, in her hair, and in a suitcase on which she sat the whole time.

As soon as the robbers left, they looked out the window again only to see a house on fire about twenty feet away. Since most houses in the town were built in rows nearly a mile long with the wall of one serving as the wall for the next, they began to pray for a south wind to blow.

Amid flying bullets, they ran to their school, carrying what baggage they could, only to be stopped by another robber band. These robbers took everything visible including the coats, hats, and watches they wore. Finally, after safely reaching their destination, they watched the city burn throughout the remainder of the night.

How thankful they were when morning came to discover that God had indeed answered their prayer. The mission home stood unharmed amidst desolation everywhere. Inside they found the money in the suitcase just as Sister Sheets left it; outside, many of their other valuables were found among the rubble.

The news of Japanese atrocities during the capture of Nanking in World War II reached the ears of Brother and Sister Sheets in Lui Shui long before they felt the repercussions of war. For a period of two months the looting, burning, killing, and raping continued. At least thirty or forty thousand people were killed and the rape cases averaged one thousand per day according to an American eyewitness. Eighty percent of the business section's buildings were looted and burned and fifty per cent of the people were burned.

In 1937, all over the Kwongtung Province the terrible bombing began. The Sheetses were kept by the hand of God through these horrible years; their motto was, "Hitherto hath the Lord helped us." Martial law, air raids, and bombings continued day after day. Just ten miles away the city of Canton suffered the loss of many lives and terrible destruction.

Brother and Sister Sheets agreed to care for a mission in Tsung Fa, located seventy-five miles northeast, for another missionary couple home on furlough. Therefore, they made regular trips to this town even though their lives were in danger. Often they had to get off the bus and hide while the bombers flew over. The Lord blessed their efforts with wonderful results. In one jail service alone fifteen men and two women turned to God.

One time Brother Sheets got caught in an air raid. He had to walk five miles amid falling bombs in order to catch the boat home. He saw the horrible devastation taking place right before his eyes: mangled bodies and ripped-off limbs were everywhere. One bomb burst just over a block away from him, killing more than five hundred people. On another trip, just after they left Tsung Fa to return home, twenty bombs were dropped on the city and the mission building was blown apart.

In one town a bomb fell on the roof of a Pentecostal church and bounced off without doing any damage. Another Pentecostal church in China held service on Sunday morning with several hundred Christians in attendance. The pastor told them not to be afraid when they heard the sound of bombers approaching. Moments later, a six hundred pound bomb fell less than forty-five yards away. It made a crater twenty-five feet deep and approximately forty feet across, severely damaging the building. But God cares for His children; not one was killed and only three even sustained any injuries.

On December 8, 1941, a band of one hundred Japanese soldiers marched into the mission. They informed Brother and Sister Sheets, "We have come to take over you and your property." For one week every door was guarded and the Sheets were not even allowed to go downstairs to the mission.

Finally, the Japanese moved out, but the Chinese puppets moved in the next morning. Using the prayer room as a police station, they guarded Brother and Sister Sheets, making sure they did not escape. Night and day the Sheetses had to be eyewitnesses to cruel torturings. Often they could hear groanings all night long from downstairs. This continued for months. Eventually all mail ceased and supplies ran out.

The Japanese officials came on February 19, 1943 to inform these two faithful missionaries that they would be taken to a concentration camp within the next few days. By this time Sister Alice, having lost sixty pounds from illnesses and poor nourishment, could barely walk, but she carried on packing for both Mary and Sally in addition to herself and Brother Sheets. The two girls left at this time to escape into Free China.

After traveling for two days by chair, army truck, foot, boat, and train, they finally arrived at Honan Island where they were interned for seven months. They joined fifty-seven other American and British missionaries, where it seemed as if they were "buried alive" since there was no contact with the outside world. The highlight of each week became the one Sunday service that Tokyo allowed; the missionaries took turns conducting the service.

Twice during their imprisonment the guards brought in a Chinese and cruelly tortured him to the point of death right before the missionaries' eyes. Following these incidents the guards threatened the fifty-seven missionary prisoners with the same treatment if they caused any problems.

At first the food supply seemed an improvement over

the past few months, but as time dragged on, things proceeded to get worse. The food became so scarce near the end of the internment that they bought the wheat that their Japanese guards used as horsefeed. Everyone helped to pick it over, grain by grain, sorting out the dirt, chaff, stones, cheat and worms before it was washed and ground. This wheat became their mainstay for the next several months.

Finally, on September 20, 1943, the consulate informed them that their dream of repatriation would come true. Seventy-two days later they stepped out of the boat onto American soil and freedom.

A few years following Brother and Sister Sheets returned to the States, they once again journeyed to Arizona. At this time they opened a work in a part of North Phoenix known locally as Sunnyslope. The church building that they erected still exists today as a United Pentecostal Church. Additions have been made over the years to accommodate growth, but the original building stands as a monument of this hardworking, dedicated couple. Sister Alice commissioned an artistic Pentecostal evangelist to paint the baptistry mural from a picture she brought from China. This same painting still greets the saints as they gather to worship the Lord today.

The Sheetses moved to Prescott, Arizona in 1957 and accepted the pastorate of the church there. They continued working for God in this capacity until Brother Sheets heart failed in 1962. Their longtime friend, Sister Oma Ellis, succeeded him as pastor at this time; and in March, 1965, Brother Sheets departed from this life.

Brother Paul Box, the Foreign Missions Secretary, came to preach the funeral, held in the north Phoenix church where they had labored so faithfully. At the close of the service, Sister Alice stepped up to the head of the casket—to everyone's complete surprise—and sang, without music, "We Will All Rise to Meet Him." How the glory of God fell!

On October 16, 1977 a young couple, Dale and Katherine Lewallen, began attending the Prescott church. Katherine received the baptism of the Holy Ghost two services later, but Dale could not seem to get it even though he sought earnestly. They came from the charismatic movement and were so afraid of not really receiving the Spirit, but just speaking in the mechanical, imitated tongues that they were used to already.

Not long after this they moved into Sister Sheets's home. One evening in December, Brother Dale was putting eyedrops in Sister Sheets's eyes as she lay on the couch. They were just talking when she began to worship and praise the Lord. Dale joined in and it was not long before he was seeking the Holy Ghost. Dale's wife, Katherine, says that Sister Sheets was like a butterfly from a cocoon. She seemed just like a young prayer warrior, instead of ninety-four-year-old saint, as she prayed him through to the Holy Ghost right there in the living room.

Katherine also remembers the wonderful writing ministry that this lovely saint of God undertook daily. All day long Sister Sheets wrote to people all over the world. Some of these people were not Christians; others received words of encouragement as they labored for the Master.

The end came to Sister Alice's ministry on September 12, 1979 at the age of ninety-six. Brother Harry Scism, the Director of Foreign Missions, came to Phoenix to preach her funeral, and she was laid to rest by her husband's side who had preceded her by fourteen and one-half years. She left this message behind to echo down through the years of her tremendous faith in God:

I may not understand just why
He leads by paths that dreary seem,
Where trials dark, like spectral forms,
Around my upward footsteps seem;
Where hurtful snares beset my way,
And spiteful foes my soul would test,
But still I know though trials there be,
His way is best; His way is best.

Alice Kugler's graduating picture 1905.

Dan and Alice Sheets' wedding picture, 1926.

Missionaries to China, 1933.

Sally Ann Sheets, 2½ years old.

Alice Sheets traveling in South China.

Alice Sheets and Oma Ellis in 1969.

Church in Lui Shui dedicated in 1940.

Bro. & Sis. Sheets with Chinese friends.

Chinese wedding, Sheetses in center.

14

THE STORY OF
Elizabeth Stieglitz

by Nona Freeman

"Is that my China?" asked twenty-year old Elizabeth as she peered through foggy swirls of a dark mass barely visible in the early morning mist. The older couple she traveled with joined her at the rail.

"This is Shanghai, Elizabeth," Brother Ramsey told her. "We'll stay here until our freight comes or maybe longer to get the feel of things. Then we'll go north to establish our mission."

Joyfully, Elizabeth and the Ramseys stepped from the boat in China on June 28, 1910. After a few days in a hotel, an independent missionary invited them to accompany her on a trip to the hills. A devout Chinese lady they met prepared a sumptous meal for them. During dinner she told her guests how she arranged for segments of uninterrupted prayer.

"I tie a white handkerchief on the door knob of my room, and everyone knows not to disturb me while I pray. Madame Chiang Kaishek is my daughter. She and her husband are often in peril; I must pray constantly for their protection and sometimes, deliverance for them.

The missionary trio left Shanghai in October for Shansi in a two-wheeled springless cart pulled by mules that shook, jerked and jolted them without mercy. "Oh, my poor head!" Elizabeth moaned. "How can I bump both sides of it at once?" Then she said to herself, "To survive I must divert my thoughts away from this misery—let me consider again the chain of events that has brought me to China.

"I suppose it began with the tent meeting Mrs. Woodworth Etter preached at my hometown, Muscotine, Iowa, in 1902. My mother dispaired of raising me because of severe convulsions for the first four years of my life. I felt tender towards God, believing He alone had spared me and went to the tent. I saw miracle after miracle happen that encouraged me to go through the prayer line. Although I was only thirteen years old, I had a large goiter. After prayer it disappeared immediately.

"Deeply moved, I fell on my knees and promised the Lord if He would heal my mother, I would dedicate the rest of my life to Him, to do whatever He wanted me to do. My mother suffered from serious heart disease, internal disorders and tuberculosis that had already destroyed one lung. The doctors said she would die in a few days.

"When I asked her to go to the tent she answered, 'I've tried everything else, I might as well try this. I only want to live long enough to raise my family.' Jesus instantly gave her two new lungs and made her completely whole.

"In 1908 someone said, 'Brother William Durham is having wonderful meetings on old Ninth Avenue in Chicago. Why not go?' We went. When I heard about receiving the Holy Ghost with the evidence of speaking in other tongues, I covered my face with a songbook to hide a torrent of tears and at the altar call I sought God until I was utterly exhausted.

"Still seeking, a week later, a worker took me to her room and said, 'Lay on the bed. You are too tired to pray.'

" 'But, I want the Holy Ghost.' I answered and started to kneel.

" 'It's not the position of your body that counts, but the position of your heart,' she insisted. 'Rest. God will fill you.'

"I slept and had barely awakened when it came. Waves of God's Spirit swept over me and I spoke in other tongues for hours.

"I went to a Bible school in Reliance, Ohio, for a few months. It was during this time as I spent an hour alone with the Lord one morning that He first spoke to me about China. 'I could never go there!' I thought. He reminded me of my promise and gave me a passage of Scripture:

"Hearken, O daughter and consider, and incline thine ear; forget also thine own people, and thy father's house; so shall the King greatly desire thy beauty: for he is thy LORD; and worship thou him" (Psalm 45:10-11).

"I left school, went home and got a job, confiding in

no one. I thought, 'This undertaking will require money.' Brother and Sister F. S. Ramsey, who were on their way to China, came to our area and visited our home, as they had done in the past. I felt strongly impressed to go with them to China, but stubbornly I refused to tell them. I remember how God dealt with me as we all sang together at home on a Sunday morning (we had only evening services). I fled to the garden with my Bible, but everything I tried to read said 'Go'!

"A month before they left, the Ramseys told me they wanted to talk to me. 'We want you to pray about going to China with us.'

" 'No need to pray,' I answered. 'I already know I must go.'

"Then they asked me to promise that I would never mention needs, personal or for our mission. 'We will strictly trust God,' Brother Ramsey said.

"I quit my job and started getting ready to go. On leaving day, I packed my trunk at 11:00 a.m. with only $5.00 in my purse. I left on the train at 11:00 p.m. with my fare miraculously provided, though it came by bits and pieces. When my mother kissed me goodby, I questioned her. 'Mother, why didn't you tell me you knew all along that God had called me to China?'

" 'Child, if I told you,' she answered, 'you might have gone because Mother said. Now, you *know* that God has called you and it's up to Him to take care of you.'

"Well, I am in China, and this is rough traveling, but I believe God. . . ."

Brother Ramsey interrupted her reverie. "Elizabeth, we are stopping for the night in this Chinese Inn." They got acquainted with Kongs, the stone beds of the Orient, heated by internal Elves. Stiff and cold from the long day's cart-ride, they asked the innkeeper to fire the Kong very warm. They found continual rotation necessary to keep from roasting the downside of their bodies. Wearisome and rough, plodding ride by day, and the night on a Kong became a pattern. It took them a week to reach Tat'ung.

The driver took them to the Swedish Holiness Mission. The men missionaries made room for the Ramseys; a mission across town gave Elizabeth a tiny room until they could find their own place. She celebrated her twenty-first birthday on November 15, 1910, with a day of prayer, still waiting.

The Boxer Rebellion, started by a secret Chinese Society in 1900, indiscriminately slaughtered Chinese Christians, missionaries and all the foreigners they could find. They burned houses, schools and churches and left a bitter legacy of mistrust to confront missionaries as an impenetrable wall, in spite of amnesty.

"We'll go forward with prayer," Brother Ramsey planned when the Lord provided a beginning site for their mission. He hired an interpreter for a daily morning service and a cook to allow more time for prayer and language study.

A few months later revolution interrupted their efforts; the American consulate ordered them to the coast. In the troublous days that followed, the dynasty fell and Dr. Sun Yatsen came to rule the new Republic of China in 1912. An "all clear" soon gave them permission to return to the mission for a fresh assault on the "wall." Slowly, the number attending the services increased from the original handful. In the third year of patient teaching and constant prayer without visible results, a hunger for God moved the people to assemble three times a day. "We must pray," they said.

A year later, W. W. Simpson came by and offered to preach a few days. Pentecost came! Li Ching Poo, the cook and his wife first received the Holy Ghost, then a flood of God's Spirit descended on the seekers. The prayer meetings evolved into three glorious services a day, and at least four people received the Holy Ghost daily over the next four years with few exceptions. If it did not happen, Brother Ramsey called for fasting and all-night prayer until confession of sin and true repentance restored the flow of the Spirit.

Elizabeth received a package at Christmas, 1914, with a portion of Frank Ewart's *Meat in Due Season* stuck in the corner. She read about baptism in Jesus' name and rebelled against it until the Lord spoke to her: "You are kicking against My name." Feeling an urgent need to obey the truth, Brother Ramsey baptized their native minister Li Ching Poo (once the cook) in the name of Jesus, then Li Ching Poo baptized Brother Ramsey, who in turn baptized Sister Ramsey and Elizabeth and all of the church. From that time on Brother Ramsey expected everyone immersed in the name of Jesus to come out of the water speaking in tongues if they did not already have the Holy Ghost.

Financial needs came as regular as sunrise. Elizabeth learned to make-do or do without until her urgent prayers brought answers. The building of a church to house the rapidly expanding congregation brought it one financial crisis after another. The trio led the believers as they fasted, wept, prayed and worked. They had to find the most economical construction possible, so they burned, handmade bricks on the site, Chinese-style. Elizabeth became adept at removing hot bricks from the kiln and tossing them up to bricklayers working on high scaffolds.

Evangelizing villages from the Tat'ung base they would strap their bedding on mules, crawl on top and take off. Her feet drug the ground on the diminutive animals. She kept on asking for a larger mule and learned that the bigger ones invariably proved more treacherous. After a big mule pitched her head first into a large umbrella, she could ride her small beast without complaint.

A migration of people, mostly farmers, from the south came by the mission, driven from their homes by famine. They came by the bunches with stomachs pitifully swollen from malnutrition and stretched out hands begging for food. "Stiegie," as her colleagues now called her, would say, "You may pause here for a rest on your journey, and we will divide with you the food God provides. You do not have to become a Christian, but we would like for you to hear the gospel of Jesus Christ."

Stiegie measured out Chinese staples, oats and millet with earnest prayers for the salvation of the transients. Only heaven kept a record of the lives transformed by the gospel. Some of them collapsed at the mission and had to be nursed back to health before they could move on. The mission had twenty sick cases before they learned that they suffered from spotted typhus.

An old man died. Stiegie came along just as some of her helpers dumped him into a crude coffin. She turned the body over scolding them, "He's not an animal!" Two more succumbed, lice crawling away from them as they died. Worn to exhaustion from nursing the ill and feeding the hungry, she only realized the misplaced lice had infected her with typhus when the dread disease laid her low in 1917.

The Ramseys wrote her parents they did not think Stiegie could possibly live. By God's mercy and their prayer, she survived, though her skin peeled off in flakes from head to toe. She returned home on furlough when she recovered enough to travel, though still desperately weak.

Shortly after her departure, younger missionaries volunteered to man the mission while the ailing Ramseys took a furlough. The Ramseys could not return to China; the privations they suffered, coupled with age, ended their missionary service.

Stiegie came back to China to discover a cruel disappointment. Misdeeds by the ones left in charge put the church, built by sacrifice, into the hands of non-Pentecostals, and the Holy Ghost revival ended in confusion. Li Ching Poo, his wife, and two believers rallied to Stiegie with joy and the small nucleus went to an untouched area and made a new start. God graciously poured out His Spirit on the hungry-hearted who came.

In that age, missionaries streamed to China moved by an allwise God who knew the time of closed doors lay ahead. When Mae Iry, her daughter and son-in-law, Robert Sonnenberg, reached China in 1921, Stiegie said, "I think too much of China is unreached, and too many missionaries have gathered in one place. Let's go farther north and break new ground!"

Mae and her family agreed and they traveled on filthy, over-crowded buses and trains across a mountain range to Taiyoh. After a lengthy stay in a Chinese inn with minimum comfort, they completed remodeling a cluster of delapidated buildings into a mission compound and moved in. Then came the painstaking struggle to gain confidence and listening ears. Miracles helped. A demon-possessed man received deliverance and salvation in the name of Jesus and became a fervent witness. Several slaves to opium found liberty in Jesus.

Their schedule of service every night and three services on Sunday continued fruitfully for many years. Though large numbers turned to the Lord and destroyed their idols, the unevangelized masses of China haunted the missionaries. Their burden moved Stiegie and Mae a year later to Kwo Hsien, sixty miles away, where they opened another mission, working profitably together for several years. All summer long they rode mules, taking the gospel to faraway villages, and had special services in the mission during the bitter-cold months when people from forty different villages came together.

On a village jaunt, Stiegie's mule frequently stumbled. If she pulled the reins tightly soon enough, he regained his balance. Once when her attention strayed however, he went down, sliding her onto his neck. A deep chasm on one side of the narrow path and a craggy mountain wall on the other gave no space to climb off and remount correctly. Not a single helper could be seen ahead or behind her. Nothing remained but to ride the mule's neck for several miles until she found a wide spot in the trail and someone to help.

When Stiegie returned from furlough in the mid-twenties, Mae went to Taiyoh to relieve her daughter and son-in-law for furlough. Because they never returned to China, Mae took full charge of Taiyoh leaving Stiegie to work alone in Kwo Hsien. As long as the uneasy national peace lasted, the two friends shared outreach, special meetings, and brief, refreshing times of fellowship.

Spasmodic outbursts of civil war made China a dangerous place to live in the thirties, a fact ignored by Stiegie when she sailed from Vancouver, Canada, in January, 1933, for a third missionary term. She waited a few days at Tientsin for Ardley Reynolds, a young man coming from San Francisco to help Mae, thus saving her friend an extra trip. Right away, Stiegie and Mae made a daylong journey to two villages of more than five thousand homes. They started meetings in a building, but huge crowds forced them to the streets where thousands heard the gospel in three days of continous services.

"Sisters Stieglitz and Iry are enjoying a very unusual outpouring of God's Spirit in China," Brother W. T. Witherspoon reported in the *Pentecostal Outlook,* April, 1934.

Stiegie wrote in June, 1935:

Twenty-five years ago today I first set foot in China. I look back and see how the Lord has showered me with blessings and led me step by step. At death's door, through trials and testing, in the dark, every way closed and not knowing which way to turn, I have stood still and seen God open doors. He has never failed. I would not want to change my place for an easier one, for I have learned to know Him better.

The people in the villages are calling—they want to hear more of the gospel. I send out native workers and go myself as often as I can. Yesterday, another opium smoker came to be delivered and follow Jesus. Our meeting place is too small for the winter services. Pray that the name of Jesus will be exalted and that none will be turned away.

Brother and Sister Garland Leonard, Brother Ardley Reynolds, and two native preachers came to Kwo Hsien for a week of special meetings in December 1935. The believers bought a three and half foot wide kettle with nine tiers of steamers to cook food for their guests. During the sacrifice offering to pay for them, a lady gave her treasured gold earrings, and someone dropped in a squash seed. A wicked man who had persecuted the saints bought it for twenty cents, then said, "I can't eat it because it is precious." He put it back in the offering basket to be sold and resold again and again. Folks came from more than thirty-two villages and took a Pentecostal blessing home with them when the week ended.

Mae returned from furlough with re-enforcements in 1936; two young ladies, Kathryn Hendriks and Virginia Weddle, came to help.

"My heart aches and there is a cry in my soul when I look on the whitened harvest field." Stiegie wrote of her deepening burden in June, 1937. And as a shadow of ominous things to come, she penned, "Soldiers are moving again and being stationed in homes and villages."

Completely engrossed in their work and without a telephone, a newspaper or a radio to keep them posted, the missionaries in their isolated compounds did not realize the devastation in the wake of advancing Japanese troops or the scope of the invasion until fleeing eyewitnesses told of looting, rape and death and warned the Kwo Hsien compound to run and hide. Chinese officials had everyone make dug-outs under their buildings with mounds of dirt for protection. The mission diligently called on the name of Jesus while they dug and blackened windows.

Concerned about their daughters, ages ten, twelve and fourteen, Stiegie's Bible woman and her preacher husband, Li Ching Poo asked them to seek safety in a mountain cave. She agreed, but the Lord spoke to her in the night, "If you go out of My will, you will have no protection." An awful darkness gripped her soul and filled the room. She walked the floor weeping and praying for two hours. Finally the gloom retreated before the presence of the Lord. "Oh, Jesus," she prayed, "I want something to stand on." He gave her Proverbs 3:23-26.

> *"Then shalt thou walk in thy way safely, and thy foot shall not stumble. When thou liest down, thou shalt not be afraid: yea, thou shalt lie down, and thy sleep shall be sweet. Be not afraid of sudden fear, neither of the desolation of the wicked, when it cometh. For the Lord shall be thy confidence, and shall keep thy foot from being taken"* (Proverbs 3:23-26).

Kwo Hsien nestled securely behind walls wide enough for two teams of horses to pass on top. The Japanese on the northern mountains began a continual cannonball exchange over the city with the Chinese army on the south. Shrapnel fell like rain. Japanese planes dropped bombs within the walls in daylight hours. Stiegie knew the mission compound made a conspicious target with its freshly white-washed walls and building, but she clung to God's promise. Windows shattered from the blasts. However, the mission escaped a direct hit.

After seven days and six nights the seige ended in victory for the Japanese. The first two Japanese soldiers that came to the mission held a gun against Steigie's chest, "Who are you?" one barked.

"American missionary," she answered without flinching. They left, only to return with twenty-five more soldiers. "We have orders to search the compound."

Stiegie motioned toward her domain, "Go ahead." She prayed silently, "Lord, show me when to be stern and when to submit."

She looked up to see most of them go in the women's quarters and went after them. "What are you doing in here? This is the women's rooms and you are not allowed here." They looked at her in amazement. Hands on hips, she stared back. "I mean it! Get out!" They did.

Shortly after they left, a short, chesty Japanese colonel with a sword buckled at his waist stopped in her gate with an insolent swagger. Stiegie had told everyone to stay out of sight and stood silent before him. He advanced one step with an emphatic "Harumph!" clearing his throat. She stepped nearer, mimicking the sound he made. His face growing red, he came forward with a mighty "Harumph!" Though her heart pounded, she answered with the same vehemence, "Harumph!" Standing toe to toe she thought she saw a twinkle in his eye as he pulled out all the stops on a terrific "Harumph!"

She put everything she could muster into her echo. Unblinking stares held sway for the next few seconds, then he touched his cap briefly and turned away. Stiegie locked the gate.

The Lord impressed her with two verses, Nehemiah

6:3, 11; one for each foot to stand on, meaning she should remain at her post as long as possible. The local Chinese expressed their love with furtive gifts of rice; this and her prolific garden sustained the mission family, though they chafed under house arrest. Japanese soldiers often supplemented their scanty food by stealing from Stiegie's garden.

"Japanese coming in the compound!" Stiegie responded to the call without taking time to dry her wet hands. An army official backed by a platoon of soldiers stood in the courtyard. She looked him squarely in the eye, "What do you want?"

"We have come to take over this property for us a place to live," he answered.

"You will not do anything of the kind," she retorted. Her mission family listened with bated breath. They knew she spoke to the commanding general who had conquered that part of China. Stiegie neither knew nor cared.

"This property does not belong to you. It belongs to God. Where do you think my people will live if you put them out? And while I'm at it, you tell your soldiers to stop climbing over the wall to steal from my garden."

She won enough respect from her captors to establish an uneasy truce. One day the weeping Bible woman ran to her for help. "Soldiers are holding guns on Ching Lee and trying to take away our three daughters."

Stiegie confronted them with her usual spunk, "What are you doing here?" she demanded, ignoring their gun. "These are my people. Get out!" They went. The soldier set to guard the compound by the Commanding General watched as she gathered the women and girls to take them to her apartment for safety. She heard footsteps behind her and turned to see the guard's sword about a foot from her back.

"All right!" she dared. "Finish what you've started. I'm not afraid to die. I'm ready to go." Intimidated by her courage, he wheeled around and returned to his post at the gate.

A stream of misplaced persons, in numerous stages of misery coming or going, made continual traffic through the mission. Stiegie and her helpers sometimes worked for days without a chance to change clothes, snatching a nap here or there to survive. They dispensed first aid (limited by short supplies), comfort, food (as God provided), prayer, the Word and love.

Stiegie delighted in every service and Bible lesson, appraising each one a score against oppression, and they continued in spite of pressure and frequent interruptions.

In the second year of occupation, several women came to her room after church to see why she did not come. They found her almost lifeless, unable to open her eyes or speak, with the left side of her body completely paralyzed. They quickly sent a man with a lantern to call a doctor and took turns massaging her extremities with vigor.

Neither of the two doctors could be found. Word came to the general and he sent a nurse, who worked with her for two hours before she could feel her pulse. When the old doctor came at 6:00 a.m., he found the patient still in a critical condition. She hovered between life and death for two weeks.

Recovery came slowly. Rejoicing filled the compound on the day Stiegie took her first faltering steps after the stroke ordeal.

Early in the invasion a farmer brought several large

bags of millet and oats. "Please store these in your cellar
for me. If I do not return, use the grain. I would rather
you had it than the Japanese." He did not come back and
the stored grain kept them alive during the acute shor-
tage of food caused by war.

Brother Witherspoon received a letter from an
English Baptist missionary in Kwo Hsien early in 1939.
The letter said:

*I wonder if in America you give Victoria Crosses as
in England? No one has ever deserved one more than Miss
Stieglitz of this city. For one solitary woman to remain
in this terribly war-afflicted city was bravery of the first
order. But if you knew what that has meant to the folks
of her own church, as well as ours, you would see my point
about the Victoria Cross.*

*As one who has known Miss Stieglitz, and as secretary
of our Shansi Mission, I want to say a big "Thank you!"
for her splendid work. She needs a change and a holiday
badly. We want you to know how we of the Baptist Mission appreciate her splendid service.*

Reports of how Chinese soldiers left their uniforms
in the streets of the main cities and fled from the advancing Japanese army made Stiegie understand the extent
of the invasion. A warning from the Lord prepared her
for the gruff verdict brought by three military police in
March, 1942.

"Pack your things; you are leaving." She felt release
for the first time, even though she had no idea of her
destination. Taking only a duffle bag and a trunk, the missionary left most of her possessions and her heart in Kwo

Hsien and meekly got on and off trains as her military escort directed.

Somewhere along the protracted journey she found out she would be exchanged for a Japanese prisoner. What a way to go on furlough! After she endured a long wait at Tientsin, they took her to a modest hotel in Shanghai. The constant, watchful eyes, and sharp manners of the military police irritated Stiegie, but glimpses of fellow missionaries gladdened her heart. Though assigned different places of abode, missionary families Frank Wheeler and Ralph Bullock waited as she did—waited for whatever. Here, they learned about the existence and the extent of World War II.

Rumors flew, stating either "We'll never leave Shanghai," or "We'll be leaving soon." Counting her blessings, Stiegie thanked God to have nourishing food once more, and prayed for patience. She heard in the middle of June that the Japanese had chartered an Italian liner, *The Conte Verde* to transport them to a port of exchange in East Africa.

They left Shanghai June 29, 1942. While she went numbly through the exhausting hassle to board the liner and locate her alloted berth, Stiegie thought, "Surely, I'm dreaming." Reality came into focus with a four-day delay in the Java Sea off the coast of Singapore, waiting for more refugees and surrounded by emotionally depleted, seasick and financially ruined humanity. More than fifty planes with the big red dots under their wings roared low over the waiting boat with a last terrifying salute the passengers could have done without.

Moving again, the muffled growl of the boat's machinery and the pounding waves merged days into wearisome nights until Stiegie lost track of time. On July 22, she heard someone yell, "A ship flying an American flag!" and hurried to see for herself. The ship's crew alongside cheered, waving handkerchiefs and clothing as the ship's whistle sounded the victory signal over and over. The refugees cheered and waved in answer with tears streaming down their faces, and with sobs of joy.

As they docked in Lourenco Marques, Portugese East Africa, (Maputo, Mazambique) alongside the *Gripsholm* (a Swedish boat), her crew tossed apples and oranges, the first they had seen in many months, to the American children on board the *Conte Verde*. Pale, undernourished American refugees marched to board the *Gripsholm* with their belongings in bundles, Chinese baskets and cardboard boxes. The Japanese exchange prisoners descended another gangplank at the same time, well-fed, well-clothed and carrying expensive luggage.

The *Gripsholm* sailed on July 28, crowded to capacity. After a two-day pause in Rio de Janeiro, Brazil, and tricky navigation through waters that held the threat of enemy submarines, the ship reached New York on August 25, 1942.

Stiegie often wondered during the journey how she would pay her $500.00 fare, considering the weakness that had persisted since her stroke. On arrival she learned that Hilda Reeder, Missions Secretary for the Pentecostal Assemblies of the World, with the help of Elder Robert Tobin's church in Indianapolis, had paid her fare. Carl Hensley, missionary to China, who had returned earlier, met the boat and took Stiegie and the Wheelers to the home of Brother Andrew Urshan on 92nd Street in New York City. They arrived in time for the evening service.

The war brought Stiegie one decided benefit—a chance to rest and regain her strength, although she felt anxious to return to China long before she fully recovered. She contacted Kathryn Hendricks, the young lady who went to China in 1936 to help Mae Iry. Tuberculosis sent Kathryn home to Skiatook, Oklahoma, in 1939, before the Japanese warlords clamped down on churches and missionaries. (After Kathryn's departure from China, Mae suffered internment in a concentration camp.) Now, fully recovered, Kathryn lived with one desire and one prayer. "Oh Lord, let me go back to China!"

The two ladies joyfully made plans to go, ignoring the inconvenience of war. They shipped numerous supplies for their work in China to the West Coast, but a few days before their scheduled departure, the United States Government called in all passports.

Kathryn passed the enforced waiting time in college, preparing herself for greater usefulness. Stiegie crisscrossed American and Canada, visiting churches and encouraging a burden for missions with her stirring account of the revival in China. She seldom mentioned the horrors except to ask prayer for the believers.

Stiegie graced our home in Rosepine, Louisiana, with a two-week stay in 1944. During that time I cooked pumpkin for pies. She followed Brother Freeman outside when he went to discard the pumpkin peel and seeds.

"Give me those seeds," she said. "I'll eat them."

"How can anyone eat pumpkin seeds?" my husband asked.

"If you had ever been as hungry as I've been," she retorted, "you would know how!"

When the seeds dried, she demonstrated to an interested audience how she cracked them with her teeth and extracted the nutritious kernel inside with chopsticks. When the head of the house marvelled at her dexterity with chopsticks, she leaned over and pinched his arm firmly with them and laughed delightfully at his responding "Ouch!"

The ladies did not waste time when the war ended. They sailed from San Francisco on October 18, 1946, having added medical supplies and many barrels of canned food to the stored freight already collected for China. The boat stopped briefly at both Hawaii and Manila, before going on to Shanghai, and they gazed in horror at the devastations of war, especially in Manila.

In Shanghai harbor, custom officials viewed their baggage, crates and barrels with suspicion and eagerly dumped all of the contents on the dock for a minute inspection of every article. Years of unloading coal on this dock had left a thick accumulation of coal dust which quickly adhered to the persons and possessions of the missionaries. Customs turned on their heels and left at the end of their detailed search and the ladies nearly collapsed before they got it all shaken off a bit and repacked.

Sad news came on the heels of this ordeal. They could not return to their missions in Shansi province. With the departure of the Japanese, a sweep of China by Mao Tsetung had made considerable progress. He now headquartered at Taiyoh mission and Kwo Hsien mission housed Communist forces.

After prayer for direction, the ladies felt led to locate in Peking, the most populous, modern and bustling city in China—a sharp contrast to the village work both of them did regularly before. They helped in other missions until intensive search helped them find a suitable compound. Fortunately, both Kathryn and Stiegie could adeptly use a hammer, saw, mop and broom. Long days of strenuous labor preceded their spiritual work, but soon they touched many lives with the gospel.

The discreet helpers Kathryn and Stiegie sent to Shansi brought reports that both gladdened and dismayed them. The Communists outlawed Christianity, closed churches and committed atrocities on their own people far in excess of those perpetrated by the Japanese. The ladies grieved over former students and helpers tortured to death, but rejoiced to know they died true to the faith, refusing to denounce Jesus Christ. Some had fled and a remnant secretly gathered in mountain caves to worship and pray.

Stiegie received a letter from pastor Li Ching Poo, now in Suiyiian, reporting blessed special meetings in several areas and twenty-seven baptized in the name of Jesus. In July, 1948, the National army helped a young saint to get his wife and small children out of Kwo Hsien. She brought word of secret meetings in the city and its suburbs held by the faithful.

Refugees streamed into Peking. Thievery and murder increased, food prices skyrocketed, and riots exploded constantly. The Communists infiltrated the university, and fomented their doctrines through every level of the schools, turning children against their parents. The present ruler, Chiang Kai-shek, and his demoralized National Army had no chance against the ruthless Communist scourge advancing on the city. The Communists told the young people that their elders had caused all of the misery and poverty in China and made them witness their system of "justice" when they dragged the elderly from their homes and stoned them to death.

The fierce battle for possession of Peking escalated until staying became impossible by December, 1949. The National Army could no longer protect the missionaries, and all avenues of escape closed except by air. The director of the Lutheran Mission in Peking sent Stiegie and Kathyrn word that their board would try to land a plane in Peking and evacuate as many missionaries as possible.

Early on the morning of December 14, Kathryn and Stiegie carrying a small handbag each, climbed on a Shell Oil Company truck profusely decked with American and British Flags. Two trucks loaded with missionary personnel and two consulate cars started toward the airport, which had been bombed by the Communists and deserted by the National Army.

Dead soldiers, dead horses and shattered buildings, evidence of last night's bombing, bordered their way. The ten miles to the airport took over two hours with guards stopping the procession about every fifty yards. Everyone on the truck knew well they faced the dangers of being turned back, imprisoned or killed. The American and British officials got out each time they were halted to talk and bluff their way through.

According to a prearranged signal, they spread four sheets on the runway at the airport. Suddenly, Communists shelled the airstrip and everyone dived under the trucks for safety. Shelling came intermittently all afternoon. They saw the C-47 plane coming, and everyone cheered, but as the pilot began his descent shelling resumed, and he had to pull up. Stiegie and Kathryn wondered if they would really get away; however, the plane returned after a few minutes and landed safely. As the waiting group scrambled aboard, shelling came again, slow-moving passengers got yanked inside, scattering luggage on the runway. The plane rose skyward swiftly, with the door still open, in the middle of gunfire.

Brave pilots took the *St. Paul* back to Peking for two more scary, rescue missions before a complete takeover by the Red Army. The ladies spent twelve days at Tsingtao that spanned a special Christmas of thanksgiving, though lonely for the believer family left behind. An unspoken question haunted both of them: "Will we ever see those dear saints again?" They stayed in the only available accommodation, the Lutheran Hospital, though not as patients.

On December 28, the *St. Paul* took Stiegie and Kathryn 995 miles to Canton and a new world. Once more they found a room in a hospital with spare rooms to rent. Planks topped by a thin straw mattress made their beds. They had to sleep under nets for protection from myriads of blood thirsty mosquitoes unheard of in the north. Worst of all, no one could understand their North China language, so different from the Chinese spoken in the south.

Missionary families Daniel Sheets and G. Kelley heartily welcomed these helpers, in spite of the language handicap. Almost immediately Stiegie and Kathryn took charge of the Sheets' mission while Brother Sheets took his wife to the United States for surgery.

The ladies found idolatry more entrenched and devoted in South China than in Shansi. Along with several carved idols, a shelf in their homes often displayed the revered bone of an ancestor, or an urn in the garden con-

345

tained bones. The people considered no hardship or sacrifice too much in their devout worship of the dead. The ladies could not help but contrast their sacrificial devotion to powerless gods with the haphazard, careless worship of the one true God by American churches.

Having left all of their personal belongings in Peking, Stiegie and Kathryn cheerfully suffered lack of comfort and rejoiced in the privilege of service. They could empathize with refugees that soon flowed into Canton before the Red Army's relentless drive south.

One day several missionaries rode in three rickshas on a ricksha path beside a deep moat, going to transact business and ask advice of the American consulate about staying in Canton. They met a Communist tank division rumbling down the other side of the street. Suddenly, one of the tanks pulled out of line and swung across the street. Someone yelled, "Jump!" All of them scrambled out, falling to the path, barely missing the edge of the moat. The rickshas lay in splinters in the street, but the drivers and missionaries escaped with minor cuts and bruises.

Conditions grew worse and the consulate advised them to leave the city, and missionaries who ignored that advice suffered greatly later on. Stiegie and Kathryn listened, once again left all and moved to Hong Kong after only a year in Canton. They found the British Colony had a measure of Western progress. However, importunate Chinese, many among them literates and professionals, had fled from Mao's exterminating forces and huddled in vast shambles of poverty, having lost everything, even hope.

The ladies unreservedly threw themselves into a ministry of compassion, alleviating misery wherever possible and sharing the unfailing gospel of hope with the unfortunates. Stiegie could not ignore need and keenly felt the refugees' plight. Four wars had capsized her life in varying degrees of intensity and the stroke she suffered left a legacy of debility. All of it together contributed to her complete collapse early in 1950.

For two weeks, Kathryn, other missionaries and friends battled death, in constant prayer for Stiegie before they called a doctor. He ordered her to the hospital, later saying she had a serious heart condition that he called "heart-block." One valve of her heart had deteriorated completely and the other three tried to beat separately instead of together. He said, "It is imperative that Miss Stieglitz retire immediately to a very quiet life, and she must return to America as soon as she is able to travel."

Nearly three months of therapy and rest followed before her friends could book a hospital bed for her on the *President Wilson* bound for America. She wrote the Hensleys, then working in Hawaii, the liner's time of arrival, stating, "My heart is so bad, I'll not be able to disembark, but I would love to see you."

Mable Hensley met the boat at 8:00 a.m., but the authorities allowed no one either on or off. One told her they had word that drugs were concealed on board, and a search must be concluded before she could enter. She waited. They finally gave Mable permission to board at noon and she walked into Stiegie's room.

"Bless your heart, Mable!" she exclaimed joyfully. "I thought I wouldn't get to see you, and I was so disappointed."

Mable explained the delay and the pair chattered away, bringing each other up to date on all that had

transpired. Though short of breath at times, Stiegie seemed to benefit from the telling of harassment, uncertain-
ties and narrow escapes.

The nurse took Stiegie to the deck in a wheel chair
to have tea, then wanted to put her to bed. "No," she
told the nurse, "I don't want to waste a minute of this
chance to visit."

"You'll be more than glad to get to bed if you stay
up much longer," the nurse answered.

"Maybe so," Stiegie retorted, "but I'll sleep better
tonight from the time spent with my friend." She stayed
up until time for the boat to sail.

Amazingly, the liner brought Stiegie to California in
June, 1950, exactly forty years from the time she arrived in China to begin her missionary career. She really
wanted to go back to Iowa, but she did not have the
strength. Long time friends she first met in Canada
prepared a comfortable cottage for her in Pasadena,
California, and installed a communication system that
someone promptly reported as illegal.

"Take it out!" an official ordered.

"If it comes out, you'll have to do it. I'll go to court,
but I won't touch it," her friend answered. "This lady has
been a missionary for forty years. Now, she is weak and
sick, and should be able to call for help when she needs it."

Stiegie's heart deteriorated to a minimum function
that barely kept her alive. She developed Parkinson's
disease, perhaps from the privations she had suffered.
Now, other foes engaged the soldier in battles that seemed
to her unending; debility, pain, helplessness and varied
inconveniences. God's mercy sent a friend's tender touch
or an act of love, now and then.

348

When one benefactor reached his limits of ability, another one came forward—the list is too long to mention names, but a faithful God will reward. After robberies made living in a cottage impractical, Stiegie took turns in nursing homes and hospitals. Brother and Sister Paul Box visited her and Sister Box remembers the trembling hands that placed a ginger snap in her plate. Those of us who received those wavery notes written painstakingly by a shaky hand wept, realizing the effort it cost. One of them said:

All I want to do is go home. I don't know why God extends my life, but it must be to keep prayer going up continually for my beloved China that needs Jesus now as never before.

The alloted time for prayer and loving ended. A nurse closed the nearly blind eyes in the aged face of a nearly eighty-six year old body on May 7, 1975. She may have thought, "Another old one out of her misery."

She could not know the splendid service, brilliant mind, valiant life and unswerving dedication represented by that worn-out body. Perhaps the nurse shivered in the presence of something she neither saw nor understood—the royal welcome of a beloved daughter by the King, who greatly desired her beauty.

The young Elizabeth Stieglitz.

Elizabeth Stieglitz in late 1920's.

1946, Elizabeth Stieglitz and Kathryn Hendricks in California before sailing to China.

Elizabeth and Kathryn with Chinese workers on way to Tong Po, South China.

Elizabeth Stieglitz in 1948.